UNINTENDED CONSEQUENCES

UNINTENDED CONSEQUENCES

The United States at War

Kenneth J. Hagan and Ian J. Bickerton

REAKTION BOOKS

For Joshua, Montgomery, Finn and Tynan
and
For Carolyn and Melissa
May They Know Peace

Published by Reaktion Books Ltd
33 Great Sutton Street
London EC1V 0DX, UK

www.reaktionbooks.co.uk

First published 2007

Copyright © Kenneth J. Hagan and Ian J. Bickerton

Printed and bound in Great Britain by
Cromwell Press, Trowbridge, Wiltshire

British Library Cataloguing in Publication Data
Hagan, Kenneth J.
Unintended consequences : the United States at war
1. Nation-building – United States 2. Postwar
reconstruction 3. United States – Foreign relations
4. United States – Military policy
I. Title II. Bickerton, Ian J.
327.1'1'0973

ISBN-13: 978-1-86189-310-9
ISBN-10: 1-86189-310-8

CONTENTS

'Wars begin when you will,
But they do not end when you please.'

Niccolò Machiavelli

'War is not, and I repeat, war is not "the continuation of politics
by other means". On the contrary, it represents the catastrophic
failure of political skill and imagination – a dethronement of
peaceful politics from the primacy which it should enjoy.'

Kofi Annan, Secretary General of the United Nations,
11 August 2006

This book is in every respect an equal collaboration by its two authors.

PREFACE

President George W. Bush went to war against Iraq on 19 March 2003, in order, he said, 'to defend our liberty and to save our lives'. Less than two months later, on 1 May 2003, on the aircraft carrier USS *Abraham Lincoln*, he triumphantly announced: 'Major combat operations in Iraq have ended.' Presumably the president thought he had achieved the ends for which he went to war. Nonetheless, Americans continued to fight and die in Iraq for the rest of 2003 and for the subsequent three years. The administration, its supporters and its critics began to debate and unravel the proclaimed justifications for invading Iraq in the first place. As they did so, the war's effects unfolded in ways that had not been anticipated or predicted by the president or his spokesmen in 2003. The most remarkable immediate aftermath of the invasion was the descent of Iraq into internecine guerrilla warfare, much of which was directed at the United States, the country that ostensibly intended to bring western-style democracy to the beleaguered people of Iraq.

As the months rolled into years of continued conflict, it became clear that the war had led to a large number of unintended and catastrophic consequences. This painful realization caused the present authors to examine the extent to which previous American wars have been accompanied by unintended consequences that are so profound as to raise doubts about the wisdom of the initial decision for war, however justified it appeared at the time. This book is the result of that examination. It demonstrates that Iraq is only the latest example of an American war whose unintended consequences dwarf the original justification and expectations of those who led the nation into belligerency. It is offered as a cautionary tale for those who would rush to arms in order to solve unpleasant problems.

The idea of the book is simple but profound. Most people think that wars end when hostilities cease and armistices and treaties are signed. This is not the case. The unappreciated reality is that while the wars the United States has fought may have ended formally, in fact they continued, producing profound and unexpected consequences. After the cessation of hostilities, American wars were most often followed by extended periods of US military, political and economic involvement in the 'defeated' country. This continued enmeshment invariably exerted widespread effects on the American victor and on the vanquished country.

Despite the historical pattern, Secretary of Defense Donald Rumsfeld claimed at the beginning of the current Iraq War: 'The United States does not do nation building.' On the contrary, occupation and nation building are precisely what the United States has done after most of the wars it has fought, from the war in which it gained independence, through Vietnam to the war in Iraq. These and other consequences of America's wars are analysed in this book.

No one should be surprised at the appalling developments in Iraq. This book's historical review of the wars fought by the United States reveals that America's wars routinely produced unintended consequences that outweighed the intended consequences. The fighting of the wars radically altered foreign policy, military strategy and domestic life. This book sets out the stated aims of each war, points out critical turning points in the conflicts, and explores the consequences that flowed from them. Most of the wars embarked upon by the United States, when measured against this criterion, were not only catastrophic and destructive for the participants, they were avoidable, unnecessary and unpredictable in outcome.

This book develops the thesis that every US war transformed the national policies that led into the war. This inevitable transformation occurred as a result of decisions or events that took place during the war, after which the initial policies and goals were rendered largely obsolete or irrelevant. A conclusion of the war on the terms initially envisioned by the national leadership became impossible.

One of the reasons this reality has not been widely recognized is that all too frequently military historians and others who have sought to assess the success or failure of American wars have failed to evaluate the outcomes of the conflicts against the stated aims. These nationalist, triumphalist historians, looking for and tracing the victory of American arms, have measured outcomes not only with the benefit of hindsight but on the assumption that the outcomes, almost invariably described as successful, were those intended. Another reason the universality of disastrous unintended consequences has not been appreciated in the United States is the prevailing influence of the nineteenth-century Prussian soldier and military theorist Carl von Clausewitz. In his book *On War* (1832), Clausewitz set out the classic formula on war's function: 'war is merely the continuation of policy by other means.'[1] Clausewitz saw war as a rational and legitimate means of furthering national interests. He argued that no nation went to war unless it knew what it was fighting for, although he did acknowledge that 'the fog of war' made unpredictability of the course and outcome inevitable.

The present book demonstrates that the magnitude of the unintended consequences resulting from 'fog' and 'friction' invalidates Clausewitz's basic proposition. War turns out not to be a continuation of existing policy; war produces an entirely new policy – often quite at odds with the original policy embarked upon. Unintended or unforeseen consequences are invariably more long-term than the intended outcomes and more often than not work in ways that counteract the original reasons for embarking on the war in the first place.

This transformation means simply that Clausewitz's book is obsolete as a guide to policy-makers, just as war is obsolete as an instrument for achieving their ends. Clausewitz was not only wrong, he was seriously wrong. War does not continue policy, it radically alters it.

INTRODUCTION

This book is a study of the unintended consequences of the wars fought by the United States. We look at what presidents and the Congress said they were doing when they made the decision to go to war, and we describe how the events turned out. We reveal that the nation's leaders did not know or realize the full consequences that would flow from their decisions, and that many of the consequences of those actions were often quite different from – even contrary to – those intended. Policy-makers did not accurately predict the outcomes of the wars they were about to embark upon. Nor indeed could they, given the confusions created by the fighting during the wars themselves. We also show that these unintended consequences and their ramifications were, more often than not, more far-reaching than the original, intended, goals. That is the point of this book.

When we speak of 'unintended' consequences we are referring to those events that could only have occurred as the result of war: that is, without the war the events would not have occurred. We do not refer to events where wars were merely a precondition, rather than a cause, of their happening. Nor are we talking about unwanted events that it was known would occur as the result of the war (for example, casualties), but which did not prevent the war from taking place. That is, we are talking about unforeseen or unpredicted events that were the consequences of war, as opposed to foreseen events or consequences. Hannah Arendt observed that politics is the realm of unintended consequences.[1] She was drawing attention to the distinction between the predictable world of mechanics and computers and the world of politicians, who cannot accurately predict the consequences of their actions. If this is true of politics, it is even more true of war, which is why the notion that war is merely policy by other means is nonsense. Because of the intensity, death and destruction intrinsic to warfare, the outcomes of wars, regardless of the intentions, aims and motives of those who enter them, are far more unpredictable than non-violent political actions.

We should note immediately that when we speak of war in this book we are referring only to the use of military force authorized and identified by presidential or Congressional declarations to achieve national goals. We do not discuss what we regard as the misapplication of the term 'war' that has come into wide use in such examples as the 'war on drugs' or the 'Global War on Terrorism'.

In this extended essay we document the multitude and profundity of the unintended consequences of America's wars, focusing primarily on the malignant effects of war. These unintended consequences changed both the world in which the United States acted and the domestic character of the United States itself. We are aware that our list of unintended consequences is incomplete and that many may disagree with our selection. That is fine with us. We do not demand or require the agreement of our readers – nor, we hope, do they of us. Our purpose is not to convert; it is to provoke discussion. In an essay, 'Why History Matters', introducing 'Teddy' Roosevelt in *Time* magazine's *The Making of America* series, managing editor Richard Stengel stated that being an American is based upon 'accepting an uncommon set of ideas'.[2] In this book we are setting out an uncommon set of ideas that we hope are of value in understanding how to grapple with current issues of war and peace. Of course, not all the unintended consequences of us wars were undesirable. The United States has been positively transformed by its major wars. From the first war of 1775–83, America's wars have been engines of economic growth. Wars have broken down class, ethnic and gender barriers (at least briefly), and have caused the greatest demographic shifts in the nation's history. The destruction of slavery was clearly an unintended but positive consequence of the Civil War. Wars have also revitalized the role of the Federal government as the planner and shaper of American society and life.

The tragedy is that it has taken wars to bring about these changes. It is one of the great ironies of modern history that a nation that sees itself as a beacon for all mankind, a nation that contains within itself the genius, the creativity, the drive to capture the imagination of peoples around the world for the past two centuries has not always been able to harness that energy without resort to war. In addition, there are many aspects of American life that were, relatively speaking, little changed, or processes that were merely accelerated by war. Perhaps the clearest examples of continuity, despite several wars, concern US attempts to secure maritime commerce, amicable relations with Native Americans, and the regulation of territorial expansion throughout the nineteenth century. We highlight the undesirable, unintended outcomes because these are most quickly overlooked and forgotten in the retelling of America's wars and in describing the lessons allegedly learned from past wars.

One of the principal tenets of the ideology and mythology of the United States is that, as a pacific democracy, it has never entered into war lightly or unjustly. This self-image or belief has been upheld and carefully nurtured by every administration in US history. It is an essential element of American patriotism. No value is more highly prized than the belief that the United States stands as a beacon for mankind, 'a city upon a hill', representing all that is good and admirable in human experience. From the first handful of settlers, seventeenth-century nonconformist refugees seeking freedom to worship without persecution, to the present 300 million inhabitants, Americans have claimed to prize peace above all. Equally, however, they have demonstrated that they are not afraid to resort to war when they believe their national interest demands it.

War is not only the most momentous decision the nation's leaders can make, it is also the most risky. Apart from the cost in lives lost and the chaos and uncertainty of the battles themselves, there is no certainty that when the fighting is over the resultant outcome will be the one intended. Our underlying message in this book is that war is folly. In going to war, US leaders did not know, indeed could not know, or appreciate the dangers they were embarking upon and therefore did not adequately plan or prepare for the unwanted eventualities that resulted. Whether or not the leadership (and/or the American public) would have gone to war had they known in advance the undesirable consequences of committing US forces, we cannot say. What we can say is that the use of force has proven inherently problematical – even unnecessary – and it has created problems for the attainment of US policy objectives. This book therefore encourages sober re-evaluation of the decisions to go to war.

Throughout American history, victory has proven far more elusive to the United States than most historians and policy-makers concede. Even the conditions wherein the United States claimed itself victorious often proved temporary. The intended consequences were rarely attainable; the unintended consequences inevitable. A fuller recognition of this normal progression of affairs should make leaders less sanguine about the achievability of their war aims.

Even in short, apparently victorious wars, the consequences of going to war can be wide-ranging and far from those anticipated. War aims are notoriously vague, frequently ad hoc, and made under pressure or on the run. Even when specific goals are well thought-out and unambiguously articulated, few wars produce the clear-cut and decisive result hoped for. Rarely do the intended military outcomes of war last long. Treaties ending wars often turn out to be merely truces. In addition, the consequences of war that are the most unexpected and troubling are frequently those felt at home. The impact on American domestic political and economic life was especially profound and utterly unanticipated in the case of the Civil War, World War I, World War II and the Vietnam War. However, our emphasis is primarily on US foreign and military policy. We do not extend our analysis to the domestic consequences of the wars we examine, other than to note major shifts in American life and the impact they had on US foreign relations.

The decision to resort to armed force raises many more challenges than simply winning the conflict. There is not only the question of achieving the peace settlement hoped for; war raises numerous domestic as well as international issues. War planners are primarily preoccupied with military operations and their immediate outcomes. Because so many contingencies flow from war, planners cannot anticipate or plan for all of them. When he asserted that war is merely policy continued by other means, Carl von Clausewitz did not take into account the broad ramifications that flow from war. Most of war's consequences are unpredictable and, therefore, unintended. The only intended consequences of war are those narrowly defined in military or diplomatic terms, and even these are most often unforeseen, unpredicted and unintended. It is amazing how many American wars display these characteristics and, judging from how often the mistakes are repeated, how quickly this is forgotten.

Mention of Clausewitz will evoke several conflicting responses, especially from alleged experts. Some will argue that Clausewitz saw war only as a last resort. We do not agree. It certainly was not the case for eighteenth-century Prussia or for Napoleon Bonaparte, both of which were his standards. He does argue that the goals of war should be clear, and in that respect we 'agree' with him. He also says that the 'fog' and 'friction' make the outcomes of war unpredictable. What we are saying in this book is that the changes are so great and fundamental that it is nonsense to say that war is in any rational way an extension of policy.

The goals of war are changed by the unfolding events of the conflict. Frequently the goals of wars that begin as 'a war to resist aggression' or as 'a war to restore freedom' undergo a transformation to become little more than a war to avoid defeat. We see a clear example of this in the current war in Iraq. What began as an apparently straightforward goal – the overthrow of Saddam Hussein, the discovery and demolition of his weapons of mass destruction, and the creation of a democratic Iraq – has ended up as a United States-led coalition fighting an insurgency in Iraq to avoid defeat, to demonstrate to the world that the United States fulfils its commitments. The goals of the war have become an 'image' issue; the war has become almost an imaginary enterprise. The war in Iraq is only the most recent example of this phenomenon. The same kind of transformations took place in the Vietnam War, the Korean War and the Civil War, to mention the most obvious examples. Moreover, we are saying that a post-war period is a continuation of war because of changes brought about during the wars. There will always be students of Clausewitz who disagree with our argument. They do so because they think he is a useful guide to war. We think he is important mainly because he perpetuates reliance on war by nations, and this perpetuation is deplorable.

Most discussions of wars assume that the outcomes or results were intended, or expected or planned. Thus it is accepted that the 1775–83 war with Great Britain was fought for American independence, the 1846–48 war with Mexico for the acquisition of the Southwest, and so on. Very little attention is given to the question as to what outcomes of wars were intended and what were not. This book explores that question, and focuses on the outcomes that were not intended. Viewed from this perspective, to take two examples, it becomes apparent that the independence of the thirteen colonies and the establishment of the United States were unintended consequences of a war begun in 1775 to redress colonial grievances over taxes imposed by the mother country; that the Civil War was an unintended consequence of the war with Mexico. We draw attention to similar examples of unintended outcomes through examining ten American wars. Our conclusions lead us to rethink the reasons the United States went to war in the first place, and the efficacy of the wars in achieving America's stated goals.

Our methodology is simple and direct. We look closely at the reasons presidents have given when they have embarked upon America's major wars, and then we examine the outcome of those wars in light of the avowed or stated reasons given for resorting to military action. We take the messages of the presidents to Congress and Congressional resolutions authorizing the use of force as evidence of the intentions of the United States in going to war. We do not rewrite the causes of the wars the United States has fought, although it becomes evident in most instances that there was a considerable gap between the rhetoric and the reality of going to war. Rather, we accept that in going to war US presidents have carefully set out what they wanted Congress and the American people to believe were the true and accurate reasons for the impending conflict. We then selectively trace the fighting of the war so as to illustrate the transformation of goals wrought by the unpredictable nature of the way in which the war was actually fought, including the impact of factional and other political-economic divisions in Washington. Lastly, we examine the circumstances ending the wars to see to what extent they fulfilled the aims outlined for resorting to war.

Carrying out such an investigation reveals that, in almost all cases, the outcomes of the wars fought by the United States were far removed from the stated objectives in entering them. We demonstrate that, if their statements accurately reflect their state of mind, US presidents have often pursued warfare with little clear notion of the consequences that might result. This may come as something of a shock to a nation accustomed to seeing itself as successful in achieving its goals. In fact, of course, as our study reminds us, presidents have not always accurately or fully revealed their intentions when embarking upon war. This may startle those citizens who believe that the foundation of democracy is public trust and that their government does not lie to them. They realize that public honesty is basic and essential if the United States is to function as a democracy. Furthermore, a failure by presidents to state their intentions fully and truthfully is damaging to democratic government in that the falsehood is aimed not at the enemy but at Congress and the American public. Secrecy is closely related to lying, and presidential secrecy surrounding the reasons for going to war is a betrayal of the people's trust. Once presidents allow secrecy and lies to replace truth in stating their intentions to go to war, politics is reduced to a species of public relations. History has shown that restrictions of civil liberties inevitably soon follow.

We do not intend to examine all the conflicts involving US armed forces. Most Americans are probably unaware of the number of conflicts in which their country has engaged: the US has fought more than 250 overseas military engagements since independence. That is more than one engagement a year. If one includes the longest running war fought by the United States – the US Army against Native Americans, which lasted for more than a century – the United States was at war for almost the entire nineteenth century, the so-called century of peace. Part of the reason for the lack of awareness of these US military actions among Americans is that when they think of America at war most of them think of large-scale conflicts fought by thousands or millions of citizen soldiers supported by a fully mobilized home front. In every decade from the Civil War to the present, those who fought in the great wars – the Civil War, First and Second World Wars, Vietnam – passed on their memories of those wars as epic events. Recent US interventions in places like Kosovo, Bosnia or Afghanistan barely qualify as a 'war' in the popular imagination. But as Max Boot has pointed out in his valuable book *The Savage Wars of Peace*,[3] most of the wars engaged in by the United States have been relatively small wars fought by a small number of professional soldiers. These are not the wars with which this book is concerned. We limit our analysis to the following major wars: the First Major War (for Independence), the War of 1812, the War against Mexico, the Civil War, the War against Spain, the US in World War I, the US in World War II, the Korean War, the Vietnam War, and the two wars against Iraq.

In these wars, Washington frequently embarked on war with only the broadest of post-war goals. As Russell F. Weigley noted in his seminal study, *The American Way of War*, until the end of World War II, 'the United States usually possessed no national strategy for the employment of force or the threat of force to attain political ends, except . . . directly in pursuit of military victories as complete as was desired or possible.'[4] Even the meaning of military victory was not always entirely clear. In some cases it was limited to achieving conquests on the frontiers of the enemy's country; in other cases it was to seek the complete overthrow of the enemy. The Civil War and the genocidal 'Indian' wars of the late nineteenth century firmly embedded the notion that the defeat of the enemy and the destruction of his military power was the object of war. World War II confirmed the primacy of this goal over all others. Weigley has called this conception of war 'the strategy of annihilation', and he regards it as the distinguishing feature of the American way of war.[5] Donald Rumsfeld's comment in 2005 on the war in Iraq illustrates Weigley's thesis: the Secretary of Defense was reported to have stated: 'We don't have an exit strategy, we have a victory strategy.'[6]

Finally, this book does not concern itself with the unintended consequences of regime changes brought about by the United States through means other than wars. Regime change through covert actions and coups are the topic of *Overthrow*, by Stephen Kinzer.[7] That book amply covers the unintended consequences of these actions. The great value of Kinzer and Boot is that they encourage the American public to subject American military and foreign policy to the kind of critical examination we undertake in this book. The self-perception of most Americans is that their country is a peaceful nation, yet not only does it have the largest war machine in the world, it outpaces all other nations in military expenditures.

* * *

The unintended consequences of a war are the result of two major factors: the uncertainties that lead to the initial decision to go to war and the formulation of its goals, and the chaos and unpredictability generated by the conflict itself – called by Clausewitz 'the fog of war'. Obvious examples of intertwining of these two factors and the unintended outcomes they produced in the wars of the nineteenth and twentieth centuries include the occupation of the territories or nations conquered by American troops for decades after the cessation of hostilities. They permanently occupied all territories captured from Native Americans, and following the Civil War Union troops remained in the South for twelve years during the period known as Reconstruction. The US military remained in the Philippines from 1899 to 1946 (47 years), in Haiti from 1915 to 1933 (18 years) and in Nicaragua from 1910 to 1933 (23 years). Following World War II and the Korean War, American troops stayed on in Germany, Japan, Italy and South Korea for more than half a century after fighting had ceased. Five years into the 'Global War on Terrorism' it appears that US troops will remain in Iraq and Afghanistan for some time to come.

The occupations were unintended outcomes, and the character of the US troop presence differed. US soldiers often acted as social workers, peacekeepers and colonial administrators. It might be argued that American troops occupying post-war Japan and Germany did not face insurgents blowing up US personnel, as they are currently experiencing in Iraq and Afghanistan, suggesting that in the former case the occupation was not such a bad thing. It might equally be argued that the populations of Germany and Japan, following the wholesale devastation of their populations, cities and infrastructure and faced with overwhelming occupation forces, were in no position to mount anything resembling an insurgency to indicate their hostility to their conquerors or so-called liberators.

Frequently major wars led to further – less vital – entanglements. The Spanish-American war, for example, led to the protracted and violent war to suppress Filipino nationalists. It also led to expeditions against the Chinese Boxers in 1900 and to a series of 'Banana Wars' in the western hemisphere. Fought in Cuba, the Dominican Republic, Haiti and Nicaragua, these neo-colonial police actions plagued the United States on and off for the remainder of the twentieth century and on into the present century. These wars, it was argued by Washington, were fought to protect American nationals or territory, but they scarcely fit into traditional, realpolitik, conceptions of 'vital' national interests.

The wars fought by the United States have frequently caused serious domestic dissent and divisions. There was far from unanimous support for the War of Independence, the Civil War and even World War I, as well as many of the so-called lesser wars. There was certainly almost universal support for World War II after December 1941, but not before, and the nation is still recovering from the domestic trauma created by the Vietnam War.

In some ways this book begs the question, 'what if' the United States had not gone to war in such-and-such a case? The objection might be raised that the question suggests counterfactual history. But what is wrong with that? Planning for war involves asking 'what if' questions. The decision to go to war rests upon hypothetical predictions, and obviously not all such predictions turn out to be correct. In the majority of cases, if war planners had thought more carefully about the consequences of their actions before going to war, perhaps they would have chosen a wiser course of action. Three obvious examples suggest themselves. By choosing not to seek a declaration of war against France in 1800, President John Adams created the conditions that led directly to the Louisiana Purchase three years later, surely one of the least expensive acquisitions of territory in history. Had President William McKinley accepted Spain's peace offer in 1898 instead of going to war over Cuba, many thousands of lives, American and Filipino, would have been saved with no appreciable disadvantage to US ambitions in the Caribbean or Pacific Ocean, or East Asia. If President Lyndon B. Johnson and his two immediate predecessors had thought more carefully about the role of the United States in East Asia in the 1960s, and had they not committed the nation to war in Vietnam, Vietnam would have been unified years earlier with far less loss of life, and with far greater economic and diplomatic benefit to the United States. We will resist the temptation to engage in counterfactual speculations in this book, however; there are just too many variables and possibilities. We will stick with the historical record; it offers ample evidence in support of our case for the unintended consequences of US wars.

ONE

THE FIRST MAJOR WAR, 1775–83

*Credulity and want of Foresight, are Imperfections
in the Human Character, that no Politician can sufficiently
guard against.*
John Adams to Abigail Adams, April 1776[1]

The first major war fought by the united English colonies was against Great Britain. It was a result of the British Parliament's persistent attempt to compel the thirteen North American colonies to bear their share of the costs for the Seven Years' War (1756–63) and the post-war expenses of policing the colonial frontiers. In October 1774 the thirteen colonies openly defied British authority when the First Continental Congress adopted a Declaration of Rights and Grievances in protest against the impost of taxes by the British government, especially the taxes on molasses and tea, and the quartering of English troops in the colonies. In April 1775 hostilities between British troops and local Massachusetts militiamen broke out in the 'battles' of Lexington and Concord. Stunned and bloodied by the colonials, the British regulars retreated to Boston, where they were besieged by what soon became a regular army. On 10 May 1775, in Philadelphia, the Second Continental Congress met for the first time to form the Army of the United Colonies. For sectional balance it appointed as commander-in-chief a Virginia soldier with substantial if undistinguished combat experience in the Seven Years' War, George Washington.

Independence was not the initial objective of the colonists. Time and again those fighting in Massachusetts stated they sought merely to guarantee themselves the historic 'rights of Englishmen' – particularly the right to be ruled and taxed by representatives of their own choosing and the right to govern their own internal affairs. Leaders such as John Adams, Thomas Jefferson and Benjamin Franklin claimed they were fighting against a 'history of repeated injuries and usurpations, all having in direct object the establishment of an absolute Tyranny over these States'.[2] In June 1775 George Washington told the New York Provincial Congress that his aim was 'the re-establishment of peace and harmony between the mother country and the colonies'.[3] The colonial legislatures, the militiamen and Washington were all quarrelling with the British Parliament, not the king. By January of the following year, however, Washington had come to the conclusion that the forcible expulsion of the British from the continent and complete severance of relations and independence from the mother country were the only viable outcomes of the conflict. He had been radicalized by George III's rejection of the colonists' final petition for redress of their grievances and by the simultaneous publication in January 1776 of the bestselling pamphlet, *Common Sense*, by Thomas Paine, a former British excise officer who had arrived in Philadelphia in 1774.

Six months later, in Philadelphia, Virginia delegate Richard Henry Lee introduced a resolution stating that 'these United Colonies are and of right ought to be free and independent states'. The Second Continental Congress responded on 4 July by adopting the Declaration of Independence, which was drawn up by Jefferson, Adams and Franklin. In declaring its independence from the British Crown, the Congress claimed it was acting 'in the Name, and by the Authority of the good People of these Colonies'. The delegates appealed 'to the Supreme Judge of the world for the rectitude of our intentions'. Finally, the signatories mutually pledged to each other 'our Lives, our Fortunes and our sacred Honour'.

But independence was a long way off and victories were scarce. The year 1776 was, in the words of historian David McCullough, 'a year of all too few victories, of sustained suffering, disease, hunger, desertion, cowardice, disillusionment, defeat, terrible discouragement, and fear'.[4] The Declaration of Independence was little more than a rhetorical gesture against an overwhelmingly stronger military force. Nor were the revolutionaries supported by all the colonists. Many remained loyal to Great Britain and were horrified by the idea of separating from a liberal, protective government they regarded as benevolent and beneficial. This was not a war fought against an oppressive, evil empire. According to McCullough, the colonists enjoyed a higher standard of living than their rulers – or indeed any Europeans.

The revolutionary, and initially unintended, decision to declare independence changed the nature of the armed conflict with Great Britain, giving it some aspects of an international war. The colonial revolutionaries sought to capitalize upon this situation by seeking foreign military assistance, and they actively pursued this goal with France. For two years the French monarchy gave only limited and largely clandestine aid, but the Battle of Saratoga in September–October 1777 convinced France that the colonists could achieve independence with French military and naval assistance. A treaty of military alliance was signed in February 1778, and the war became one of a Franco-American coalition against the diplomatically and militarily isolated British. This treaty was the consciously sought result of the Americans' strategy, and it led to the culminating victory at Yorktown in September 1781. It also had far-reaching unintended consequences once the colonists won the war.

THE WAR

One man and two battles determined the nature and consequences of what became a war for independence. The man was George Washington; the battles were those at Saratoga, New York, in 1777, and at Yorktown, Virginia, in 1781. George Washington became the epicentre of the war against Britain the moment he assumed command of the Continental Army surrounding Boston on 3 July 1775. He was facing British regulars who were attempting to break through the colonial militia's emplacements around the city. On 17 June, under the operational direction of General William Howe, a highly regarded field commander, the British had frontally attacked American militiamen holding the high ground on Breed's Hill, immediately in front of a somewhat higher promontory named Bunker Hill. The well-drilled and disciplined British soldiers 'went down like wheat before the scythe all along the line'.[5] On the third desperate charge Howe's men took the hill, but only because the defenders were running out of ammunition. In what became known as the Battle of Bunker Hill 50 per cent of the British force was killed or wounded. Howe never fully regained his offensive spirit, while the colonists acquired confidence in the ability of irregulars to defeat a proud professional army. This conceit fed the spirit of resistance, inclining it more and more toward outright independence, a decision formally made by the Continental Congress on 4 July 1776.

Colonial hubris following Bunker Hill also made Washington's task of organizing a regular army more difficult, but from the outset he understood better than anyone else that only by building and preserving a national army could he ensure the success of the American cause. His army therefore became the critical Clause-witzian centre of gravity, and the British generals never fully under-stood this fact. As a result, they were too timid and indecisive in their efforts to engage Washington decisively in a battle of their choosing. During seven years of fighting, Washington rarely arranged his army in formation for frontal engagements; on the few occasions when he did so the outcome was not favourable to the Americans. His preference was to elude the main forces of the British army and make stinging, ungentlemanly, guerrilla-like raids, sometimes in the dead of night. In this manner he compelled the British generals to include his army's existence in the calculations for their next offensive. So long as Washington's regulars and militia-men remained in the central states – New Jersey and Pennsylvania – the British could only fight on the periphery; they could not enjoy interior lines of communications at the strategic level. Thus, in a real sense, Washington was a part of every battle, whether or not he was physically present. At Yorktown, where he was personally in command of a large coalition army, he won the war.

The long road to Yorktown began in Saratoga in October 1777. Lieutenant General John Burgoyne of the Royal Army had recently come from London with a plan for defeating the colonists with a two-pronged attack to split off and isolate the New England colonies, the heart of the revolution. He would descend from Canada to Lake Champlain; General Howe would head north from New York to rendezvous with him. Simplicity itself, but Howe did not comply. Orders directing him to march north were mislaid in London by the Secretary of State for the American Department, Lord George Germain. Howe in any case preferred to attack the rebels' political centre. He thought the people of Pennsylvania were increasingly 'disposed to peace, in which senti-ment they would be confirmed by our getting possession of

Philadelphia'.[6] He occupied the capital on 25 September, after skirmishing with Washington, but possession proved irrelevant to a war in which the soldiers in the field were the only real American centre of gravity.

Abandoned by Howe, 'Gentleman Johnny' Burgoyne and 8,000 formidable troops, by whom he was 'universally esteemed and respected', marched south into the waiting arms of the savage, forest-smart colonials.[7] The militiamen felled trees to slow his advance and cut supply lines in his rear. At Bemis Heights, on 7 October 1777, they joined the regulars commanded by Benedict Arnold, a charismatic leader possessed of 'boundless energy and enterprise', and Washington's surrogate, Major General Horatio Gates, to rout much of Burgoyne's force.[8] Rather than preside over the complete wrecking of his army, Burgoyne did what a sensible and honourable eighteenth-century commander should have done: he surrendered the entire army intact. The formal surrender came at Saratoga on 17 October: 7 generals, 300 officers and 5,600 soldiers withdrew from the war. New England was saved for the Revolution as the rebels had hoped, but the monumental unintended consequence of Burgoyne's capitulation was a war-winning military alliance between republican America and monarchical France.

News of Burgoyne's surrender reached the American representative in Paris, Benjamin Franklin, on 4 December. Two days later, King Louis XVI approved the concept of a military alliance with the United States. The king and Franklin recognized that the magnitude of the American victory at Saratoga could transform the relationship between their two countries. Since early 1777 France had been clandestinely shipping arms and ammunition to the revolutionaries. The Catholic Bourbon monarchy was seeking revenge for Protestant England's victory in the Seven Years' War, and it hoped for restitution of some of the North American territories lost in that imperial war. In the words of the Comte de Vergennes, France's foreign minister, American independence would 'diminish the power of England and increase in proportion that of France'.[9] Prior to Saratoga, however, the American military record had been mixed, and France had been cautious; now it was clear that the unorthodox combination of militiamen attacking from the sides and rear and Continental regulars standing in line could force the surrender of an intact British army. This was a previously unimaginable military catastrophe of high symbolic importance. France suddenly had the opportunity to greatly increase the American prospects for winning independence.

Vergennes and Franklin signed a treaty of military alliance on 6 February 1778. This first pact with a European power recognized the United States as a sovereign nation. It ensured the new nation of a steady supply of war materiel. Most importantly, the alliance brought French naval power into play as a check on the Royal Navy's monopolistic sway over the coastal waters and maritime approaches to North America. The British government retaliated by going to war with France on 11 March, and within two years England was fighting alone against a coalition of Holland, Spain and France. 'Thus, at Saratoga', writes British historian J.F.C. Fuller, 'the sword of Damocles fell, not only on Great Britain, but, because of the fervour of the American Revolution, upon the whole of the Western World.'[10] Saratoga and the continued existence of Washington's army presented the British with a stalemate in the northern and central colonies. Lord George Germain therefore decided on an offensive against the south, where Loyalists were in greater abundance. By capturing Georgia and the Carolinas – and continuing to occupy New York City – London hoped to frustrate the revolutionary leaders so thoroughly that they would agree to remain within a reformed imperial system. The campaign began in late 1778 and continued through 1780. Initially it went well for the British. The Americans surrendered two armies, one of them commanded by the victor of Saratoga, General Horatio Gates, who turned over his force on 16 August 1780.

Gates's loss proved fortuitous. Under Washington's prodding, Congress now placed Major General Nathanael Greene in command of the Southern Department. Rated as 'one of the greatest of small war leaders', Greene faced the perfect foil: Lord Charles Cornwallis, whose aggressiveness made him something of a rarity among British generals. By the time of Greene's appointment, the excessive brutality of the British soldiers and their loyalist allies was turning much of the population against the Crown. Guerrilla bands, 'the backwoodsmen of the Alleghenies', had begun to harass the British troops, and Greene exhibited an extraordinary ability to coordinate their attacks and those of militiamen with his field army's manoeuvres.[11] Unlike Washington, who would not 'divide the Army . . . into detachments contrary to every Military principle', Greene broke his into segments.[12] He lured the pursuing Cornwallis into doing the same with his units. In vain, 'Cornwallis lunged after Greene in a twisting, back-country campaign that wore down British strength and patience.'[13] Greene tersely described his operational strategy: 'We fight, get beat, rise and fight again.' He commonly ran 'as fast forward as backward, to convince our Enemy that we were like a Crab, that could run either way'.[14]

By June 1781 Cornwallis had given up the chase and moved his campaign from the Carolinas to the sea coast and then north into Virginia, hoping still for a Loyalist uprising. At that point General Sir Henry Clinton, his nominal superior based in New York, ordered him to the coast so that he could send reinforcements from his army to New York, which British intelligence believed Washington and the French would soon attack. Refusing to detach soldiers from his army, Cornwallis marched his army of 7,000 men to Yorktown, Virginia. With the Marquis de Lafayette's 5,000-man contingent of Continentals nipping at his heels, Cornwallis established a defensive position where he could communicate with the Royal Navy, which could carry him safely out of harm's way so long as it commanded the offshore waters. In this manner, Nathanael Greene's unorthodox warfare, intended only to expel the British from the Carolinas, had driven a British army to the brink of a disaster that would end what had become a war for American independence.

Yorktown resonates through American history as George Washington's greatest triumph, but it was the French naval connection rather than his own calculations that drew him there instead of to the main British position in New York City. By 1780 Washington, more than any other colonial war leader, had come to understand that a conclusive military victory over the British depended on achieving at least transitory command of the seas. 'In any operation, and under all circumstances,' he wrote, 'a decisive naval superiority is to be considered as a fundamental principle, and the basis upon which every hope of success must ultimately depend.'[15]

The rebels lacked the resources to build, equip and man a fleet of warships, so Washington turned to his allies. In early 1781 he thought that French men-of-war might establish temporary supremacy over the Royal Navy off New York City. However, French Admiral Comte de Grasse and French General Comte de Rochambeau saw Cornwallis's army at Yorktown as the more promising target, in part because its southerly location would facilitate de Grasse's quick return to the West Indies once the hurricane season ended in the autumn. Persuaded by his comrades-in-arms, Washington joined them in drawing up a plan to trap Cornwallis between the Franco-American armies and de Grasse's fleet at the mouth of the Chesapeake. It was a bold stroke, and it succeeded in September and October 1781 because of allied good luck and countervailing mismanagement by the British in New York.

De Grasse, sailing from the West Indies, had the good fortune to arrive when there were no Royal Navy warships in the Chesapeake. He disembarked 3,000 men and supplies to aid Lafayette, who was barely containing Cornwallis until Rochambeau and Washington could arrive with 6,000 more soldiers. Surprised at anchor by British Admiral Graves's small fleet, de Grasse fought them off in the inconclusive and poorly conducted Battle of the Chesapeake on 5 September. On 10 September another French fleet arrived with eight ships of the line, siege artillery and military stores. Outnumbered and outmanoeuvred, Graves sailed for New York; Cornwallis was cut off from reinforcement or escape by sea; Washington and Rochambeau, now commanding more than 16,000 men, arrived on 17 September. They began preparations to annihilate Cornwallis's army.

A month later, on 17 October 1781, the fourth anniversary of Burgoyne's surrender at Saratoga, Cornwallis repeated his countryman's sad act. He sent a note to Washington proposing 'a cessation of hostilities for twenty-four hours . . . to settle terms for the surrender'.[16] Rochambeau and Washington agreed. Cornwallis had saved his army to fight another day, in another war. Except for a few military formalities and some intense diplomatic negotiations in Paris and London, the American phase of this war was finished. The men who first took up arms in 1775 now had to cope with the consequences of their successful insurrection.

UNINTENDED CONSEQUENCES

After an eight-year-long war, and the loss of around 25,000 American lives, in April 1783 British and American representatives signed the Treaty of Paris granting independence to the United States. On 19 April, eight years to the day after the militiamen ambushed the British regulars at Lexington, all hostilities ceased. A colonial people had been transformed by war into a sovereign people, and the consequences were profound at every level. The former colonists now had to maintain military security throughout their spacious segment of North America. They intended to trade freely with all the nations of Europe, and they insisted on sending their merchantmen into the Mediterranean despite the dangers posed by the Barbary 'pirates' of North Africa. The newly independent people also expected to trade within the British Empire, where formerly their merchant vessels had been welcomed. Very quickly it became apparent that the weak and decentralized government of the Articles of Confederation could not guarantee safety on the frontiers, could not conduct foreign policy with unity and coherence, and could not protect United States merchant vessels and the men aboard them from assault by the North Africans. These crippling political, economic and military-naval weaknesses had not been anticipated in 1775, or even in 1783.

A solution was sought in the Constitution of 1787, an enabling document that strengthened the central government at the expense of the states' partial autonomy. Upon ratification of the Constitution in 1789, a new federal government was seated in Philadelphia, with George Washington as the first president of the United States of America. His inauguration coincided with the totally unexpected French Revolution, the result of which would be more than two decades of almost uninterrupted war between France and Great Britain. This desperate Anglo-French war presented the new constitutional government of the United States with insurmountable problems in the arenas of self-respect as a nation state, military-naval security and commercial expansion.

Unintended consequences had materialized even before the signing of the Treaty of Paris in 1783, formally ending the conflict. Benjamin Franklin, John Adams and John Jay, the three US diplomats entrusted with negotiating the treaty, violated their instructions of Congress forbidding them to sign a treaty with Britain without French consent. By negotiating independently of Vergennes they gave the British a chance to drive a wedge into the Franco-American alliance, the continued existence of which would soon threaten the United States with unwanted entanglements in European diplomatic and military machinations. A separate peace treaty with the British also enabled the three Americans to minimize French and Spanish claims to any part of the broad territorial domain stretching north to the St Lawrence River and Great Lakes, westward from the Appalachians to the Mississippi River, and southward to the top of Florida. British recognition of American independence in the preliminary and final treaties of 1782 and 1783 in effect consecrated a status already accepted by France in the treaty of alliance of 1778. Vergennes, a master of duplicitous diplomacy, told the Americans they had 'managed well'.[17] The trick now was to manage the new nation in the face of unprecedented and unanticipated conditions.

The immediate unintended consequence of the initial hostilities was the severing of colonial ties with Great Britain. A number of closely related unexpected outcomes followed. The first was the failure of Britain's northernmost colonies in Canada to join with the thirteen colonies in driving the British from North America to gain independence and form a unified new nation. What eventuated, in fact, was to be repeated in all future wars: repressive measures were introduced against dissenting voices. Of the 2.5 million people who made up the population of the thirteen colonies, around half a million remained loyal to the Crown. Loyalists who took up arms, estimated at around 60,000, and those who refused to swear allegiance to the rebel cause, as was demanded in almost all colonies, were imprisoned, confined in detention camps, tarred and feathered, summarily deported, and had their property confiscated. Thousands were murdered, and following the end of the conflict many thousands more fled to open up new settlements in Canada rather than face the persecution that awaited them in the newly liberated democratic United States.

Perhaps the most disturbing unintended consequence of the war for the former colonists was that they discovered that American shipping remained subject to the same restrictive British Navigation Acts that had prompted the war. Not only that, leaders of the newly independent nation found that United States ships were the prey of the French as well as the British when war broke out between those two countries in 1793. They also felt obliged to embark upon an unintended series of naval operations to protect US traders who were being attacked by pirates off the Barbary Coast at the mouth of the Mediterranean.

The achievement of independence brought unintended consequences. One of the most celebrated in the United States was the transformation of a group of ideologically driven insurgents into national heroes. These leading participants have assumed the status of demi-gods in the pantheon of heroes of US history. They have gained iconic status representing public virtue, political wisdom, statesmanship and heroism. They are viewed as embodying freedom in the civil religion that constitutes United States nationalism. However, the iconic status of the participants, and the central place the war for independence occupies in the foundation myths and national identity of the United States, has complicated the making of distinctions between the intended and unintended consequences of the war.

The Founding Fathers (or Parents) may have been demi-gods, but they had not anticipated the constitutional requirements of the new nation, nor did they manage them well at first. When the states' delegates met in Philadelphia to frame a constitution in 1787, few had imagined the enormity of the task of writing a constitution to fill these needs. At first they were content to rely upon constitutional arrangements that were in many respects the same as those that had existed prior to the conflict. Little had changed in terms of arrangements concerning the distribution of powers between the states and the federal government, local government powers, and power over foreign and military affairs. They simply moved the central government from London to Philadelphia, transferring the taxing powers to an American legislative body, the Congress. Furthermore, they failed to address a number of issues that haunted the United States for decades after. These unintended and inadequately addressed issues included the future of slavery, relations with Native Americans, the expansion of settlement into frontier areas and relations with Europe.

Nor did the framers of the Constitution envision a modern democracy, in the sense of political parties contesting elections.

Delegates wanted representatives to Congress to be elected, but they did not want factional or party divisions. Those who had fought against Great Britain believed that it was the corrupting influence of parliamentary parties that had misled George III. They wanted an elected powerful chief executive independent of a national legislature (to be two houses of Congress), unhindered by, and above, factional divisions. Political parties were unintended and did not emerge until 1800 with the election of Thomas Jefferson as president.

Few inside or outside the United States expected the territorial expansion or the remarkable economic and military achievements of the nation. This growth surpassed even the most optimistic of those who took up arms against Great Britain. There emerged what most commentators, domestic and foreign, came to define as a republican ideology that shaped the political, economic and social institutions of the new nation. Most of these changes were unexpected. The colonists initially had gone to war to prevent change rather than to promote it. They had sought to preserve the values and institutions of the past, not to initiate new ones. When asked by his wife, Abigail, to 'Remember the Ladies' who also sought to have a say in the laws under which they were governed, John Adams replied, 'As to your extraordinary Code of Laws, I cannot but Laugh.' He went on to lecture her that the revolutionary struggle had loosened all the traditional bonds of authority throughout the colonies. Children, apprentices, slaves, Indians and college students had all become 'disobedient' and 'insolent'. Everyone, including women, 'had grown discontented'. But, he assured his wife, 'General Washington and all our brave Heroes' would fight to resist the changes in domestic life being demanded.[18]

Few of his compatriots were more involved in drawing up the Constitution than John Adams. But few were more disillusioned by the outcome. Prior to the outbreak of war Adams had been a true believer. 'America', he had written as early as 1765, 'was designed by providence for the Theatre, on which Man was to make his true figure, on which science Virtue, Liberty, Happiness and Glory were to exist in Peace.' He believed that war, independence and the newly created Republic would astonish the world. Instead, the war had unleashed a whirlwind of unwanted passions throughout the continent. There was 'so much Rascality, so much

Venality and Corruption, so much Avarice and Ambition, such a Rage for Profit and Commerce among all Ranks' that he did not know where it would all end. By the 1780s, in Adams's view, the new nation was 'more Avaricious than any other nation that ever existed'. Any hope of an emerging Republic based on virtue had disappeared.[19]

Adams could blame himself in part for the way things had gone because he was a signatory to the Constitution, one provision of which was the provision for a standing army headed by the executive. This highly unintended consequence of the war and its aftermath was to shape American history significantly. Standing armies had been widely regarded as an evil, especially in a republic, and were condemned in the Declaration of Independence. Colonial experience of the British army stationed in the colonies following the end of the Seven Years' War in 1763 confirmed this view. However, the newly formed confederation was reluctant to abandon a peacetime army. The young nation immediately faced the need to defend itself without the aid formerly provided by the mother country. Following the British surrender at Yorktown on 19 October 1781, the French and the Spanish saw an opportunity to regain the eastern Mississippi Valley lost in earlier colonial wars. At war's end, George Washington argued for the establishment of a small, permanent, well-trained, adequately armed and properly led army educated in 'Military Art', in place of the voluntary, untrained, colonial militias. He had in mind the raising and support of a permanent standing army to protect Americans against foreign foes and domestic disorder. The Indians and the British would have to be conquered to the west, and American commerce would have to be defended on the oceans. The Constitutional Convention put no limit on the size of the standing army, requiring only that the legislative branch of the government would have to provide appropriations for it every two years.

The desirability of an army was brought home by another, unintended, incident. Not all colonists had benefited from the war. Many farmers and town merchants found themselves in debt as a result of inflation caused by speculation, paper money and a post-war economic slump. In 1786 an impoverished group in western Massachusetts led by a former army captain, Daniel Shays, raided the armoury at Springfield to forcibly close down the court system.

Shays's rebels were easily repulsed by a volunteer cavalry regiment. But by 1787 some state officials were lamenting that revolutionary violence seemed to have become a permanent condition, and that the population believed that power was seated 'in' the people. The confusion brought about by the breakdown of established social and political stability, together with conflict with Native Americans on the western frontier, further convinced many members of Congress that an army was necessary.

The states did not wish to give up their local militias, seeing in them protection against attack and a symbol of state sovereignty. The only solution was to allow the militias to remain but to place them under the control of the president as commander-in-chief. This was a novel and unexpected outcome: to have military responsibility and political leadership in the hands of the one person was a departure from the accepted pattern of British constitutional monarchy familiar to the colonists. The result was a constitution in which the president was both political leader and commander-in-chief. As commander-in-chief, the president swore to protect the states against 'foreign invasion and against domestic violence', an obligation that enabled him to authorize military intervention in the states to prevent anarchy or despotism. The exact extent of the president's war powers, the circumstances in which they could be used, the president's relationship as commander-in-chief with Congress and the states, and the boundaries between presidential power and that of the chief of the armed forces were not made entirely clear. Many believed that rather than fulfilling the aspirations of those seeking independence and freedom, the Constitution drawn up at Philadelphia merely replaced one threat of military dictatorship with another. At the beginning of the twenty-first century that threat remains a clear and present danger.

Somewhat unexpectedly, during the Paris peace negotiations ending the war, the British decided to abandon the northwestern frontier of the colonies. These lands were settled by veterans who were granted one-hundred-acre parcels in the region that later became the five states of Michigan, Ohio, Illinois, Wisconsin and Indiana. This opening of the West to settlement was another of the unexpected consequences of the war. The British had prohibited settlement in this territory in 1763, without avail. By the end of the war there were 25,000 settlers living on the frontier, and following the war thousands more migrated there. They would also require protection, of course, and within a day of the disbanding of the Continental Army on 2 June 1784, the Confederation Congress recommended the creation of a 700-man strong militia under the secretary of war to protect the Pennsylvania frontier and the Ohio River valley.

Another unintended consequence of independence concerned Native Americans. Among the complaints against George III in the Declaration of Independence was that he encouraged 'the merciless Indian savages, whose known rule of warfare is an undistinguished destruction of all ages, sexes and conditions', to attack colonial frontiersmen and women. The British had encouraged Native Americans to remain loyal to the Crown during the war. The majority of them did so because the British traded with the best and cheapest goods, and the colonists were constantly encroaching upon their lands. The Americans hoped that the Native Americans would remain neutral, and in 1775 the Continental Congress set up a committee to handle 'Indian affairs' along the New York frontier. However, each state negotiated its own arrangements with Native Americans, thereby preventing the development of a unified national policy. Reluctantly, the tribes began to take a more active role in the war, for the most part on the side of the British. American forces soon took to committing the same atrocities against their Native American enemies that they claimed were being used against them: scalping, indiscriminate murder, and the destruction of homes and crops. The officers toasted their victories: 'Civilization or death to all American savages.'[20]

In the treaty ending the war, Native Americans found that they had been betrayed by their British allies. There was no mention of Native American land rights, and the British granted the entire Northwest to the Americans. Native Americans continued to fight, but the European Americans saw the end of the war with the British as providing a new opportunity to move westward into Native American territory. Nor were the boundaries of the new nation formally agreed upon. They remained imprecise and ill-defined. Thomas Jefferson, always a dreamer, predicted, 'as a certainty that not a foot of land will ever be taken from the Indians without their own consent'. Secretary of War Henry Knox more accurately foretold the bloody future when he wrote to President

Washington: 'the Indians being the prior occupants, possess the right of soil. It cannot be taken from them unless by their free consent, or by the right of conquest in a just war.'[21] As historian Michael Rogin demonstrates, over the next thirty years American settlers and local governments found ways by intrigue, deception and violence to create the conditions for what they called a defensive and 'just war' – an all-out war – against Native Americans to acquire their territory. In doing so they not only engaged in the genocide of Native Americans but they ensured that conflict and hatred between European and Native Americans would continue for the next two centuries. Many of the policies adopted in later wars – widespread destruction of homes and crops, removal of populations, detention camps, torture, use of biological weapons, to name a few – were first employed against Native Americans.

Violence continued unabated on the frontier, and the British continually provoked Native Americans to resist the westward movement of European Americans. The armed forces provided by Congress were unable to maintain peace and law and order in the disputed and conflicted territories. As a result, in 1812, barely twenty-five years after the Constitutional Convention, the United States and Great Britain again went to war to settle the future of the frontier, including Canada.

TWO

THE SECOND WAR AGAINST GREAT BRITAIN, 1812–15

*If there was any disagreement between the Indians and our
Government, why were not discreet commissioners sent to treat
with them first, let them know that our Government was willing
to do them justice?*

Obadiah German, US Senator from New York, 13 June 1812[1]

The war of 1775–83, although it achieved American independence, left the new nation far from secure. The states jealously guarded their independence from the intrusion of federal control and, compared to the nations of Europe, the United States remained economically undeveloped and militarily weak. Periodically, in the years between 1783 and 1812, American merchant vessels had been attacked by ships of warring Britain and France, as each sought to enforce its blockades and trade embargoes and prohibit neutral countries from trading with its enemy. In addition, pirates from the Barbary Coast of North Africa demanded tribute from American trading ships entering the Mediterranean.

In 1812 President James Madison, prompted by congressional 'War Hawks' from the South, decided he would use British impressment as an excuse to launch an attack upon Canada and to force the Indian populations out of the northwestern frontier. In his message to Congress of 1 June 1812 seeking a declaration of war against Great Britain, Madison spelled out very specific and limited war aims. The war was to be fought to restore American maritime rights and put an end to impressment of American sailors by the Royal Navy. Madison began with the statement that since 1803 Britain had instituted 'a series of acts hostile to the United States as an independent and neutral nation'.[2] He then detailed continuing incidents and tension over British harassment of American shipping, the impressment of American merchant seamen into the Royal Navy, British interception of neutral (US) ships, and the arming of Indians who attacked American settlers.

British violations of the American flag on the high seas fell within the definition of war, he stated. Madison continued, 'thousands of American citizens, under the safeguard of public law and of their national flag, have been torn from their country and from everything dear to them.' He complained: 'Without the presence of an adequate force and sometimes without the practicability of applying one, our commerce has been plundered in every sea, the great staples of our country have been cut off from their legitimate markets, and a destructive blow aimed at our agricultural and maritime interests.' Americans knew that British warships required an enormous annual replacement for lost manpower during the war with France, which had been dragging on since 1793, but they were unsympathetic to the fact that in England's fight for survival, the 'wooden walls' of the Royal Navy stood as the principal bulwark against invasion from Napoleonic Europe.

During all this time, according to Madison, the United States had 'in vain exhausted remonstrances and expostulations', and had acted in a conciliatory manner. Finally, Madison blamed the British for the warfare 'just renewed by the savages on one of our extensive frontiers – a warfare which is known to spare neither age nor sex and to be distinguished by features peculiarly shocking to humanity.' He was, he said, forced to conclude: 'We behold, in fine, on the side of Great Britain a state of war against the United States, and on the side of the United States a state of peace toward Great Britain.'

The choice, he explained, was either to continue passively accepting these 'progressive usurpations', or 'to commit a just cause into the hands of the Almighty Disposer of Events' and use force in defence of the nation's rights. The president ended by stating that he was confident that 'the decision will be worthy of the enlightened and patriotic councils of a virtuous, a free, and a powerful nation'.

A bellicose Congress had previously voted for military preparations and, in April 1812, a 90-day embargo. The House of Representatives voted for war on 4 June, but the Senate debated for more than two weeks and did not sanction war until 17 June. In a regionally divided vote, Congress declared war on Britain the following day. The war lasted until August 1814, and a peace treaty was signed on Christmas Eve 1814 at Ghent, Belgium. The peace treaty, ratified by the Senate by a vote of 35 to 0 on 17 February

1815, in the view of one historian 'settled nothing of importance'.[3] The treaty called into question the wisdom of the United States' declaration of war in 1812, a declaration whereby the nation reached beyond its capacity to achieve its ends by force. The United States accepted a treaty that confirmed the status quo antebellum and did not so much as address its war aims.[4]

THE WAR

The War of 1812 was fought at sea and on the northern frontier. The naval battles on the Atlantic gave rise to heroic tales of glory, but the combined military-naval combat along the inland lakes had greater significance for the consequences of the war.

At the outbreak of the war the US Navy's fighting strength consisted of nine frigates mounting between 36 and 44 guns each and eight smaller vessels. The Americans were dwarfed by the Royal Navy's 1,000 plus ships, including 120 ships of the line and 116 frigates. Foolishly undaunted, the senior American naval officer, Commodore John Rodgers, convinced the secretary of the navy to arrange this meagre force into two squadrons, with Rodgers in command of one of them. The commodore set sail from New York immediately upon learning of the declaration of war, and for two months cruised the eastern Atlantic. He opportunistically hunted for a large British convoy from Jamaica, hoping for enough prize money to make himself wealthy. He vaguely had in mind the depredations of John Paul Jones along Britain's coasts during the Revolutionary War. Presumably secure at sea, the British Admiralty chose to ignore Rodgers, much as the US Navy would disregard Confederate cruisers in the Civil War.

Rodgers returned home in August 1812, empty-handed and embarrassed. The two squadrons were disbanded, and the frigates went to sea individually, in search of Royal Navy frigates to engage and merchant vessels to capture. In a series of hard-fought one-on-one engagements with British frigates in late 1812 Captains Isaac Hull, Stephen Decatur and William Bainbridge forced their opponents to surrender. Thereafter the Admiralty forbade its frigate commanders to engage in single-ship actions with American frigates. As a result, in the remainder of the war the only other notable frigate action occurred in the South Pacific, where two British vessels ganged up on Captain David Porter's 32-gun *Essex*, forcing Porter to strike his colours. Defeated but not disgraced, Porter and his single frigate had previously captured a dozen whaling vessels as prizes, hurting the profitable English industry and encouraging the expansion of the New England whalers. Madison realized that Porter's indirect support of a major maritime industry could help him defuse the virulent anti-war sentiment of New England, just as commerce raiding by us naval vessels and – more importantly – privately financed privateers could contribute to making the English mercantile class weary of the war. For Madison, however, the heart of the war was not on the high seas.

Fighting Great Britain provided an opportunity to establish dominance over the Native Americans of the old Northwest by ending what the president claimed was English incitement of armed Indian confrontations with Americans. In deciding for war, Madison was stirred by the recent battle at Tippecanoe Creek, in modern Indiana, where the territorial governor, William Henry Harrison, barely defeated the Shawnees. A warmonger from Kentucky depicted the way in which the Indians attacked Harrison's sleeping men at night: 'with the silent instruments of death, the war club, the scalping knife, the tomahawk . . .'.[5] By attacking and defeating the British in Canada, many War Hawks in Congress hoped to incorporate the vast region north of the Great Lakes into the American republic. This defensive-offensive objective and mercantile New England's opposition to the war explain why the most important early military campaigns of the War of 1812 took place in upper Ohio, in the Michigan Territory around Fort Detroit, and in the Canadian peninsula that separates Lake Erie from Lake Huron.

The first engagement, and the first us defeat, occurred at Fort Detroit on 16 August 1812. General William Hull, a veteran of the Revolutionary War, had marched across Ohio from Dayton to Fort Detroit at the head of an insoluble mixture of regulars, volunteers and militiamen. When he crossed over into Canada, the militiamen exercised their constitutional prerogative of refusing to sortie beyond United States territory. Hull lost his nerve. He retreated to Fort Detroit and wrote despairingly to the secretary of war that 'the entire northern hive of Indians [was] swarming in every direction'.[6]

Terrified by the likelihood of Indian mutilation and massacre of his accompanying family, Hull surrendered Fort Detroit and 2,000 well-emplaced men to British General Isaac Brock without a fight. 'It was', historian Geoffrey Perret notes derisively, 'the biggest capitulation between the Revolution and Bataan.'[7] Hull was court-martialled and condemned, but Madison commuted the death sentence.

The War Hawks' plans to annex Canada had been checked at Detroit, a little over a month after the declaration of war, but this setback did not mean the land war in the northwest was finished. Seeking to regain Detroit, President Madison ordered the Kentuckians and the 'Army of the Northwest' to march out from Fort Defiance in the Indiana Territory. The American commander, James Winchester, sought to do the president's will. He got as far as Frenchtown, on the lower east coast of the Michigan peninsula, where he was momentarily victorious. But on 22 January 1813 the British and Indians under Colonel Henry Prevost counterattacked. Winchester surrendered; Prevost promised all prisoners safe treatment and scurried eastward. The abandoned US prisoners of war were tortured and tomahawked to death by the Indians. Winchester's debacle had again shown that attacks in the northwest would not easily liberate Canada. While Winchester was meeting defeat, William Henry Harrison, his second-in-command, had lagged behind in order to exterminate as many Indians as possible; Harrison's reward was to be elected president of the United States in 1840, after running under the sanguinary sobriquet 'Tippecanoe'.

Two strategic realities were quickly dawning on Madison and his cabinet officers. First, naval control of Lakes Erie and Ontario was essential to prevent the British from defeating invasions by the United States. As a corollary, only a strong American naval presence could forestall a British thrust into Ohio and south toward the Ohio and Mississippi Rivers, a potential catastrophe that would cut the United States in two. Thomas Jefferson articulated the second reality with characteristic clarity: 'It would probably have been best, if it had been practicable in time, to have concentrated a force which could have seized on Montreal, and thus at one stroke, have secured the upper Province [Canada], and cut off the sap that nourished Indian hostilities.'[8]

The president now evinced a broad understanding of grand strategy. 'The command of the Lakes by a superior force on the water', he wrote, 'ought to have been a fundamental part in the national policy from the moment the peace [of 1783] took place.'[9] He chose Commodore Isaac Chauncey to wrest Ontario and Erie from the British. Chauncey headed north to Sackett's Harbour, on the eastern shore of Ontario, just south of the egress point of the St Lawrence River. In short order he established a naval base as his headquarters and initiated a shipbuilding frenzy. By November he had chased a handful of enemy warships into refuge in the British naval base at Kingston. Winter stopped him from doing more.

The British Admiralty at this point came to a Madisonian realization that the defence of Canada depended on control of the lakes. Their lordships ordered 30-year-old Captain Sir James Lucas Yeo to take command of the small fleet at Kingston. He arrived in May 1813 and immediately began a shipbuilding duel with Chauncey. The naval race lasted until the war's end, at which time each side was constructing line-of-battle ships mounting nearly as many guns as Horatio Nelson's legendary HMS *Victory*. There was to be no decisive naval battle on Ontario, but by per-petually contesting the British for mastery of the lake Chauncey prevented its use as a route for supply of the English soldiers and Indians to the west, or as an avenue of military approach to upstate New York.

On 10 September 1813 American naval superiority on Erie was dramatically established by 27-year-old Master Commandant Oliver Hazard Perry. Perry's opposite number, Captain Robert H. Barclay, was a one-armed veteran of Trafalgar. Barclay's squadron numbered fewer ships with less firepower than Perry's, but the Briton was compelled to seek battle in hope of ending the American interdiction of the maritime supply lines that sustained the British forces occupying Detroit and the invading British army attacking along the Sandusky River in Ohio. Barclay found Perry at Put-in-Bay on the morning of 10 September 1813, and the squadron action began at 11.45 am. In early afternoon Barclay surrendered on board the *Niagara*. Perry sent a message to the secretary of the navy evan-gelically reporting: 'It has pleased the Almighty to give to the arms of the United States a signal victory over their enemies on this lake.'[10] The US Congress was not confused about whether the deity or man should receive credit. It authorized a gold medal for Perry and lesser ones for his men.

Small in scale, brief in duration and remote in geography, the Battle of Lake Erie had monumental strategic significance. It forced the British to withdraw from Detroit and northwestern Ohio, and it opened Canada to an American invasion. William Henry Harrison seized the opportunity. He occupied Detroit and pursued the retreating British northeastward into Canada, along the Thames River. On 5 October 1813, at the Battle of the Thames, he defeated a demoralized and numerically inferior British army. Harrison thereupon returned to Detroit. He had stung the British on their own territory; by leaving Canada he terminated the American offensive in the region. All along Harrison had been primarily interested in massacring Indians for the sake of security on the frontier, and at the Thames he had killed the very embodiment of Indian resistance. Tecumseh, the transcendent Shawnee chief and leader of an intertribal Indian confederation stretching from Canada to Florida, had fallen. His death removed the fiercest and most implacable opponent of American settlement between the Alleghenies and the Mississippi. It shattered the already shaky Anglo-Indian alliance, one of the root causes of Madison's decision for war in 1812. Coupled with the unanticipated failure to occupy Canada north of Lake Erie, the collapse of unified Indian resistance redirected the inexorable American migration more to the west than to the north.

After the victories of Perry and Harrison, the war's centre of gravity shifted to the east. For two years the Americans 'had overlooked the fact that the historic front door to Canada was to be found on Lake Champlain and not at Detroit or Niagara'.[11] Now it was too late to take the offensive along the Champlain-Richelieu River axis towards Quebec. On 4 April 1814 the Emperor Napoleon had abdicated his throne, and at the end of May Great Britain initiated a blockade of the entire United States coastline. British commanders prepared for offensive operations as the Duke of Wellington's veteran troops poured across the Atlantic from the Iberian Peninsula.

By August 1814 Lieutenant General Sir George Prevost had assembled an army of more than 11,000 men. The largest British force ever mustered in North America, Prevost's force was greater than the one that hapless John Burgoyne commanded in 1777, when he had attempted the same offensive from the St Lawrence up the Richelieu River toward Lake Champlain and the Hudson River Valley. As in Burgoyne's time, the lake held the key to the success or failure of a British invasion. If the British won control of Champlain their lines of supply and communications to Quebec would be inviolable; the Americans would be doomed. If US forces held the lake, they would retain New York. Prevost decided to await a naval victory before assaulting strategically located Plattsburg and the surrounding forts. The army beheld a stunning defeat of a Royal Navy squadron inflicted by a superb young American tactician, Thomas Macdonough.

The battle began very early on the morning of 11 September 1814, and soon became a melee, as was usually the case in the age of sail. The British struck their colours at 10.45 am. Prevost witnessed the Royal Navy's humiliation from a high point above Plattsburg. He ordered his army to halt its advance.

Macdonough's brilliant accomplishment approached Perry's in strategic importance, but it did not surpass it. America's foremost advocate of fleet engagements and command of the seas, Captain Alfred Thayer Mahan, later wrote, 'The battle of Lake Champlain, more nearly than any other incident of the War of 1812, merits the epithet "decisive".'[12] The English government offered the military command of Canada to the venerated Duke of Wellington. He declined: 'That which appears to me to be wanting is not a General . . . but a naval superiority on the lakes . . . The question is whether we shall acquire this naval superiority. If we can't, I shall do but little good in America . . .'.[13] As a matter of strengthening US national defence, therefore, the victory at Lake Champlain takes top honours. But as a purely defensive contest it did nothing to further the objective of taking Canada, which Jefferson and others thought should result from operations in this theatre.

While Macdonough was saving New York, the British were sacking Washington, DC. On 24 August, in retaliation for an earlier American burning of two Canadian cities, the redcoats torched the White House and Capitol. The conflagration was accentuated by the commander of the nearby Washington Navy Yard, who destroyed two new US warships to keep them out of English hands. Satisfied by their ability to strike at will, British Admiral Alexander Cochrane and Major General Robert Ross retired to their ships and headed farther up the Chesapeake to attack Baltimore. Maryland's major seaport was a notorious haven for privateers. At a time when the politically decentralized United States was economically dependent on overseas trade, the loss of Baltimore would be far more crippling than the destruction of the national capital. The attack failed because the British could not overwhelm Fort McHenry, which protected the city. Admiral Cochrane withdrew and sailed to the Royal Navy's base at Kingston, Jamaica, to refit and reorganize. His next target would be New Orleans, the choke point regulating the entire agricultural export trade of the Mississippi River.

Cochrane arrived at Kingston on 1 November 1814. Wasting no time, he revitalized his sailors, replenished his ships, embarked several thousand soldiers, and sailed for New Orleans. The army's commander, Lieutenant General Sir Edward Pakenham, was a brother-in-law to the Duke of Wellington. Conditioned by European warfare to think in terms of massed frontal attacks, Pakenham adopted the strategy he knew best. He assembled a large force of soldiers and attacked the defending American army en masse. His opponent, Andrew Jackson, transformed Pakenham's traditional mode of operations into a fatal error. Jackson had enlisted a polyglot force including free blacks from San Domingo and pirates of the infamous Jean Lafitte clan. More to the point, perhaps, Jackson commanded fierce Kentucky and Tennessee sharpshooters who would unleash a torrent of precision rifle fire on the advancing British.

Early on the morning of 8 January more than 5,000 redcoats marched through marshy terrain straight towards Jackson's 4,700 Americans. Shielded by an earth-and-log barricade and a canal, the riflemen met the advancing British infantry with fusillade after deadly fusillade. Within an hour 2,000 British soldiers had fallen, Pakenham was cut in half by a cannon ball, and his next two senior officers were severely wounded. A truce was called to bury the dead, and the British army withdrew to the sanctuary of Cochrane's ships. The British never again attacked United States soldiers anywhere in North America.

The Battle of New Orleans cost the Americans thirteen casualties and elevated Jackson to the status of America's leading military hero. In 1828 he was elected president of the United States. As for its effect on the war, the battle had none. On 24 December 1814, unbeknownst to Jackson or Pakenham, American and British negotiators meeting in Ghent, Belgium, had signed a treaty of peace. The US Senate approved it on 17 February 1815.

UNINTENDED CONSEQUENCES

The most remarkable unintended consequence of the War of 1812 was that it achieved none of its proclaimed goals. The efforts by the Madison administration to redress its maritime grievances against Great Britain by the use of armed force in 1812 was transformed by the ensuing war into an attempt to annex Canada. Neither goal was achieved. Instead, the war accentuated tensions between the nation's sectional interests, which threatened the Union. The war glorified the resort to arms, sanctified the nation's military heroes and strengthened the power of the central government. It unleashed an insatiable drive for more territorial expansion and destroyed any lingering chance there might have been for a non-violent resolution to borderland issues with Native Americans and foreign nations. The appalling legacy of the genocidal policy adopted towards Native Americans lives on today, as does the residual border hostility between Mexico and the United States.

The Treaty of Ghent only indirectly addressed the issues raised by Madison, yet the president and the Senate ratified the treaty, and the war was widely praised at home as a victory for the United States. The treaty did not, however, put an end to the practice of impressment or blockades. Instead, it was peace in Europe that eliminated Britain's need to blockade and impress; there would not be another major European war until 1914. The Treaty of Ghent did not compensate the United States for its losses. Nor did it add any territory to the United States. It nevertheless preserved the sovereignty of the United States. In view of how badly the war had been going in August 1814 – US credit had collapsed, the British had occupied Pensacola and burned Washington, the northeastern states had declared their neutrality – this was a major achievement.[14]

A key intention of fighting against Great Britain during the years 1812 to 1814 was to expel the British from North America, conquer Canada and incorporate it into the United States.

Attacking Canada was also seen as one way of forcing British compliance with Washington's demands to respect its maritime rights. But few in the United States or Great Britain really wanted a war, and neither the American political nor military leaders grasped the full extent of their own national goals. As a consequence, the war failed to force the British to give up Canada, and the United States remained vulnerable to invasion from the north. Despite an increase in size authorized immediately after the cessation of hostilities in 1814, neither the army nor the navy was sufficient to defend the nation's boundaries if attacked by Great Britain.

The foreign threat was not the only one left unresolved by the war. It had created considerable disunion within the United States. Madison's rallying cry of free trade and freedom of the seas appeared to favour the interests of coastal merchants. However, the prospect of war appealed more to frontier settlers looking covetously at fertile land in Ontario, and to Southerners who wanted to take over Florida from Spain. In fact, the conflict was bitterly opposed by the New England states. The restrictions on trade nearly devastated its maritime-based economy; by the time the war concluded at the end of 1814 the region was on the brink of secession. Beginning in December 1814 delegates from five states (Massachusetts, Rhode Island, Vermont, New Hampshire and Connecticut) held a series of meetings in Hartford, Connecticut. Profoundly unhappy with the war's destruction of their maritime commerce and the administration's military blundering, they rightly felt that the Federal Government was unable to protect them from British attack. In a direct challenge to the Constitution, the delegates at the Hartford Convention proposed that the states should assume their own defence and 'a reasonable portion' of taxes raised by the United States Government should be retained by the states for defensive purposes.[15] Luckily, the war ended within weeks, but the spectre of dissolution of the Union had been raised, an unintentional consequence of the war that would re-emerge with deadly virulence in 1861.

Facing intense domestic criticism, Madison immediately ratified the Treaty of Ghent. To put the best face on what was far from a military victory, on 4 March 1815 he issued a proclamation calling for a day of thanksgiving. The president grandiloquently wrote: 'He [God] reared them [the United States] into the strength and endowed them with the resources which have enabled them to assert their national rights and to enhance their national character.'[16] Madison believed the United States had been successful in at least 'asserting' its national rights. The offensive British 'Orders in Council', imposing blockades, and impressments were discontinued. As that was what the US had sought, the administration was satisfied. Madison was also aware that Britain relinquished its initial demand that the United States cede nearly a third of its territory to create an Indian state. The 'peace', he believed, was honourable. In securing from Great Britain a more complete recognition of her political independence and power, the United States had rebuffed British claims and demands. One historian has noted: 'the War of 1812 thus passed into history not as a futile and costly struggle in which the United States had barely escaped defeat and disunion, but as a glorious triumph in which the nation had single-handedly defeated the conqueror of Napoleon and the Mistress of the Seas.'[17]

Enhanced chauvinism, ambitious jingoism and patriotism were unintended consequences of the war. These popular currents were fostered by President James Monroe (1817–25) in what has been dubbed the 'era of good feelings'. After 1815, historian Bradford Perkins argues, the United States displayed an assertive foreign policy and posed a major threat to any European power with interests in the western hemisphere.[18] The war had drastically altered the course of American history.

In other areas of the world the United States had not increased its stature, as was demonstrated by one important matter covered by the Treaty of Ghent but not mentioned by Madison in his war message. By the terms of Clause X of the treaty both parties agreed to 'use their best endeavours' to abolish the traffic in slaves stretching from Africa to the New World.[19] The British Parliament had outlawed the Atlantic slave trade in 1807, and the United States Congress had done likewise in 1808. However, rising cotton production in the South, and a huge increase in demand for Cuban sugar and Brazilian coffee, expanded the market for slave labour. But the small American navy lacked the power and desire to enforce the legislation. Nor was the United States ready to cooperate with Great Britain against the slave trade. Britain was far in advance of the United States in interdicting slave traders: British warships enforced the 1807 Parliamentary act by conducting routine patrols in African waters. Following the War of 1812, London continued to insist on its right to search American transports for cargoes of slaves. It was generally believed throughout the United States that the practice constituted a thinly disguised obstruction of legitimate American trade with Africa; it definitely impeded cooperation between United States and British African naval squadrons from 1820 to 1861.

At home, the war had completely transformed the United States from a barely self-sufficient agricultural country guided by Enlightenment principles into a rapidly changing nation with a moderately strong military, a reasonably centralized government, booming cities, high taxes and finance capitalism, and the emergence of a dominant ideology of fundamentalist Christianity. Manufactures had grown in the three years of the war as much as they had in the previous twenty years. The northwest frontier was more secure, the fear of attack from Native American buffer states under foreign control had evaporated. Settlers would be protected by regularly paid soldiers. Speaking of the transformation the war had brought to the United States, Geoffrey Perret concludes: 'There was hardly a corner in American life in 1815 that did not give off a whiff of gunpowder.'[20] This was certainly true on the southern frontier.

The War of 1812, like the Revolution, had included a massive assault upon Native Americans. Because most people in the United States viewed Native Americans as incorrigible and non-reformable savages, the assault continued and intensified after the war. The US Army ostensibly protected both frontier farmers and Native Americans from reciprocal and vengeful attacks. In fact, however, the army invariably provided the white settlers with a military advantage over the Native Americans, who no longer had British allies. One historian, Russell Thornton, claims that the United States fought more than 40 Indian wars from 1775 to 1890, reportedly resulting in the deaths of some 45,000 Native Americans and 19,000 European Americans.[21]

The war weakened the resistance of Native Americans in the northwest and in the south; in so doing it unintentionally provided tremendous political benefits for those who fought and survived. Among the offices subsequently held by veterans of the Battle of the Thames River were the presidency of the United States (William H. Harrison), the vice presidency, three governorships and lieutenant governorships, four seats in the US Senate and twenty in Congress. General Andrew Jackson emerged as the towering war hero, equal in public esteem to George Washington, and destined for the presidency in 1829. These men made their careers at the cost of 2,200 American lives lost in the conflict.

The subsequent Indian wars witnessed an unexpected adoption of a genocidal policy of total annihilation of Native Americans that intensified throughout the nineteenth century as the United States fought many wars to gain title to Native American lands. In addition to the use of infantry and cavalry in direct hostilities against Native Americans, the US Army employed germ warfare, the destruction of crops and houses, ethnic cleansing involving the transfer (removal) of entire communities, and the massacres of women and children to overcome Native American resistance to American expansion into their territories.

In the period immediately following the War of 1812 the policy of removal, if not extermination, of Indians was most ruthlessly carried out by Andrew Jackson. The Treaty of Ghent required the return of Creek territory ceded in the Treaty of Fort Jackson, signed on 9 August 1814, which had brought the war against the Creek Nation to an end. The Creeks had ceded 23 million acres of land in present-day Alabama and Georgia to the United States. However, Jackson, at the time a major general of the Tennessee militia, disregarded a directive from the secretary of war, and refused to return Creek land. That was not entirely the end of the story. On 22 March 1816 the United States signed and ratified a treaty with the Cherokees acknowledging that the Creeks had unlawfully ceded Cherokee land in the Treaty of Fort Jackson. Jackson once again refused to return the land. In a letter to Secretary of State James Monroe on 12 May 1816, Jackson asserted that the Cherokee Nation 'never had the least semblance of claim' to the disputed territory. In 1818 he once again threatened the Cherokees with war. His threat persuaded them to sign a treaty ceding two million acres.[22]

This extortionate treaty inaugurated Jackson's ultimate 'solution' to the 'Indian problem', which he thereafter aggressively pursued: removal of all southern Indians. At least 6,000 Cherokees were relocated in lands west of the Mississippi within two years after the signing of the treaty. In the same year, 1818, in the First Seminole War, Jackson invaded Florida, taking control of Spanish forts and executing two British nationals. He invaded and took over the Spanish fort at Pensacola, Florida. This action heightened international tensions, and the United States feared another war with Britain. Afterwards, Jackson was accused of acting without authorization and threatening the peace of the United States.[23] He nonetheless maintained a similar policy of terrorist threats directed against the Chickasaws the same year. In 1820 Jackson threatened the Choctaws that if they did not accept a treaty their 'nation will be destroyed'. They signed a pact on 20 October 1820. Jackson had set the United States on a course of expansion through Indian removal that he would accelerate as president (1829–37). The brutal sweep would carry Americans westward toward Texas and war with Mexico.

THREE

THE WAR AGAINST MEXICO, 1846–48

It is our unparalleled glory that we have no reminiscences of battle fields, but in defence of humanity, of the oppressed of all nations, of the rights of conscience, the rights of personal enfranchisement.
James L. O'Sullivan, 'The Great Nation of Futurity'[1]

The war against Mexico has been somewhat neglected by Americans. In large part, this is because there was and remains a certain moral uneasiness about the origins, conduct and outcome of the war. If one overlooks the invasion of indigenous lands and incursions into Canada during the War of 1812, the war against Mexico was the first war fought by the United States on foreign soil, and it was a war of conquest. The inescapable feeling lingers that a general settlement might have been reached with Mexico that would have achieved the goal of acquiring California without a war had President James K. Polk been more patient. It was also a war during which the United States helped bring about 'regime change' and left the enemy nation mired in a long period of political instability that lasted another half-century. Finally, the war was badly mismanaged. In those and other respects, the Mexican War resonates with the present conflict in Iraq.

The battles were relatively small, involving relatively few numbers of troops, and the war was short. The fighting, however, took a heavy toll. In terms of casualties the Mexican War was, proportionally, the deadliest war the United States has ever fought. According to historian John S. D. Eisenhower, US forces suffered a cumulative mortality rate of 153.5 per thousand troops per annum, as contrasted with 98 per thousand for the Union in the Civil War.[2] More than 42,500 regular army troops fought in the war, with an additional 73,500 others in volunteer units. Total US casualties, including those who died of disease, amounted to more than 11,900. Almost 10,000 troops deserted despite the threat of, or perhaps because of, severe floggings with rawhide whips.

Fighting the war cost $58 million, plus $15 million paid to Mexico under the treaty. All this was quite unexpected by the Polk administration, which had anticipated a quick and easy war.

The war against Mexico resulted from a failure peacefully to resolve long-standing differences with Mexico over the future of Texas – and California. The commencement of war in April 1846 was actually an indirect consequence of the Battle of San Jacinto, a small, sharp encounter between Texans and Mexicans that took place late in the afternoon of 21 April 1836, less than two months after Texas had declared its sovereign independence. During the early 1830s the Mexican government had unsuccessfully sought to prevent Texas from separating itself from Mexican rule. Following the engagement at San Jacinto, on 5 May the victorious Texan Sam Houston forced the defeated Mexican General Antonio Lopez de Santa Anna to sign the Treaty of Velasco, by which Mexico recognized the independence of Texas and the Rio Grande as the border between the two states. That was a fateful decision for Mexico, because previously the more easterly Nueces River had been considered the western boundary of the Mexican state of Texas. Subsequent to – and despite – the Treaty of Velasco, the Mexican government continued to insist that the line of demarcation between newly independent Texas and Mexico remained the Nueces River. This stance would provide an American president with the pretext for provoking war with Mexico.

At first the United States was happy to acknowledge the independence of Texas : on 3 March 1837, the last day of his presidency, Andrew Jackson signed a congressional resolution so doing. But by early 1845, Congress voted by joint resolution to annex the fledgling republic. By this vote, Congress accepted the Texas claim that its border was the Rio Grande, not the Nueces. On 4 July 1845 a Texas convention voted to accept the possibly unconstitutional invitation extended by Congress to enter the Union, despite repeated warnings from Mexico that it would regard such a step as an act of war. Texas was admitted to the Union on 29 December 1845.

James K. Polk of Tennessee, elected president in 1844, came into office determined to acquire California. He assumed that Mexico was so weak and poor it would readily give up its territory. In the hope of intimidating Mexico into agreeing to his proposals, Polk reinforced a naval squadron in the Gulf of Mexico and in mid-June 1845 sent General Zachary Taylor and some 3,500 volunteer troops to Corpus Christi on the Nueces River. Mexico, meanwhile, was in turmoil as rival militia factions fought to establish a stable government. In response to a request for negotiations from the then president, General Jose Joaquin Herrera, Polk sent an envoy, John L. Slidell, to Mexico in December 1845. But when Herrera discovered that Slidell had been instructed to offer Mexico $40 million to purchase California and New Mexico, he refused to continue negotiations. (At that time, New Mexico included much of what is now the southwestern United States, not just the present state of New Mexico.) Herrera and General Mariano Paredes, who overthrew Herrera in January 1846, were determined to defend Mexico against US expansionist demands. They rejected Polk's offers. At that point Polk, encouraged by Slidell and a jingoistic and racist press, decided to engineer a situation he knew would almost certainly provoke Mexico to war. In mid-January 1846 he ordered Taylor to move his troops to 'positions on or near the left bank' of the Rio Grande.

President Polk claimed the move was a defensive measure. He was persuaded to act, in part at least, by the urging of an exiled Mexican, Colonel Atocha, representing exiled former President Antonio Lopez de Santa Anna, who told Polk that, if faced with US military pressure, Mexico would capitulate. Democratic newspapers in the United States applauded the president's action. Whig newspapers said that the movement was an invasion of Mexico rather than a defence of Texas. Mexican officials protested the movement of the US troops to the Rio Grande, stating that it was Mexican territory. The troop movements, they said, were an act of war. For almost a month US and Mexican soldiers kept their positions. While newspapers in Mexico called for war, General Pedro de Ampudia warned, 'If you insist in remaining upon the soil of the department of Tamaulipas, it will clearly result that arms, and arms alone, must decide the question.'[3] On 23 April 1846 Mexico declared that a state of war existed. Two days later, on 25 April, as Polk expected, hostilities broke out. Mexican cavalry attacked a small US contingent on the northern side of the Rio Grande, killing eleven soldiers and capturing several others. Taylor notified the president that war had begun. News of this skirmish reached Washington on 9 May. With the unanimous endorsement of his cabinet, Polk sent a disingenuous war message to Congress on 11 May; war was declared two days later.

In his message to Congress on 11 May, Polk outlined the 'deplorable state of relations between the United States and Mexico'.[4] The president stated that:

> after reiterated menaces, Mexico has passed the boundary of the United States, has invaded our territory and shed American blood upon American soil. She has proclaimed that hostilities have commenced, and that the two nations are now at war . . . As war exists, and, notwithstanding all our efforts to avoid it, exists by the act of Mexico herself, we are called upon by every consideration of duty and patriotism to vindicate with decision the honour, the rights, and the interests of our country.

Polk's message recounted the history of relations between Mexico and the United States since March 1845. In what had become, and was to remain, the pattern of presidential addresses seeking congressional authorization for war, Polk told a story of persistent injuries suffered by the United States at the hands of an unreasonable, dictatorial regime. The culprit, in this case Mexico, refused repeated appeals by an aggrieved and innocent United States bent on avoiding conflict until at last it had no choice but to respond with force, thereby finding itself enmeshed in unavoidable warfare.

The president provided Congress with what he described as 'a succinct statement of the injuries which we had suffered from Mexico, and which have been accumulating during a period of more than twenty years.' He said that the issue was one of settling boundaries between the two states. At all times the United States 'had shown a readiness to regulate and adjust our boundary and other causes of difference with that power on such fair and equitable principles as would lead to permanent relations of the most friendly nature.' For that purpose the president had sent an envoy to Mexico to negotiate. However, 'The Mexican Government not only refused to receive him or listen to his propositions, but after a long-continued series of menaces have at last invaded our territory and shed the blood of our fellow-citizens on our own soil.'

There was, Polk continued, much more to the dispute than mere geographical lines in the ground – as President John Tyler had described the boundary in 1843. The security of Texas was at stake. Polk told Congress that he had ordered troops to occupy the left bank of the Del Norte (the present-day Rio Grande)

> to meet a threatened invasion of Texas by the Mexican forces, for which extensive military preparations had been made. The invasion was threatened solely because Texas had determined, in accordance with a solemn resolution of the Congress of the United States, to annex herself to our Union, and under these circumstances it was plainly our duty to extend our protection over her citizens and soil.

Polk denounced the Mexican government, stating that Mexico had 'repeatedly threatened to make war upon us for the purpose of reconquering Texas'. He added: 'In the meantime, we have tried every effort at reconciliation.' Despite his efforts to prevent it, he said, hostilities had broken out on 25 April, and so the two countries were, in effect, at war.

Polk's narrative, like all previous and subsequent 'carefully considered' presidential pre-war accounts of 'facts and opinions', was highly selective. It omitted as much as it included. In the first place, Polk's claim that the Del Norte was the boundary of newly annexed Texas was highly dubious. In the second place, Polk failed to mention that prior to his sending Taylor to the Rio Grande, Mexico had no intention of going to war with the United States over the border issue or over the annexation of Texas. Polk knew that. Taylor's presence opposite Matamoros was an act of war in itself and showed contempt for Mexico. As a further provocation, Polk had secretly ordered Commodore John D. Sloat to capture Californian ports if Mexico attacked Texas. In doing so he ignored the Congressional prerogative of acquiescing in warlike decisions made by the executive branch of the government.

Polk had two goals clearly in mind: acquiring the Mexican provinces of New Mexico and Alta (Upper) California, and extracting the government of Mexico's formal agreement to United States possession of Texas. A Jacksonian Democrat from Tennessee, Polk was sometimes referred to as 'Young Hickory'. No less avid an expansionist than his mentor, he ascribed to the racist dogma of 'Manifest Destiny', a popular ideology proclaiming that 'Providence' had allotted the North American continent to white Americans 'for the free development of our yearly multiplying millions'.[5] As with all politicians who see themselves guided by God's hand, Polk also understood the profit motive. By the 1840s California had long attracted Boston merchants trading in otter pelts and hides cut from cattle raised by the superb horsemen of quasi-autonomous California. The state was ripe for economic penetration and domination by the United States.

At 6.30 pm on 11 May 1846 the US House of Representatives overwhelmingly passed a bill authorizing President Polk to raise up a force of fifty thousand volunteers to prosecute the 'existing War between the United States and the Republic of Mexico' to a 'speedy and successful termination'.[6] The vote was 174–14 in favour of war. The fourteen who voted against the bill were chiefly northern anti-slavery Whigs led by John Quincy Adams. Twenty congressmen abstained. Opponents of the bill regarded the war as unconstitutional and fraudulent, improperly begun by Polk without Congressional approval in order to extend slave-holding territory. On 12 May the Senate voted 40–2 in favour of the bill: the next day Polk declared war.

THE WAR

The war was fought in two phases, first as a peripheral campaign to surround Mexico by land and sea, and in the process to take California. Secondly, when Mexico remained adamantly resistant to Polk's demands for its territory, the United States struck directly at the enemy's heart, occupying the national capital and forcibly changing regimes until it found one ready to agree to national dismemberment.

President Polk and his advisors mistakenly assumed that the United States would easily and quickly break the Mexican will to fight. In consultation with Secretary of War William L. Marcy and Major General Winfield Scott, Polk devised a strategy of attacking along the periphery rather than at the enemy's vital political centre. The US Army's principal field of operations was to be northeastern

Mexico, with Zachary Taylor in command. A smaller army would march through Santa Fe and into California. Simultaneously, the US Navy's Pacific Squadron would seize Monterey and other coastal cities. In the Gulf of Mexico the navy would establish a blockade of the Mexican coast and make harassing coastal raids. The Mexicans were expected soon to tire of the uneven contest and accept the American demands. These arrogant premises guided the conduct of the war from May until October 1846.

Taylor had begun his part of the campaign to dismember Mexico five days before Congress declared war. On 8 May, acting under a Mexican declaration of defensive war provoked by Taylor's move to the Rio Grande, Major General Mariano Arista attacked Taylor at a place called Palo Alto, near today's Brownsville, Texas. Arista commanded 6,000 regulars; the opposing US army was a composite of regulars and volunteers. After four hours of seeing his frontal charges bloodily repulsed by American artillery fire, Arista threw in the towel. He began to retreat, with Taylor in pursuit. The next day, at a dry wash of the Rio Grande called Resaca de la Palma, Taylor's men broke the Mexican line and a rout ensued. The Mexicans lost 600 men killed or wounded; United States casualties numbered 200. Taylor kept moving southward through Mexico, winning battles and occupying towns as he went: Matamoros on 17 May, Camargo on 14 July, Monterey in September, and Saltillo in November. Along the way he became a national hero and the likely 1848 presidential nominee of the Whig Party, many of whose members had opposed the war as an infernal machination of slave-owning Democrats. But Taylor's offensive in an area far removed from the Mexican capital had done nothing to advance Polk's war aims.

The US Army's second major offensive was intended to win possession of New Mexico and California. Under Polk's orders, Colonel Stephen Watts Kearny, a hardened veteran of the War of 1812 and the subsequent Indian wars, led 1,800 regulars and volunteers on a 700-mile forced march from Fort Leavenworth, Kansas, to Santa Fe, the political and trading capital of New Mexico. He arrived on 18 August. Unopposed, Kearny entered the city, got himself promoted to brigadier general, and established US civil governance with a territorial constitution. He headed west to seize California, only to learn that the state had already fallen into US hands. In July insurgent

Yankees and the US Navy had removed most of the state from Mexican jurisdiction, including the port city of Monterey, the capital of Upper California. The United States now physically controlled much of California, but the war was far from over.

While insurgents, soldiers and sailors were capturing California for Polk, the president was reconsidering his strategy, but not his territorial goals. After six months of fighting, the Americans had demonstrated that they could take Santa Fe and California. The army had penetrated northern Mexico and overwhelmingly won almost every battle; the navy had blockaded the coast of the Gulf of Mexico. What the United States could not do was coerce the intransigent Mexicans into recognizing the conquests by treaty. Until that happened, the territorial acquisitions remained outside the pale of international law. To compound Polk's distress, in the fall Congressional elections the Whigs gained control of the House of Representatives and were actively boosting General Taylor as their next presidential candidate. Taylor had to be brought to heel, as did the principal Mexican thorn in the Americans' side, General Antonio Lopez de Santa Anna. Charismatic and duplicitous, Santa Anna repeatedly deceived and bewildered the Americans with promises of concessions and peace. In late 1846 he was raising an army of perhaps 15,000 men with which he planned to attack Taylor.

Stirring this volatile brew of military success and political failure was Major General Winfield Scott, a highly regarded veteran and general-in-chief of the US Army. Since the war's beginning he had insistently pressed Secretary of War Marcy and President Polk to authorize him to emulate the 1519 invasion of Spanish conquistador Hernán Cortés. Scott wanted to make a large amphibious landing at Veracruz, on Mexico's east coast, and then march directly inland. He would seize the capital of Mexico City and dictate a peace legitimizing the US conquests. His plan represented a major reorientation of US strategy away from attacking the periphery to assaulting the political and military heart of the enemy. It made sense militarily. For Scott, it promised fame and possibly a Whig presidential candidacy of his own. Polk resented Scott's political ambitions, but he saw no better way to terminate a stalemated war. He approved the plan in late October and selected Scott as the commander on 19 November 1846.

A vainglorious soldier and meticulous planner, 'Old Fuss and Feathers' scrutinized every logistical and tactical detail of what would become the largest amphibious assault by the United States prior to the Pacific landings of World War II. His planning paid off. On 9 March 1847 Scott's specially designed 'surf boats' disgorged almost 10,000 men in successive waves. They faced no opposition, and there were no casualties. Scott regrouped his men and laid siege to the city from the landward side, while Commodore David Connor's Home Squadron maintained a blockade offshore. The city capitulated on 29 March, and Scott hastened to move inland to escape the pestilential yellow fever soon to blanket the coast and lowlands. He was headed for the enemy's centre of gravity.

Scott advanced along the mountainous 'national road' with never more than 10,000 soldiers, and he faced a determined opponent. General Santa Anna had been badly mauled when he attacked Taylor near the town of Buena Vista on 22 February, but in facing Scott he enjoyed the advantage of being able to erect strong defensive roadblocks along a narrow road. Santa Anna lost the first engagement in a mountain pass at Cerro Gordo on 12 April, but Scott was in operational extremis. About one-third of his veterans took off for home because their enlistments had expired; another 1,000 were seriously ill with fevers. Scott had only 7,000 men left, too few to garrison forts or depots along the road. He made two crucial decisions: he would await some 2,000 reinforcements commanded by Franklin Pierce, and he would cut himself from his base of supplies at Veracruz. Upon learning of the decision to live off the land, the Duke of Wellington said, 'Scott is lost . . . He can't take the city, and he can't fall back upon his base.'[7]

In August Scott began an offensive characterized by brilliant reconnaissance on the part of young West Point graduates, such as Robert E. Lee, and by deft flanking movements. Santa Anna, who in May had become president of Mexico, was out-fought and out-manoeuvred. He lured Scott into an armistice that the somewhat gullible American thought was a prelude to capitulation. When Santa Anna resumed hostilities just outside the capital Scott fought one of his rare frontal battles, at the fortified castle of Chapultepec on the outskirts of Mexico City. Artillery fire, scaling ladders and pickaxes brought American troops triumphantly to the top of the castle; they raised the US flag; Santa Anna decided not to fight further for his city and withdrew to Guadalupe Hidalgo on the outskirts.

The next day, 14 September 1847, Scott's army swarmed into the capital; he set up headquarters in the national palace. For the first 36 hours the conquerors had to contend with guerrillas sniping at them from windows and roofs. The Yankees reacted mercilessly with grapeshot, and the resistance ceased. For the next six months Scott sat in occupation of Mexico's capital while his handmaiden, the diplomat Nicholas P. Trist, negotiated a peace treaty without achieving all that Polk wanted.

The Duke of Wellington expressed his awe. He declared Scott to be 'the greatest living soldier' and the campaign to be 'unsurpassed in military annals'.[8] The restrained and indirect way Scott fought from Veracruz to Mexico City became a model for military analysts repulsed by the excessive bloodshed characteristic of the Civil War and its twentieth-century counterparts. What these admirers of Scott have failed to publicize is that during his extended occupation of Mexico City he set a damning precedent for regime change. Subsequent generations of US military occupiers of foreign countries would not overlook this brutal facet of Scott's generalship.

UNINTENDED CONSEQUENCES

The Mexican War came to end with the Treaty of Guadalupe Hidalgo, signed on 2 February 1848.[9] Under its terms the United States was to purchase New Mexico and California for $15 million, and pay $3 million in damage claims that Mexico owed to American citizens. Mexico was to recognize the US annexation of Texas and the Rio Grande as the border with Texas. A final territorial adjustment between Mexico and the United States was made by the Gadsden Purchase in 1853. The United States' territory had been increased by a third. Few Americans, however, gained immediate economic profit from the conquered lands. What they thought they had gained was security, as their land now stretched from sea to shining sea.

The United States did gain 529,017 square miles at a cost of 48 cents an acre. Nevertheless, the territorial gains of the war that Polk had anticipated were far less than the success of US arms might have led the administration to expect. What the United States in fact had gained from the war was unintended: less territory than expected, a habit of paternalistically intervening in the internal affairs of Mexico, and a reluctance to compromise over the extension of slavery that would lead to a war that tore the nation apart. Quite simply, the Polk administration had seriously overestimated the impact of US military success and occupation on Mexico's determination to resist Washington's demands – much as the Bush Administration did following the invasions of Afghanistan and Iraq.

Despite the US military victories, the escalation of the war failed to produce the treaty desired by Polk. He had miscalculated the stubbornness of his enemy. United States military superiority and occupation could not force a Mexican government to negotiate seriously or enable the United States to impose its will on the defeated enemy. Military commander Winfield Scott resorted to the threat of regime change to achieve American demands. In January 1848 Scott promised to protect the new government of Jose Manuel de la Peña y Peña from revolution if it signed a treaty, threatening dire consequences if it did not. With Scott's promise of protection, the Mexican peace commissioners went ahead and signed the Treaty of Guadalupe Hidalgo on 2 February.

The two sides then worked out the details of who would rule the country after the cessation of hostilities while awaiting ratification of the treaty. Although Mexican generals had hoped for an armistice and resumption of power by the Mexican military, they acquiesced simply to a general suspension of hostilities. It was agreed that United States occupying forces would not interfere in elections for the Mexican Congress to be held on 2 April. Santa Anna was to be permitted to leave the country, and he departed Mexico on 5 May. Later that month the American occupiers indirectly shaped the Mexican government to their taste. In late May the Mexican Congress elected the candidate preferred by the United States, General Jose Joaquin Herrera, to the Mexican presidency. Herrera had favoured Texan independence prior to the war and had been willing to negotiate with Washington, but he had been deposed because of his willingness to give up Mexican territory.

Polk accepted the Treaty of Guadalupe Hidalgo, he told the cabinet, because it was 'made upon my own terms, as authorized in April last', and if he rejected it the probability was that 'Congress would not grant either men or money to prosecute the war'.[10] He sent the peace treaty to the Senate, which reluctantly voted 38–14 to approve it on 10 March 1848. It was accepted by the Mexican Congress on 25 May after a month-long debate. Ratifications were exchanged on 30 May, bringing the war to a formal end. The last United States troops left Mexico on 2 August.

The war had not gone as intended. In May 1846 Polk and his supporters had looked forward to a quick war and a successful peace achieved with the loss of few American lives. Although it enacted some appropriations bills for the fighting, Congress was not ready, and did not welcome, raising the men and money for a major war. In rhetoric that bore a strong resemblance to the tenor of debates during the Vietnam War, Polk devoted two-thirds of his annual message to Congress of 8 December 1846 to justifying the war. He sharply criticized the growing and articulate anti-war dissent as giving aid and comfort to the enemy. In turn, he was attacked for his 'artful perversion of the truth . . . to make people believe a lie'.[11] Polk was also berated for illegally strengthening executive power by approving the civil governments in New Mexico and California. In April 1847 the Massachusetts legislature denounced the conflict as 'a war of conquest, so hateful, in its objects, so wanton, unjust and unconstitutional in its origin and character, [that it] must be regarded as a war against humanity, against justice against the Union . . . and against the free states'.[12] On 3 January 1848, by a vote of 85–81, the House of Representatives approved a resolution declaring that the war was unnecessary and unconstitutionally begun, and calling for the immediate withdrawal of American forces from Mexico.

At the other extreme, Secretary of State James Buchanan and some in the War Department sought the acquisition of all of Mexico, but their goals were unrealized. Vice President George M. Dallas in January 1848 even proposed a toast to the New York State Democratic Convention to 'a more perfect Union; embracing the entire North American continent' (presumably including Canada). Some expansionists spoke of taking all of Mexico as a duty in order to redeem Mexico and to introduce republicanism and Protestantism.[13] By December 1847 the president had added transit rights across the Isthmus of Tehuantepec as one of the conditions for peace, but this too was omitted in the Treaty of Guadalupe Hidalgo.

Washington had not considered the long-term effect of the war on Mexican-US relations. Mexico regarded the war as an unwarranted invasion and resented attempts by the United States to influence its internal political affairs. To this day Mexico harbours a bitterness and resentment toward the United States as a result of the shame and humiliation inflicted upon Mexicans by the US invasion and occupation of their nation. For its part, over the past 150 years since the war the United States has not hesitated to disregard the territorial integrity of Mexico and assert its military supremacy over its southern neighbour whenever it has felt the need to do so. The most blatantly outrageous example of US military intervention for the purpose of regime change occurred in the presidency of Woodrow Wilson. In 1916 the arrogant Democrat sent 7,000 soldiers commanded by John J. 'Black Jack' Pershing 350 miles into Mexico on a wild and fruitless chase after the bandit hero and presidential aspirant Pancho Villa.

Domestically, the unintended consequences of the war were just as far-reaching and devastating. They culminated in the outbreak of the Civil War, the most catastrophic event in the history of the United States. The war against Mexico hastened the growing and increasingly evident divisions between rural, agricultural, slaveholding southern states and the more urban, industrial, free-trade northern states. It accelerated the growth of sectional hostilities between the two distinct entities, thereby challenging the future of the Union. Sectional and party differences over the possible admission of Texas and the conquest of Mexican territory had been brewing for years. So great was northern opposition to the creation of a new southern pro-slavery voting bloc in Congress should Texas annexation be approved, that in the early 1840s John Quincy Adams had declared that it would justify the dissolution of the Union.[14]

The Mexican War was, in reality, the first phase of the Civil War: the war against Mexico was provoked by a southern president; Major General Zachary Taylor and Major General Winfield Scott, who led the armies, were both from the South; the vast majority of the volunteer militiamen who fought the war were southern; the Texas Rangers were southern (obviously); and the war was fought to extend slavery. The acquisition of 1,193,000 square miles of new territory revived the most volatile issue in American politics at that time: would the new territories be slave or free? President Polk asked Congress for immediate permission to form territorial governments in California and New Mexico. But the question of slavery delayed quick Congressional action. In the summer of 1846 Pennsylvania Congressman David Wilmot had put forward the proviso that slavery should be excluded from any territory won from Mexico, but, although passed by the House of Representatives in 1846, and again in the succeeding four years, it was rejected by the Senate.

The discovery of gold in 1848 led to a tremendous increase in the population of California, which reached over 100,000 by 1849. California and New Mexico remained under US military rule, but that situation could not last. Tensions between North and South escalated dangerously. Southerners threatened secession should Congress pass the Wilmot Proviso into law. Texas even threatened to send a military force to enforce its border claims over land in the Colorado Rockies to prevent that territory from becoming one of free labour. Even in Congress, the threat of personal violence was never far beneath the surface and occasionally erupted.

A series of compromises, including a more stringent Fugitive Slave Act enforced by federal officials, was eventually worked out and passed by Congress in September 1850. California was admitted as a free state, while New Mexico (and Utah) remained territories, so the balance between Northern and Southern states remained unchanged. Upon passage of the Compromise of 1850, Daniel Webster wrote to a friend:

> I can now sleep of nights. We have passed through the most important crisis that has occurred since the foundation of the government, and whatever party may prevail, hereafter, the Union stands firm. Disunion, and the love of mischief, are put under, at least for the present, and I hope for a long time.[15]

Unhappily, the calm was not to last. Ideological and political battle lines had been drawn. A decade later they were transformed into military lines of battle in the most destructive war the United States has ever experienced.

FOUR

THE CIVIL WAR, 1861–65

There is many a boy here today who looks on war as all glory,
but, boys, it is all hell. You can bear this warning voice to generations
yet to come.
William Tecumseh Sherman, 19 June 1879, Michigan Military Academy[1]

Some wars have greater consequences – intended and unintended – than others. It is hard to consider any aspect of American life in the decade – or even in the generation – that followed the Civil War that was not in some way a consequence of that war. Newly elected minority President Abraham Lincoln failed to plan prudently for the outcome of a war when, on 15 April 1861, he issued a proclamation calling for 75,000 local militia to quell what he described as an insurrection against the government of the United States. Instead, approximately 230,000 enthusiastic volunteers responded to the president's call. Lincoln intended few of the things that transpired over the next four years, nor indeed over the next forty. He said publicly that he expected a short and limited war, although his general-in-chief, Winfield Scott, had already advised him that an army of 300,000 well-trained and well-led troops would take three years to conquer the Confederacy of southern states at a cost of hundreds of millions of dollars. Nevertheless, perhaps with the brevity of the Mexican War in mind, Lincoln went ahead and unleashed a conflict of unimagined brutality and destruction that reverberated throughout what remained the United States for the next century.

Lincoln went to war to retain the territory and resources of the southern states and to secure for the federal government the new territories to the west and northwest. The Civil War was not initially fought to free slaves or to attain equality for Black Americans. The war prompted the granting of freedom to African-Americans, but former slaves certainly did not achieve equality. The majority of white Americans in the United States of 1860 did not object to slavery. Most in the North and South – like most of the population in that other great nineteenth-century empire, the British – shared the prevailing racist view that Africans and other dark-skinned peoples were inferior to light-skinned Americans and Europeans. Supporters of the Union had not intended that African-Americans migrate to their states in the north; when the migration occurred they erected myriad barriers to deny freedmen their civil rights.

The causes of the conflict may have been purely domestic, but the war was nonetheless a war like those that preceded and followed it: one against a foreign foe. The Confederate States of America effectively constituted an enemy nation. In defeat, during Reconstruction, the Confederacy was treated as a defeated nation while being rebuilt and reincorporated into the United States of America. Lincoln contended that the southern states had never left the Union; since secession was an illegal act, the Union remained intact. Of course, because it caused deadly rifts between families, friends and states, the Civil War in many ways was quite unlike the wars fought against Great Britain or Mexico. But one feature the Civil War shares with all other American wars is that its unintended consequences far outweighed those envisaged by the leaders who initiated it.

The Civil War is the central event in American history. Not only did the Civil War destroy a way of life, it lives on in the memory and imagination of Americans today.[2] It does so because of the appalling number of deaths and devastation the war exacted, and because of the romance and excitement engendered by tales of the conflict, often recounted by the participants themselves. Writing in the mid-1990s, one historian noted that the toll of Civil War dead probably exceeds that of all other American wars combined. He observes that 2 per cent of the American population of 1860 were killed in the Civil War. According to James M. McPherson:

> The 6,300 men killed and mortally wounded in one day near Sharpsburg were nearly double the number of Americans killed and mortally wounded in combat in all the rest of the country's nineteenth-century wars combined – the war of 1812, the Mexican War, the Spanish-American War and the Indian wars thrown in for good measure.

The total death toll was more than 600,000, and the war cost more than $20 billion in destroyed property and military expenditures. If the United States suffered the same proportion of deaths in a war fought in the 1990s, McPherson adds, 'the number of American war dead would exceed five million'.[3]

Moreover, the war was an ideological one. The volunteers on both sides believed they were fighting for freedom. This added to the savagery of the war, and the unwillingness of both sides to end it before victory had been achieved. This prolongation was unexpected and unintended. Initially nobody thought the war would end up becoming a total, or even a long, war. In his second inaugural address Lincoln recalled that 'Neither party expected for the war the magnitude or the duration which it has already attained . . . Each looked for an easier triumph and a result less fundamental and astounding.'[4] The Union regarded suppressing the Southern insurrectionists, whom it believed to have temporarily taken over a few Southern states, more as a police action than a full-blown war. In his proclamation on 15 April 1861, declaring that war had begun following the assault by Confederate troops upon Fort Sumter in Charleston, South Carolina, Lincoln had promised Southerners that the 75,000 state militiamen that he federalized to quell the uprising would avoid 'any devastation, any destruction of, or interference with, property, or any disturbance of peaceful citizens'.[5]

Lincoln initially intended that the war should be a short one, but he quickly learned that the three-month term of enlistment for the militia was pure folly. By July 1861 he radically increased his request for troops to reflect battlefield requirements. The president stated to Congress: 'It is now recommended that you give the legal means for making this contest a short, and a decisive one; that you place at the control of the government, for the work, at least four hundred thousand men, and four hundred millions of dollars.' He described this request as modest, less than was asked for at the time of the War of Independence. He concluded: 'Surely each man has as strong a motive now, to preserve our liberties, as each had then, to establish them.' In considering the policy to be adopted for suppressing the insurrection, he added,

I have been anxious and careful that the inevitable conflict for this purpose shall not degenerate into a violent and remorseless revolutionary struggle. I have therefore in every case thought it proper to keep the integrity of the Union prominent as the primary object of the contest on our plan, leaving all questions which are not of vital military importance to the more deliberate action of the Legislature.

He concluded that although all 'indispensable means' should be employed to preserve the Union, 'We should not be in haste to determine that radical and extreme measures, which may reach the loyal as well as the disloyal, are indispensable.'[6]

Turning to the causes and nature of the conflict, Lincoln told Congress in July 1861 that southern leaders had been filling the minds of their people for the past thirty years with scandalous stories of grievances. He described the war as:

essentially a People's contest. On the side of the Union, it is a struggle for maintaining in the world, that form, and substance of government, whose leading object is to elevate the condition of men . . . to lift artificial weights from all shoulders . . . to clear the paths of laudable pursuit for all . . . to afford all an unfettered start, and a fair chance, in the race of life.

He conceded that the war had been precipitated by his election: 'Our popular government has often been called an experiment. It is now for them [the people] to demonstrate to the world, that those who can fairly carry an election, can also suppress a rebellion . . . that ballots are the rightful, and peaceful, successors of bullets.' More specifically, Lincoln blamed the war on Confederate military action. The last ray of hope for preserving the Union peaceably had expired with the first salvo. He stated: 'The assault upon, and reduction of, Fort Sumter was, in no sense, a matter of self defence on the part of the assailants. They well knew that the garrison in the Fort could, by no possibility, commit aggression upon them.' Lincoln described the issue facing the United States government in universal but highly focused terms. It embraced, he continued,

more than the fate of these United States. It presents to the whole family of man, the question, whether a constitutional republic, or a democracy – a government of the people, by the same people – can, or cannot, maintain its territorial integrity, against its own domestic foes. It presents the question, whether discontented individuals . . . [can] break up their Government, and thus practically put an end to free government upon the earth.

He raised a timeless question: 'Is there, in all republics, this inherent, and fatal weakness? . . . Must a government, of necessity, be too strong for the liberties of its own people, or too weak to maintain its own existence?' After viewing the matter, he was left with 'no choice but to call out the war power of the Government; and so to resist force, employed for its destruction, by force, for its preservation.'[7]

By the time of Lincoln's second inaugural address of March 1865, his focus on the justification for the war had shifted fundamentally. He now argued that slavery was at the heart of the conflict: 'All knew that this interest was somehow the cause of the war.'[8] He was alluding to the effects of the development of separate economies in the previous half-century – an agrarian economy in the South and an industrially based northern one. The fundamentally contrasting systems had led to disagreements over tariffs and over the rights and wrongs of slavery. The disputes arose, in large part, from the conviction of southern slaveholders that the southern economy was dependent upon slave labour. These economic and moral debates were exacerbated by political and constitutional questions surrounding the possibility of extending slavery into the newly acquired territories after the Mexican war.

These constitutional issues had come to a head in the election of November 1860, which followed closely on the heels of the admission of Minnesota and Oregon to the Union as free – that is, non-slave – states. Lincoln hailed from the free state of Illinois and was elected president with only 40 per cent of the popular vote, derived almost entirely from the eighteen non-slave states. These events heralded the end of the South's domination of national politics. Almost immediately after the election, on 20 December, South Carolina passed a resolution of secession and was soon joined by six other southern states.

In January 1861 local militias occupied Federal forts and arsenals in these states, including Fort Sumter in the harbour of

Charleston, South Carolina. On 4 February delegates from the secessionist states met at Montgomery, Alabama, and formed a provisional government known as the Confederate States of America. In early March, Lincoln called on the Confederate States not to launch attacks that would take the country into a civil war. His call went unheeded. On 12 April 1861 Confederate Brigadier General Pierre G. T. Beauregard opened fire on Fort Sumter, an act that Lincoln seized upon as a reason for war.

THE WAR

The Civil War was lost by one general and won by two others. In losing the battle of Antietam, Robert E. Lee inadvertently transformed the Union cause into a crusade against slavery, the result of which was to harden the resolve of both North and South to a point where any compromise was impossible. Ulysses S. Grant and William T. Sherman broke the deadlock and won the war by adopting a revolutionary strategy of annihilation, thereby transforming what historian Russell F. Weigley has called 'the American way of war'.[9] The unintended consequences of the actions of the three generals reverberated for decades.

The Confederate President, Jefferson Davis, was a West Point graduate, as was his leading general, Robert E. Lee. Davis would have liked to adhere to the US Army's popular strategy of offensive warfare, but he understood that the Confederacy's only chance of surviving against the industrially more advanced and much more heavily populated Union lay in assuming a purely defensive posture. His model was George Washington, who rarely engaged in large-scale battles and who saw the survival of his army as the key to wearing down the aggressor. Overall, Lee agreed with his president, but he had fought under Scott in Mexico, and he appreciated the strategic potential of well-placed offensives. Unfortunately for the Confederacy, he did not grasp the benefits to be gained from guerrilla warfare, which might well have saved the South from defeat.

In late August 1862 Lee took the offensive. He would carry the war into Maryland and possibly Pennsylvania, hoping his army's presence on Union soil in the proximity of the national capital would induce Lincoln to recognize Confederate independence. Lee had made a great miscalculation. With unshaken resolve, Lincoln ordered Major General George B. McClellan to march northwestward from Washington, locate Lee and stop his advance. The Union general commanded 75,000 men to Lee's 50,000, many of whom were visibly averse to fighting a campaign of invasion when they had enlisted to defend Virginia and the Confederacy. The armies found one another at Antietam Creek, near the village of Sharpsburg, Maryland, on 1 September 1862. McClellan attacked; Lee, his back to the Potomac River, welcomed the challenge. Historian Geoffrey Perret observes, 'It was the deadliest day of a very bloody war.' Lee's 'Army of Northern Virginia was shoeless, ravenous, and fought-out.'[10] He lost 2,700 dead, another 9,000 wounded; McClellan lost 2,000 dead, 9,500 wounded. Such a near equality of loss, if continued, would spell doom for the Confederacy, whose population of nine million (more than three million of whom were slaves) was less than half the North's. Chastened for the time being, Lee retreated into Virginia. Tragically, McClellan lacked the nerve to pursue him. Otherwise, Lee's artillery chief would have been perfectly correct when he said of Antietam, 'The end of the Confederacy was in sight.'[11]

Antietam did not spell the immediate collapse of the Confederacy, but it did transform Lincoln's goal from preservation of the Union into the destruction of slavery. Before Antietam, the president had shown no sign of supporting the abolition of slavery for its own sake. He wrote to the New York newspaper editor Horace Greeley: 'My paramount object in this struggle is to save the Union, and is not either to save or destroy slavery.' Five days after Lee's defeat, on the eve of a Congressional election, he changed all that with the Emancipation Proclamation, 'the propaganda masterstroke of the war'.[12] The proclamation, issued on 23 September 1862 and to come into effect on 1 January 1863, was made for reasons of military and political expediency. It freed slaves only in those areas still fighting against the Union. It remained legal to own slaves in states loyal to the United States until the very last months of the war in 1865. Nevertheless, with Lincoln's announcement freeing Confederate slaves, the war had shifted from a war about territory and the restoration of the Union into a war to transform the way of life of the Confederate States.

It had become a war to destroy a nation and to build another in its place.

Lee was not the only general officer to experience disaster at Antietam. In November 1862, after successfully weathering the Congressional elections, Lincoln dismissed McClellan for being insufficiently aggressive. The president was searching for a fighting general, and his quest would lead him to the West, where Union armies were chipping away at Southern defences, especially those that could be reached by river. Ulysses S. Grant had resigned his commission in the US Army in 1854 to avoid dismissal for drunkenness. He thereafter failed in every enterprise he undertook as a civilian. Returning to an army now at war, Brigadier General Grant in February 1862 used riverine gunboats to carry his men to Fort Donelson on the Cumberland River in Tennessee. Offering the defenders 'No terms except unconditional and immediate surrender', Grant captured the fort and 11,500 Confederate prisoners.[13] He had taken the first step toward winning the Civil War.

Grant had true genius for command in battle, the kind of which Carl von Clausewitz could only dream. He could intuitively assess the operational flow and decide what must be done to win decisively or to lose with minimal adverse effects. In mid-1862 Grant took command of the 65,000-man Army of the Tennessee, knowing instinctively what he must do: take the Confederate fortress at Vicksburg, Mississippi, the last obstacle to complete Union control of the Mississippi River.

Geoffrey Perret has painted Grant's strategic dilemma with deft verbal strokes: 'Vicksburg was protected by nature like few places on earth: by the serpentine Mississippi below and by the swampy land all around.'[14] In late December 1862 Grant ordered William T. Sherman to storm Vicksburg from the great river. Confederate gunfire drove him back. Other setbacks followed until, in April 1863, Grant hit on his secret for success: he would attack the fort overland, from the rear. Navy gunboats and small craft ferried his divisions down the Father of Waters, straight past the bastion's batteries to a point 50 miles downriver. Grant recalled his sense of anticipation when the troops were safely landed. 'I felt a degree of relief scarcely ever equalled since.'[15] Emulating Scott's 1847 march from Veracruz to Mexico City, Grant cut loose from his base of supplies on the river. His army would feed off the rich land without starving the inhabitants in its march toward Jackson, Mississippi, the massive fort's railroad link to the outside world. In partnership with Sherman he captured the city and headed west toward the now cut-off fortress. In late May he established a siege featuring heavy bombardment by guns borrowed from the navy and an enforced starvation of the encircled Rebels.

Lincoln was watching over Grant's shoulder like a Valkyrie. Whether a success or a failure, the president counselled his chosen general, the advance toward Vicksburg would rank 'as one of the most brilliant in the world'.[16] There would be no more costly charges into blazing Confederate rifles, a tactic the defending commander, Lieutenant General John C. Pemberton, fully expected until it dawned on him that Grant intended simply to starve him and his men into submission. On 4 July 1863, having seen what lay ahead, Pemberton surrendered his bulwark, all it contained, and the adjacent city of Vicksburg. Grant scooped up almost 30,000 prisoners and more than 50,000 muskets and rifles. The Union and its navy now entirely controlled the broad waterway down which the limitless foodstuffs of the Ohio Valley could flow to occupied New Orleans and from that transhipment point into the Gulf of Mexico and beyond to Europe. Russell F. Weigley concludes that 'few campaigns in history have accomplished so much at so low a cost in lives as Grant's for Vicksburg, against great obstacles of geography if not of enemy generalship.'[17]

Vicksburg coincided with Robert E. Lee's defeat in the Battle of Gettysburg on 3 July 1863, after which Lee taunted the commanding general of the Army of the Potomac, Major General George G. Meade, with hints of yet another offensive. Meade commanded 90,000 men to Lee's 55,000, but always he temporized rather than pressing southward. Lincoln was near despair. 'We cannot help beating them, if we have the man', Lincoln wailed to his confidant, Secretary of the Navy Gideon Welles. Echoing Clausewitz, he said, 'How much in military matters depends on one mastermind.'[18] Lincoln knew he had found his keystone in Grant, and in late 1863 he decided to give him transcendent authority to destroy Lee and the South. He persuaded Congress to authorize the promotion of Grant to the rank of lieutenant general – the hallowed rank of George Washington and Winfield Scott. In March 1864 he bestowed the three stars and a legacy of national victory on a businessman's son who had never wanted a military career. With the rank came the position of general-in-chief and command of seventeen armies totalling 533,000 men disbursed across half a continent. This was the greatest aggregation of military power the United States would assemble before World War I, but so determined was Grant's opponent that it took another thirteen months to vanquish him.

Grant's strategy to break the stalemate in the east and end the war was simple, and ruthless. First, he would concentrate his own Army of the Potomac for an unremitting frontal campaign to annihilate Lee's Army of Northern Virginia. This victory would neutralize the enemy's military centre of gravity and the political-logistical nexus of Richmond. Secondly, he would unleash Sherman against Joseph E. Johnston's army to press through Tennessee into Georgia. Sherman then would take Atlanta, the political and logistical heart of the southeastern Confederacy.

Grant's original orders to Sherman succinctly summarized the increasingly tenuous distinction between uniformed and civilian enemies. He wrote, 'You I propose to move against Johnston's army, to break it up and to get into the interior of the enemy's country as far as you can, inflicting all the damage you can upon their war resources.'[19] Grant was perfectly clear in his mind about the importance of destroying all materiel that might possibly be within reach of the Confederate armed forces. He regarded 'such supplies . . . as much contraband as arms or ordnance stores. Their destruction was [to be] accomplished without [civilian] bloodshed and tended to the same result as the destruction of armies.' He forbade 'promiscuous pillaging'.[20] The restriction would become meaningless.

The year 1864 was one of expansively ferocious warfare. Philip Sheridan won Grant's approval to render the lush Shenandoah Valley into 'a barren waste'.[21] On behalf of Grant, Henry Wager Halleck, heretofore bookish and restrained in his generalship, wrote savagely to Sherman as he was approaching Atlanta. Sherman must gather up from the towns and countryside whatever goods and equipment the 'army will require, both for a siege of Atlanta and for your supply in your march farther into the enemy's country'. Halleck would strip people of their food and 'would destroy every mill and factory within reach which I did not want for my own use'.[22] These were orders for total war, a war of annihilation.

Sherman complied. He cut down and destroyed everything in his path, burning the city of Atlanta before blazing a swath of desolation all the way into Savannah and Charleston. His way of war, his penetration very deep into the Old South, helped Lincoln to win in the November 1864 election, where the president faced George McClellan, a general turned peace advocate. Sherman himself was fully cognizant and succinctly direct about what he was doing: 'If the [Confederate] people raise a howl against my barbarity and cruelty,' he said, 'I will answer that war is war, and not popularity-seeking. If they want peace, they and their relatives must stop the war.'[23] They would stop, but only after their most beloved leader surrendered his army to the Union's most relentlessly determined general.

Ulysses S. Grant had laboured under no illusions about the price his men must pay as they started 'upon that memorable campaign, destined to result in the capture of the Confederate capital and the army defending it'. His soldiers and Lee's would experience:

> as desperate fighting as the world has ever witnessed; not to be consummated in a day, a week, a month, or a single season . . . The campaign now begun was destined to result in heavier losses, to both armies, in a given time, than any previously suffered; but the carnage was to be limited to a single year, and to accomplish all that had been anticipated or desired . . . at the beginning.[24]

Carnage it was. In May 1864, the first month of the campaign, the Army of the Potomac suffered 55,000 casualties, the Army of Northern Virginia 32,000. Undeterred by the cost in tens of thousands of lives unlived, Grant pushed on for almost a year. Finally, he surrounded what was left of Lee's army, fewer than 30,000 men, and requested Lee's surrender. The two opposed giants met at Appomattox Courthouse, Virginia, to sign the surrender document on 9 April 1865. The terms were liberal, having been drawn up during a conference between Lincoln, Grant and Sherman on 27 March. The Union would be gracious to the vanquished fighters if they simply laid down their arms and resumed their civilian pursuits. This last gesture was remarkable for a war of unprecedented violence. It had the Lincoln touch.

The liberality shown Lee at Appomattox was extended anti-climactically to Joseph E. Johnston, whose army remained intact but contained by Sherman's. There was some fear Johnston might extricate himself to fight again; there was apprehension that rebel units would take to the hills and mountains of the South and wage an irrepressible and indefinitely protracted guerrilla war. Lee rendered his last service to the United States by decrying such a desperate gambit, and on 18 April Johnston formally surrendered his 37,000 men to Sherman. Four days earlier, at Ford's Theatre in Washington, DC, a southern sympathizer assassinated Abraham Lincoln. With his death Lincoln became one of 600,000 warriors to die in the Civil War. This was the price paid to transform United States governance from loose federalism to centralized power – a clear example of regime change. The war eradicated slavery, but it also inculcated a warlike mentality in the minds of many national leaders. Finally, it set the stage for an occupation of the defeated power that dwarfed Scott's tenure in Mexico City and established a strong precedent for how the United States would treat the nations it vanquished in the twentieth century.

UNINTENDED CONSEQUENCES

The consequences of the Civil War went far beyond the defeat, occupation and reconstruction of the Confederate States. A partial list would include more than one million military casualties on both sides – an extraordinary number for a nation of 31 million people – the assassination of the victorious president, the almost total destruction of the economic, political and social infrastructure of the southern states, the emancipation – although not the equality – of slaves, the impeachment of Lincoln's successor, lingering deep-seated hostility, disagreements and suspicion between the two sections, and political chaos and corruption resulting from the so-called 'Reconstruction' of the South between 1865 and 1877. The total cost of the war – apart from the costs of destroyed homes, crops, livestock, railroads and other factors – has been estimated as in excess of twenty billion dollars, a mind-boggling figure representing more than five times the total expenditure of the Federal government up to that time. War memorials all over the country remind Americans of this most destructive conflict.

The armies of the Confederate States may have surrendered but Southerners never acknowledged they had been defeated. The war left a legacy of hostility, bitterness and division between the two sections of the re-United States that reverberates to this day. The southern states have neither forgotten nor forgiven the North for the destruction of their way of life and the subsequent century of relative poverty and second-class status they suffered as a result of their defeat. The North, full of resentment at the cost of victory over the South, sought to prevent the incorporation of the southern economy into that of the North and to deny to the South a return of regional prosperity.

In the course of the war, the Federal government disregarded the Constitution as personal liberties were trammelled and dissent punished with imprisonment in the name of liberty. As far as abolition of the peculiar institution of slavery was concerned, the war failed as a civilizing exercise. Southerners continued to defy the Union, finding countless ways to circumvent the newly enacted Fourteenth and Fifteenth Amendments of the Constitution, adherence to which had been the condition to the South's readmission to national politics. These amendments, passed in 1866 and 1870, guaranteed the protection of US citizenship, and granted voting rights to former slaves. Nonetheless, freedmen were routinely subjected to terror and discrimination. Nor did the North care too much about the racism and violence directed toward African-Americans in the South, or the denial of civil rights and inequality that flowed as a consequence of southern racism.

As a result of the war, the Federal government dramatically expanded its power. It increasingly allied with banking, transportation and business interests to foster economic growth. Spurred on by the requirements of an industrializing and demographically expanding nation, the US government greatly accelerated its destruction of Native Americans. The battle-hardened US army adopted a new strategy in its offensive against Native Americans: the quite unjust and illegal strategy of collective punishment. This approach involved holding a whole tribe responsible for the attacks of any of its members – whether approved or not approved by tribal councils or chiefs.

In the area of foreign relations, a kind of uneasy peace – a quasi-diplomatic war – had developed between the United States and Great Britain during the Civil War. In November 1861 Union Navy Captain Charles Wilkes forcibly removed from a British steamer, the *Trent*, two Confederate diplomats, James M. Mason and John Slidell, who were on their way to Europe. London's outrage sparked Union fears of war with Great Britain. British sympathy for the Confederacy had been indicated by the government's allowance of the construction of Confederate commerce raiders in British ship-yards. The css *Alabama*, in particular, was highly successful, destroy-ing sixty us merchant ships. Anglo-American relations suffered as a result. A nasty diplomatic dispute over Britain's responsibility for the cost of the *Alabama*'s depredations lasted until 1872. In the post-war years, Anglo-American relations also were strained over Central America and East Asia as American expansionists encouraged by Secretary of State William H. Seward increasingly and vigorously challenged British commercial and investment dominance in these areas. The cry to annex Canada was even heard once again.

The Civil War elevated and glorified the notion of the United States as a nation with unlimited military potential. Lincoln, as chief executive and commander-in-chief, assumed an unprecedented, personal and direct role in managing the war. The war became shrouded in universal, pseudo-moralistic rhetoric extolling the messianic destiny of the United States. The military occupation of the former Confederacy, and the election three years later of Union hero General Ulysses S. Grant as president, continued the trend seen during the war of militarizing the Federal government. In a penetrating review of Harry S. Stout's study of the Civil War, *Upon the Altar of the Nation: A Moral History of the Civil War*, Benjamin Schwarz noted that Union veteran Ambrose Bierce described the war as a murderous enterprise without uplift, with-out virtue, and without purpose. Bierce was only a little harsh. It is hard to see how the resort to arms was the wisest step for Lincoln to take or that the United States could regard such a bru-talizing war as a just war. A more prudent president or one less driven by ideology, politics and self-righteous conviction would have energetically searched for alternative policies.[25]

Beginning with the proclamation on 15 April 1861, declaring his determination to preserve the Union, and continuing for the next four years of war, President Lincoln acted in ways that were unprecedented, controversial, and which certainly produced unintended outcomes. Some of Lincoln's most controversial decisions were a disturbing extension, if not an abuse, of presidential powers, arrogating to himself greater authority than allowed by the Constitution. It is incumbent for a democracy such as the United States, especially during wartime, to retain its basic democratic character if it is not to lose the values and institutions for which its citizens fight. The Civil War, like the wars that preceded and followed it, placed great strains on the national government, and Lincoln's perception of the nation's requirements to win the war came into conflict with established constitutional conventions and individual liberties. Lincoln set precedents for the expansion of executive branch powers that future presidents were to draw upon for the next one hundred and fifty years. He recognized that the United States republican model was an experiment among nations, and fiercely sought to preserve it. However, in doing so, he felt obliged to take upon himself executive prerogatives that far exceeded the ones exercised by George III that had so enraged and offended American colonists. All this was unintended in April 1861. He, of course, could not know that he was setting an example for George W. Bush's assertion of an all-powerful unitary executive.

Lincoln's decisions overriding the Constitution have echoed down to the present administration with its suspension of habeas corpus, the use of illegal detention centres and the establishment of extrajudicial military commissions. Lincoln adopted these measures largely in response to his generals, who increasingly influenced his policy. The process of executive expansion began almost immediately upon the onset of war. Lincoln's 15 April 1861 proclamation was itself regarded by many as an illegal violation of the Constitution and an unlawful extension of presidential power. The Constitution in Article 1, Section 8, puts the power 'To provide for calling forth the Militia to execute the Laws of the Union, suppress Insurrections . . .' in the hands of Congress.[26] Lincoln not only did not convene Congress, he delayed the opening of the session by almost three months. On 21 April the president unilaterally ordered the purchase of five naval vessels, ignoring the constitutional requirement for prior Congressional appropriations. On the same day, he ordered the navy to blockade all southern ports. A blockade by definition is an act of war requiring a resolution of Congress. Lincoln, however, would not concede that this was a foreign war because to do so would legitimize the Confederacy in the eyes of foreign powers, opening the prospect of formal aid and support from England and continental Europe.

Perhaps the most ominous example of Lincoln's questionable conduct was his suspension of the writ of habeas corpus. The writ of habeas corpus protects Americans from being unjustly imprisoned; it prohibits the government from making arrests without demonstrable cause. Habeas corpus is the guarantee of the principle of equality before the law, and under the Constitution only Congress has the power to suspend it. Lincoln was the first president to suspend habeas corpus without first obtaining Congressional approval. In doing so, he enabled the military to arrest and imprison more than 10,000 civilians. In a later suspension of the writ approved by Congress more than 38,000 people were arrested and detained, often for non-existent crimes manufactured by generals. Lincoln's denial of these basic constitutional rights, like many other government actions, escaped scrutiny by the courts during the war, but once the Union had achieved victory, the Supreme Court ruled on some of the cases. Probably the most famous case involved Lambden P. Milligan, who had been found guilty of acts of disloyalty and sentenced to death by a military commission in Indiana during the war. In granting Milligan freedom in 1866, the court ruled that his imprisonment had been unlawful as the suspension of habeas corpus was unconstitutional when civilian courts were operating, and while it might be lawful to hold civilians, they certainly could not be tried by a military tribunal.

On 14 February 1862 Lincoln ended his own suspension of habeas corpus and issued an amnesty to political or state prisoners no longer deemed dangerous. His new proclamation apologetically explained that, at the early stage of the war, 'Every department of the Government was paralyzed by treason.' Congress 'had not anticipated and so had not provided for the emergency'. Lincoln explained that he had felt compelled to 'employ with energy the extraordinary powers which the Constitution confides to him in cases of insurrection'.[27] Perhaps the president believed the insurrection was all but over and that victory was in sight. The War Department closed recruiting offices a few months later. Antietam had still to be fought; elimination of slavery was not yet the president's goal.

Perhaps the major unintended consequence of the Civil War was the abolition of slavery in the United States. Although the rhetoric of the Civil War was couched in terms of fighting to preserve the Union or to preserve freedom, the war initially was not fought to gain freedom for slaves. In the half-century preceding the Civil War, the Federal government had shown few signs of enforcing the 1808 law prohibiting the profitable slave trade, but it had vigorously enforced the 1850 Fugitive Slave Act, which had required Federal law officials to arrest anyone suspected of being a runaway slave. Despite his professed personal desire to see the end of slavery, in his first inaugural address of March 1861, before the outbreak of hostilities, Lincoln was conciliatory, stating: 'I have no purpose, directly or indirectly, to interfere with the institution of slavery in the States where it exists. I believe I have no lawful right to do so, and I have no inclination to do so.'[28] Lincoln at this point interpreted the Constitution strictly: he believed he was legally obligated to preserve slavery in the states that chose it. These quasi-sovereignties included the four slave states – Maryland, Kentucky, Missouri and Delaware – that remained loyal to the Union in 1861. The republic of liberty was one in which slavery was legal.

By mid-1862 Lincoln had shown no sign of supporting the abolition of slavery for its own sake. Moreover, the Emancipation Proclamation issued on 22 September 1862 was limited in scope and political in purpose. It provided freedom only to slaves in Confederate territory not already under Union control. It was not until April 1864 that the Senate, in response to a request not by the president but to a petition signed by 400,000 antislavery advocates, adopted the Thirteenth Amendment declaring an end to slavery throughout the entire United States. In January 1865 the House of Representatives did the same, thus ending slavery in the land of the free.

The elimination of slavery was the major unintended consequence of the Civil War, but the us Army's twelve-year occupation of the South was also an unintended consequence of great and lasting significance. The assassination of Lincoln on 14 April 1865 by John Wilkes Booth, an extreme secessionist, added confusion and uncertainty to post-war reabsorption of the defeated states.

Lincoln's successor, Andrew Johnson of Tennessee, was sympathetic to the devastated and bankrupt South and, like Lincoln, hoped to impose few conditions upon the southern states rejoining the Union. He wanted their almost immediate readmission. The issue, however, was inseparable from the question of the recognition accorded by the southern states of the civil rights of freed slaves.

Beginning in December 1865, several southern states had passed a series of 'black codes' that reduced freedmen to serf-like conditions. On 16 June 1866 Congress passed the Fourteenth Amendment guaranteeing equal rights to African-Americans, and made the re-entry of the southern states into the Union dependent upon their acceptance of this Amendment. Troubled by southern avoidance of the terms of readmission, Congress increased the power and size of the Freedmen's Bureau within the War Department, and Federal agents were sent to the South to assist freed slaves. Supported by a 20,000-man army of occupation, the Freedmen's Bureau found jobs and land, built schools and protected former slaves from maltreatment. 'Radical' Republicans in Congress dominated Reconstruction policies by overriding presidential vetoes of harsh measures. The bitter conflict between President Johnson and the Congress culminated in 1868 with his impeachment. Johnson escaped conviction by the Senate and was acquitted by a margin of one vote. As a result of Johnson's incapacitation and the ascent of Ulysses S. Grant to the presidency in 1868, the US Army occupied the South until 1877. Reconstruction officially terminated with the inauguration of President Rutherford B. Hayes, a former Union general, who ended the occupation to satisfy a political compromise that ensured his election. None of these events were foreseen by the war-makers.

The political gains of African-Americans were short-lived. Neither northern nor readmitted southern states had any intention of allowing former slaves political equality. The Federal government in Washington, imbued with racist views concerning the inferiority of the former slaves, acquiesced in moves to disenfranchise African-Americans. They were to wait another century – until 1964, in the administration of President Lyndon B. Johnson – before gaining genuine legislative recognition of their civil rights.

Finally, one unintended consequence of lasting import was the broadening of hostilities to include the destruction of the enemy's morale and war-making capacity. Sherman's devastation of Georgia and South Carolina was a horrifying revelation to all. J.F.C. Fuller describes Sherman as 'the first of the modern totalitarian generals'. Sherman 'universalized the war, waged it on his enemy's people and not only on armed men, and made terrorism the lynchpin of his strategy.'[29] Russell F. Weigley has aptly characterized this strategy as one of 'annihilation'. It transcended protracted conventional warfare. It not only aimed to destroy Confederate armies, but also effected the destruction of transportation links, factories, agricultural crops and entire cities. Sherman's war of annihilation created an animosity towards the North that lingers in the South to this day. His strategy became the 'American way of war'.[30] It would reach its apogee with the 'strategic bombing' of World War II.

FIVE

THE WAR AGAINST SPAIN, 1898

*The war of the United States with Spain was very brief. Its results were
many, startling, and of world-wide meaning.*
Henry Cabot Lodge[1]

The Spanish-American War should more accurately be called the
Spanish-Cuban-Filipino-American War. This title accounts for
where the war was fought, and it identifies all the combatants. It
also acknowledges, implicitly at least, that the Cubans and
Filipinos were fighting the Spanish before the United States entered
into the fray. Including 'Cuban' in the title of this war also indirectly
draws attention to the suggestion that the United States only
entered the conflict to protect US interests in Cuba when it appeared
that the Cubans were going to win independence from Spain on
their own.

   The Spanish-American War, as it is better known, more than
any other fought by the United States, resembles the present war in
Iraq. Like the Iraq war, it was begun ostensibly to achieve regime
change, to bring democracy to a people suffering under a cruelly
repressive regime. It was initiated by an administration loudly proclaiming the moral righteousness of its cause, led by a president
widely believed by contemporaries to be easily influenced, if not
controlled, by a powerful group of aggressive foreign policy unilat-
eralists committed to extending the power of the United States on
the world stage, and controlling access to external vital raw mate-
rials while espousing free trade doctrines. In 1898 President
William McKinley, like President George W. Bush in 2002, portrayed himself as deeply religious, acting in accordance with the
will of the Almighty. McKinley was surrounded by powerful allies
and friends – Theodore Roosevelt, Captain Alfred Thayer Mahan
and Senator Henry Cabot Lodge among them – advocating a 'large
policy' of imperial expansion, as Bush was surrounded by power-

ful neoconservatives urging the use of unilateral forces to achieve the American goals of furthering the spread of democracy and market domination.

In both wars, the conventional military phase was over quickly, the victorious outcome never in doubt. And in both the consequences for the United States, mostly unanticipated, were far reaching, domestically and externally. Within a short time in both wars, the United States found itself enmeshed in a brutal war against insurgents determined to expel American forces from their land. The hoped-for market gains were not immediately forthcoming; rather than strengthening the United States economically and strategically, both wars had the opposite effect. Suspicion and fear of the United States increased among friend and foe around the world. Thucydides had warned of this phenomenon when writing of the expanding empire of Athens. When Athens became an empire, he wrote, it became a tyrant abroad and then a tyrant at home.

The war against Spain was not fought to free Cuba from repressive Spanish rule as the McKinley administration claimed. To one of its strongest advocates, Senator Lodge of Massachusetts, it was fought to gain Cuba and Hawaii, to maintain the Monroe Doctrine and assert American supremacy, and to prevent the British from extending their economic (and to some extent their military) power and influence in the western hemisphere and in the Caribbean in particular. Lodge had written to a friend as early as 1894, 'We intend to take Hawaii . . . we ought to have Cuba also unless I am greatly mistaken.'[2] He repeated this theme often in the years immediately prior to 1898. He might have added that the war was also fought in large measure to prevent the feared partition of Latin America by the European powers, which had recently divided Africa.

In 1895 an insurrection calling for *Cuba Libre* broke out against the Spanish colonial rulers in Cuba. By that year American investments in Cuba had reached some $50 million in plantations, railroads and mining; there was an annual Cuban–American sugar trade of twice that value; all of these enterprises were suffering badly in the revolutionary ferment. William McKinley of Ohio, a pro-business Republican elected president in 1896, had no intention of going to war when he assumed office. In his inaugural address in March 1897 he stated: 'We want no wars of conquest; we must avoid the temptation of territorial aggression. War should never be entered into until every last agency of peace has failed; peace is preferable to war in almost every contingency.'³ He hoped the Cuban insurrection against Spain would be resolved without American armed intervention. He said he was appalled by the methods employed by Spain to suppress the Cuban revolution, but he was not prepared to fight to protect the Cuban population.

McKinley had nevertheless run for office on a highly expansionistic political platform calling for US control of Hawaii, an isthmian canal across Central America, a larger navy, and purchase of the Virgin Islands. With surprising moderation, the Republican Party sought only independence for Cuba, not American annexation, a position congenial to the new president. To placate powerful Republican imperialists such as Senator Lodge, McKinley submitted a treaty for annexation of Hawaii to the Senate, but he resisted the extreme expansionists' cries for Cuban annexation.

In his annual address to the Congress of December 1897 McKinley denounced acquisition as 'criminal aggression', rejected military intervention and pleaded in vain for patience.⁴ Nonetheless, war came quickly in the first four months of 1898. In January the United States learned that all sides in Cuba were rejecting Madrid's gradualist offer of limited self-government. Spaniards hostile to any compromise with the Cubans rioted in Havana, and McKinley responded by sending in the USS *Maine* on 24 January. While the battleship sat at anchor in Havana, symbolizing American protectiveness and apprehension, it blew apart at 9.40 pm on Tuesday 15 February, killing 266 sailors and marines. A firestorm engulfed the United States. The sinking of the *Maine* provided a perfect warmaking opportunity for the stridently pro-war *New York Journal* of William Randolph Hearst, who had instructed one of his artists in Cuba: 'You furnish the pictures, I'll furnish the war.'⁵

The disaster led very quickly to much greater violence. Although the cause of the explosion has never been satisfactorily explained, Americans agitating for a war to free the Cuban people from governance by Madrid convinced themselves that somehow Spain was responsible. The war hawks, although comprising no more than 20 per cent of the voting public, immediately recognized the sinking of the *Maine* as an extraordinary opportunity to fan popular and Congressional winds for a war that would be just, humane and a road to overseas empire.

McKinley was desperate to retain some control over events. He demanded that Madrid order a ceasefire and open peace negotiations with the insurgents. The president also proposed American arbitration, which seemed equivalent to granting Cubans their independence. This was one demand too many for a Spanish government that was moving as fast as was politically possible to accommodate United States demands. The time for compromise had run out. On 28 March 1898, the day after McKinley sent his ultimatum to Spain, the US Navy reported that 'the *Maine* was destroyed by a submarine mine'.[6] The fully aroused nation chanted, 'Remember the *Maine*, to hell with Spain.'[7] To complicate matters, 1898 was a Congressional election year. McKinley had to prevent the Republicans from fragmenting over the issue of Cuba prior to the November elections. On 11 April he therefore sent a message to Congress asking for authority to use the US Army and Navy to terminate Spanish occupation of Cuba.

McKinley cited several factors as justification for this unprecedented military intervention into the colonial territory of a European country. He solemnly emphasized Spain's 'cruel, barbarous, and uncivilized practices of warfare' and the desperate longing of the Cubans to be a free people.[8] He placed somewhat less emphasis on the recent damage to American trade and investments and on the 'constant menace to our peace' symbolized by the loss of the *Maine*.[9] Although ready to take military action, the president rejected US annexation of the island. At the same time he remained unalterably opposed to recognition of Cuban independence. Congress responded with a joint resolution proclaiming Cuban independence, authorizing the president to employ American military and naval power to dislodge the Spanish from Cuba, and rejecting recognition of the Cuban Republic.

Passed easily by both houses early on the morning of 19 April 1898, the joint resolution incorporated an amendment introduced by Republican Senator Henry M. Teller proscribing US annexation of Cuba. Teller's amendment repudiated 'any disposition or intention to exercise sovereignty, jurisdiction, or control' over the island.[10] This self-denying ordinance had a sobering influence on American ambitions toward Cuba. Throughout the twentieth century the United States consistently attempted to control the politics and economy of Cuba, but like a sentinel of freedom the Teller

Amendment forever blocked Washington from brandishing the ultimate threat of permanent occupation and annexation.

Expansionists, businessmen and agricultural investors were pleased that their interests in Cuba would be protected by Washington's oversight. The 'Yellow Press' of Hearst and Joseph Pulitzer had contributed greatly. Following the Congressional authorization for war, Spain on 21 April broke diplomatic relations, the US Navy began a blockade of Cuba, and four days later Congress declared that war had already begun.

American leaders were mesmerized by the prospective glory of war. Theodore Roosevelt spoke for the hawks in 1897 when he addressed the officers at the Naval War College: 'No triumph of peace is quite so great as the supreme triumphs of war.'[11] He eagerly resigned his position as assistant secretary of the navy to join the 1st US Volunteer Cavalry, from which platform he launched a brief, glory-seeking military campaign in Cuba that catapulted him to the vice presidency of the United States in 1900. Upon the assassination of McKinley in 1901 he became president.

THE WAR

The US war against Spain was lopsided. Cuba lay less than 100 miles from the American coast, making it an easy target for invasion. The Spanish navy was decrepit and disheartened; the US Navy was modern and eager for combat. Leaders of both American services were veterans who remembered the combined army–navy operations of the Civil War; they were prepared to implement these techniques once again. It was no contest from the beginning.

While the army was mobilizing to invade nearby Cuba, the navy struck first in the western reaches of the Pacific Ocean. On 24 April Secretary of the Navy John D. Long cabled Commodore George Dewey with orders to attack. A Civil War veteran who had fought under the legendary David G. Farragut, Dewey now commanded the small but modern US Asiatic Squadron. 'War has commenced between the United States and Spain', wrote Long in anticipation of Congress's declaration. 'Proceed at once to the Philippine Islands. Commence operations at once, particularly against the Spanish fleet.'[12] Dewey was absolutely confident of his superiority over the Spanish. 'My squadron is all ready for war', he had written to his son on 31 March, 'and would make short work of the defences of Manila.'[13]

Upon receipt of Long's order, Dewey steamed from neutral Britain's Crown Colony of Hong Kong with his ships' bunkers full of coal. Around midnight on 30 April, with flagship *Olympia* in the van, Dewey entered Manila Bay. At dawn on 1 May he found the Spanish squadron anchored ten miles below Manila proper, in the shallow waters of Cavite naval base. Spanish Admiral Patricio Montojo had prudently chosen the location to avoid shell-damage to the capital and to enable the Spanish sailors to swim ashore from ships that Montojo glumly assumed would soon be sunk by Dewey's new and well-armed cruisers. The Americans opened fire at 5.40 am and continued to pummel the Spanish vessels until slightly after noon. When Montojo surrendered he had lost seven warships and approximately 400 sailors killed or wounded. Eight Americans were wounded; none were killed; their ships received some minor damage. Spain's naval power in the Pacific, dating back to Ferdinand Magellan's arrival in 1521, ceased to exist.

In exultation Senator Lodge introduced a resolution authorizing Tiffany's of New York to fashion a jewelled sword for the newly promoted rear admiral. Another jingo waxed poetically:

Dewey! Dewey! Dewey!
Is the hero of the Day
And the *Maine* has been remembered
In the good old-fashioned way.[14]

A major unresolved problem lurked beneath the hysteria: Manila still stood as the Spanish capital of the Philippines. Dewey could batter the city into submission, but he lacked an occupying force. He must await the arrival of the US Army, which was slowly despatched. While he waited the centre of American military and naval operations shifted to the Caribbean.

The Navy Department had begun urgent preparations for a war in Cuban waters within days of the explosion of the *Maine*. Secretary Long immediately ordered the large new battleship *Oregon* to rush from the West Coast to Cuba, a high-speed voyage of 14,700 miles lasting 67 days. 'Our great battleships are experiments', Long wrote with a mixture of anxiety and anticipation.[15] In April he and his immediate subordinate, Assistant Secretary of the Navy Theodore Roosevelt, ordered Rear Admiral William T. Sampson, commander of the North Atlantic Squadron, to blockade Cuba and lay a trap for the enemy fleet of Admiral Pascual Cervera y Topete that was steaming from Spain to reinforce the Spanish garrison on Cuba. On 6 May the pugnacious Theodore Roosevelt resigned from the Navy Department to be commissioned as a lieutenant colonel in the volunteer forces.

The American campaign to take Cuba, the strategic heart of the war, was a joint army–navy operation, although Rear Admiral Sampson and Major General William R. Shafter each reported separately and telegraphically to their respective cabinet officers in Washington, DC. As soon as Cervera's squadron took refuge in Santiago Harbour on the southeastern coast of Cuba, Sampson and his second-in-command, Commodore William S. Schley, imposed a tight blockade. Cervera commanded outmoded relics; some of his warships even lacked complete batteries of guns. He wailed to the minister of marine in Madrid, 'We are blockaded. I qualified our coming here as disastrous . . . Events begin to show I was right.'[16]

Sampson was a veteran of Union naval blockades in the Civil War. He understood that an indefinite closure required a nearby supporting naval base for storing coal and making repairs to his ships. Accordingly, on 9 June he occupied Guantanamo Bay, one of Cuba's finest harbours and a place still held by the United States despite the Teller Amendment. Now fully in command of the maritime approaches, Sampson telegraphed the Navy Department urgently requesting the dispatch of an army to assault Santiago. The War Department cooperated with orders directing Shafter to steam immediately from his port of embarkation in Tampa, Florida.

Convoyed by protective warships, Shafter and his composite army of 16,000 regulars and volunteers rendezvoused with Sampson's fleet on 20 June. Two days later the troops began to disembark at Daquiri, several miles east of Santiago. They linked up with Cuban insurgents, organized themselves for battle and began approaching the well-defended city. The entrenched Spaniards met their advance with heavy fire, killing over 200 Americans and wounding more than 1,300 in the battle for El Caney Hill. The costly action was most intense on 1 July, the day that Lieutenant Colonel Roosevelt gained immortality by leading his dismounted cavalrymen – the 'Rough Riders' – on a flanking charge up a promontory adjacent to San Juan Hill, a fortified high point holding the key to the city of Santiago. At the crest Roosevelt surveyed the carnage around him, looked to the west and marvelled, 'we found ourselves overlooking Santiago'.[17] Just over the horizon lay the vice presidency of the United States.

Shafter, a 64-year-old Civil War veteran weighing more than 300 pounds, was sick and dispirited. He was reluctant to suffer more casualties and he feared for the health of his men. The rainy season had begun, bringing the perils of malaria and yellow fever. As he wavered, he received some political spine-stiffening in a telegram from Secretary of War Russell A. Alger: 'If . . . you could hold your present position, especially San Juan Heights, the effect upon the country would be much better than falling back.'[18] Shafter promised to hang on and turned to Sampson for help, begging him to finish the job: 'I urge that you make every effort immediately to force the entrance [to Santiago] to avoid future losses among my men . . . You can now operate with less loss of life than I can.'[19]

The astounded American admiral feared more than the loss of sailors. He worried about having one of his new cruisers or battleships sunk by the shore batteries defending the city, a catastrophe he personally had experienced in Charleston Harbour during the Civil War. Sampson decided to confer with Shafter, and his flagship, the armoured cruiser *New York*, pulled away from the blockade early on the morning of 3 July 1898, heading for the general's headquarters down the coast. Cervera chose that moment to sortie for the sake of Spanish honour. At 9.31 am the battleship *Iowa* spotted Cervera's flagship, the *Infanta Maria Teresa,* charging from the mouth of Santiago Harbour. Cervera quickly turned west, hugging the shore as he fled. The Americans followed in hot pursuit, and the Spaniards either beached themselves or succumbed to the far superior American firepower. The Battle of Santiago ended in four hours. The Spanish lost 323 dead and 151 wounded; one American died and another was seriously wounded. The US Navy lost not a single ship; the Spanish lost all of theirs. Sampson telegraphed Washington: 'The fleet under my command offers the nation as a Fourth of July present the whole of Cervera's fleet.'[20]

The 'Hero of Manila Bay', meanwhile, was still waiting for the army to help him liberate Manila. Until 1898 the US Army had comprised a continental force preoccupied with fighting Native Americans and policing westward expansion. The president's mid-war decision to send troops to the Philippines was an unexpected taxation on the War Department's strategists. McKinley did not help matters by refusing to divulge to the Philippine expedition's commander, Major General Wesley Merritt, the precise political purpose of the deployment. When Merritt pointedly asked the President whether he intended only to seize Manila or to subdue the entire archipelago of 7,000 islands, McKinley responded with masterful ambiguity. He told the general that the American goal was to complete 'the reduction of Spanish power' and bring 'order and security to the [Philippine] islands while in the possession of the United States'.[21] The extent and duration of American possession was not defined, and Merritt expressed his frustration in a letter to the President: 'I do not yet know whether it is your desire to subdue and hold all of the Spanish territory in the islands, or merely seize and hold the capital.'[22] Denied clear guidance about his goals, Merritt decided to play it safe. Instead of the 5,000 volunteers proffered him by the War Department he insisted on a composite of 20,000 regulars and volunteers.

Merritt's men began to leave San Francisco in increments beginning in early June. During the trans-Pacific voyage of the first troop transports and protective warships the cruiser *Charleston* was detached to capture Guam. The surprised Spaniards thought the ship's visit was a courtesy call; they surrendered without resistance or bloodshed on 20 June. Less than a month later, to consolidate the insular line of naval and maritime communications linking California and the Philippines, the US Congress passed a joint resolution annexing American-dominated but politically independent Hawaii. The American empire was snaking its way across the Pacific in the wake of Merritt's armada.

In Manila Bay Dewey had been doing his part to hasten what he ironically described as 'the conclusion of hostilities in a war which was made to free Cuba from Spanish oppression'.[23] He maintained a blockade of Manila and kept a watchful eye on the several European warships that had dropped into the bay to witness the American conquest. The commodore was especially suspicious of the German commander, Vice Admiral Otto von Diederichs, in whom he spied imperial ambitions. Dewey also was sponsoring a cautious advance on the city of Manila orchestrated by the young Filipino nationalist Emilio Aguinaldo, whom one of his officers had encountered in Hong Kong while the squadron was waiting for the war to begin.

A leader of the anti-Spanish Philippine revolution that began in 1896, Aguinaldo had been promising American consular officers that he would grant the United States control over the lucrative customs-collection of the Philippines in exchange for arms and other help in driving the Spanish from the Philippines and establishing a republic. Since 'our purpose was to weaken the Spaniards in every legitimate way', Dewey befriended Aguinaldo.[24] He transported the revolutionary nationalist and a cadre of close associates to Cavite, in Manila Bay, on navy vessels. By early June Aguinaldo's insurgents were slowly advancing toward the Spanish blockhouses and trenches ringing Manila, while Dewey's ships threatened to bombard the city from seaward. The Dewey-Aguinaldo partnership was militarily productive, but Washington was apprehensive. Secretary of the Navy John D. Long cabled the admiral 'not to have political alliances with the insurgents . . . that would incur liability to maintain their cause in the future'.[25]

It was too late. The determination of McKinley not to make an early decision about the political future of the Philippines, coupled with Dewey's quasi-autonomous status as the senior commander in a very remote theatre of operations, had robbed the Americans of the strategic initiative. On 12 June Aguinaldo proclaimed Philippine independence; on 23 June he formed a government headed by himself. The first detachments of the US Army did not arrive until 30 June. General Merritt did not make his appearance until 24 July, fully a month after the formation of Aguinaldo's government.

One of Merritt's first manoeuvres was to bribe Aguinaldo into yielding his favourable siege positions to the Americans, after which Merritt opened direct bilateral negotiations with the Spanish governor general in the city. The Spaniard would not surrender to 'niggers', but he readily agreed to surrender to Merritt.[26] The city's defenders would mount just enough resistance to Merritt's force to satisfy the demands of Spanish honour. They would then turn Manila over to the Americans, who vowed to keep Aguinaldo's men outside the city walls.

The treacherous Spanish–American military ballet was played out on 13 August, with more casualties than had been expected. Nonetheless, the capital fell into American hands as arranged. Somewhat unnervingly, Merritt's men found themselves peering out of the city into the hostile eyes of Aguinaldo's surrounding freedom fighters, who were demanding joint occupation of the Philippine capital. An outbreak of Filipino-American hostilities was temporarily forestalled on 16 August, when news reached Manila of the 12 August armistice between Spain and the United States.

A final treaty of peace was signed in Paris on 10 December 1898. The pact was ratified by the US Senate on 6 February 1899, by a vote of 57 to 27. The terms of the treaty provided for Spain to relinquish sovereignty over Cuba. The United States was to occupy the island and determine its future. All other Spanish islands in the West Indies, together with Guam, were ceded to the United States. The whole archipelago of the Philippines was ceded to the United States, which agreed to pay Spain $20 million. All claims for indemnity or damages between the two nations and their citizens were mutually relinquished. The war had cost the United States just under 400 lives and 1,600 wounded. Many Americans joined Secretary of State John Hay in extolling the short conflict as 'a splendid little war'.[27]

UNINTENDED CONSEQUENCES

In fact, the Spanish-American War was 'little' only in a very restricted sense. Its consequences, short-term and long-term, intended and unintended, would manifest themselves for over a century. The most immediate and tragic of the war's unintended consequences was the bloody suppression of the Philippine insurrection against the United States that erupted on 4 February 1899, two days before the US Senate narrowly ratified the peace treaty with Spain.

Aguinaldo's uprising caught Washington by surprise. Of the many arguments used to justify taking all of the Philippines, perhaps the most attractive and persuasive was that of America's civilizing role. The expectation of US policy-makers, who were almost completely ignorant of the Philippines and its inhabitants, was that the Filipinos were a backward people who needed uplifting and civilizing, that they would welcome rule by the United States, and that a grateful population would celebrate the transformation brought about by the democracy and liberty the United States would introduce. All these assumptions were false, and in February 1899 war erupted in Manila. It was certainly unexpected by American leaders, who responded mercilessly to defeat the insurgents.

The administration had gone to great pains to suggest that the post-war power vacuum offered no other solution but to control the archipelago. General Merritt informed the peace commissioners in Paris, in early October 1898, that the Americans must remain in the Philippines. Dewey supported his position, and cabled on 14 October that: 'Spanish authority has been completely destroyed in Luzon, and general anarchy prevails without the limits of the city and Bay of Manila. Strongly probable that islands to the south will fall into the same state soon.'[28] Dewey considered it highly unlikely that Spanish domination could be restored. The withdrawal of the American forces would therefore not mean the re-establishment of Spanish rule but no government at all. If the United States did not take the islands, in his view, Spain would sell the islands to another power that possessed the capacity to conquer the Philippines.

In his initial instructions to his peace commissioners meeting in Paris, McKinley instructed them to seek only full rights and sovereignty over the island of Luzon. But by 26 October McKinley had decided that 'the cession must be of the whole Archipelago or none'.[29] On 13 November Secretary of State Hay telegraphed the American delegates that the United States was entitled to an indemnity for the cost of the war and instructed the commissioners to offer Spain $10 to $20 million for the Philippines. The treaty was concluded on this fiscal basis and signed on 10 December 1898.

On 21 December McKinley announced the United States would retain the Philippines as a colonial possession. He described the mission of the United States as one of 'benevolent assimilation'.[30] In the same proclamation, he named Major General Elwell S. Otis as commander of US ground forces, which were to 'extend by force American sovereignty over this country'.[31] McKinley clearly intended the United States to stay permanently in the Philippines.

Aguinaldo, who had been elected the nation's first president by the Philippine Constitutional Convention meeting at Malolos, thirty miles north of Manila, on 1 January 1899, responded by issuing his own proclamation four days later, warning that his government would forcibly resist any American attempt to take over the country. This sounded like a declaration of war against the United States, but Aguinaldo only desired that US forces leave the islands. Most Americans would probably have supported his demands (as they had supported the idea of Cuban independence) had they believed he or his supporters were capable of ruling the whole island group. Unfortunately, it appeared to most contemporary observers that the Filipinos did not constitute a nation but merely a group of peoples and tribes of differing ethnicity, religion and origin, whom the Spanish had been unable to civilize despite four centuries of colonial rule. Aguinaldo drew his main support from the Tagalog tribe, which comprised less than one half of the population of the island of Luzon. Washington believed only the American presence could bring peace, liberty and democracy to the Filipinos, and prepared to carry out the task.

On 4 February 1899, two days before the US Senate's ratification of the treaty, hostilities between US naval and land forces and the Filipino forces broke out in what would become the most deplorable unintended consequence of the Spanish-American War. An American soldier, Frank Grayson, shot a Filipino soldier who was crossing a bridge into American-occupied territory in San Juan del Monte. Historians now consider this incident to be the start of the insurrection. Open fighting soon erupted between American troops and pro-independence Filipinos. The outcome of this conflict was to prove more problematic than the war with Spain. No formal declaration of war was ever issued, and the McKinley administration subsequently declared Aguinaldo to be an 'outlaw bandit'.[32] Calling the American–Philippine War an 'insurrection' made it appear to be a rebellion against a lawful government, although the only part of the Philippines under American control at that time was Manila. The Filipinos rightly felt betrayed by their former allies.

US forces in the Philippines numbered 14,000 men, under the command of General Otis. As would be the case throughout the Vietnam War, the army wanted more. In August, Otis requested '40,000 effectives for the field'. Twelve regiments of volunteers were raised, two of which were composed of African-Americans. By mid-June 1899, following a number of more or less conventional military operations on the island of Luzon in which US forces were victorious, the fighting gradually assumed a guerrilla character. The United States had engaged in guerrilla-style fighting prior to 1899 against Indians, but lacked experience fighting combined mountain and sea operations, which involved cavalry, infantry and artillery, spread over a number of islands. In April 1900 the military organization of the American forces was changed from the traditional one of divisions and brigades to a geographical basis. Each commander was given charge of a certain area.

The Americans were lavishly armed with modern weaponry. The land forces were supported by US warships that used naval gunfire against Philippine positions. In contrast, the Filipinos were armed with outmoded rifles and worn-out pieces of artillery mostly captured from the Spanish. The Filipinos fought in small groups and generally under local chieftains. They relied upon the sympathy of some of the population and the fear they instilled in the remainder. The Americans, unable to distinguish friend from foe, trusted nobody; they fought ruthlessly, most notoriously under Brigadier General Frederick Funston.

The presidential election of 1900 served as a referendum on American policy about the future of the Philippines and Cuba. The victory of McKinley in November, by a greatly increased majority, indicated widespread approval of the outcomes brought about by the war, and gave the president four more years in which to complete military operations. On 23 March 1901 Aguinaldo was captured. The Filipino nationalist eloquently defended his actions:

After mature deliberation, I resolutely proclaim to the world that I cannot refuse to heed the voice of a people longing for peace, nor the lamentations of thousands of families yearning to see their dear ones enjoying the liberty and promised generosity of the great American nation. By acknowledging

and accepting the sovereignty of the United States throughout the Philippine Archipelago, as I now do, and without any
reservation whatsoever, I believe that I am serving thee, my
beloved country.[33]

On 19 May 1901, on behalf of the US Army in the
Philippines, Brigadier General Lloyd Wheaton reported the termination of the state of war, despite ongoing fighting with other
tribes and in other islands, particularly with the Moros of the Sulu
group. On 4 July 1902 President Theodore Roosevelt declared that
the American–Philippine war was over. The US volunteers and
many of the regulars were sent home, but some remained. Two-
and-a-half years after the peace treaty, Washington purported to
believe that the Spanish-Cuban-Filipino-American War had ended.
In all likelihood, Roosevelt simply saw a chance to cut his losses
and run, and he took it.

By that time, more than 120,000 American soldiers had
served in the Philippines: 4,324 American soldiers had been killed
and another 2,818 wounded. At least 16,000 Filipino soldiers and
between 250,000 to 1,000,000 civilians were killed; the population
was horrifically reduced from nine million people to eight million.
By the end of 1903 the Americans had succeeded in taking control
only of urban and coastal areas. In 1907 Macario Sacay, one of the
last remaining Filipino generals fighting against the Americans,
was captured and hanged. The guerrilla war did not fully subside
until 1913, when President Woodrow Wilson proclaimed a change
in policy that would lead to full independence. Nonetheless, in the
south, Muslim Filipinos resisted until 1916 – the so-called Moro
Rebellion.

Atrocities were perpetrated by both sides during the
American–Philippine war. US troops regularly used torture to
obtain information and confessions. The so-called 'water cure'
torture was administered to rebel suspects. Some were hanged by
their thumbs; others were dragged by galloping horses; fires were
lighted beneath others while they were hanging. Villages were
burned, civilians massacred in townships and their possessions
looted. In Samar and Batangas, Brigadier Generals Jacob H.
Smith and Franklin Bell ordered mass murders in retaliation
against the mass resistance. For their part, Filipino guerrillas

chopped off the noses and ears of captured Americans in violation of Aguinaldo's orders. There were reports that some
Americans were buried alive by angry Filipino guerrillas. In
response to public demand in the US for retaliation, President
Theodore Roosevelt ordered the pacification of Samar. And in six
months, General 'Jake' Smith transformed Balangiga into a
'howling wilderness'. He ordered his men to kill anybody capable
of carrying arms, including ten-year-old boys. Smith particularly
ordered Major Littleton Waller to punish the people of Samar for
the deaths of Americans. He is reported to have said: 'Burn all
and kill all. The more you burn and kill, the more you will please
me.'[34] Waller had exceeded even the standard of brutality set by
Sherman in the Civil War.

In 1901, in what many regard as an early version of the relo-
cation hamlets employed by US forces in Vietnam, all the men,
women and children of the towns of Batangas and Laguna were
herded into small areas within the *población* of their respective
towns. Houses, furniture, carts and animals were burned; the people were incarcerated as prisoners for months. The same tactics
were perpetrated by US soldiers against non-combatants from
March to October 1903 in the province of Albay, and in 1905 in the
provinces of Cavite and Batangas. All of this transpired during
Roosevelt's presidency, much of it after he had announced the conclusion of the American–Philippine war.

The army and the administration in Washington had begun
planning for the post-war government of their territorial dependencies as early as January 1899. In 1901 McKinley appointed Judge
(later President) William Howard Taft to the governorship of the
Philippines. The Supreme Court sanctioned what had been done in
decisions known as the 'Insular Cases' of 1901. The Court held
that in legislating for the territories, Congress was not bound by all
the restrictions of the Constitution, as, for instance, that requiring
trial by jury; that Porto Rico and the Philippines were neither foreign countries nor completely parts of the United States, though
Congress was at liberty to incorporate them into the Union. Taft,
Congress and the governors of the other new US possessions
enjoyed a degree of *carte blanche* that would have been the envy of
the Crown's men in colonial North America, against whom
Jefferson and the others had rebelled.

Some indication of how Washington felt about the outcome of the Spanish-American War can be seen in Theodore Roosevelt's December 1903 State of the Union message. Roosevelt wrote Congress that:

> Of our insular possessions the Philippines and Porto Rico it is gratifying to say that their steady progress has been such as to make it unnecessary to spend much time in discussing them . . . No one people ever benefited another people more than we have benefited the Filipinos by taking possession of the islands . . . The condition of the islanders is in material things far better than ever before, while their governmental, intellectual, and moral advance has kept pace with their material advance.

He made clear the direct benefits to the United States. The establishment of a naval base in the Philippines at Subig Bay, he stated, 'ought not to be longer postponed. Such a base is desirable in time of peace; in time of war it would be indispensable, and its lack would be ruinous. Without it our fleet would be helpless.'[35] He had his eye on Japan, the rising industrial-military power in the Far East.

In 1907 the US-appointed Philippine Commission was replaced by a Legislative Assembly, and under the Wilson administration the process toward independence was accelerated. The Filipinos remained loyal to the United States in both World Wars and a son of Aguinaldo served with American forces. The Philippine people eventually gained independence in 1946, a liberation that could have taken place in 1899 with the saving of thousands of lives and without so much unspeakable suffering.

Other unintended consequences flowed from the Spanish-American War. One whose disturbing significance lay dormant for almost a century was a unique, perpetual lease agreement entered into with Cuba in 1903 over an area of 47 square miles in Guantanamo, a space slightly larger than Manhattan. The terms of the lease provide that 'the United States shall exercise complete jurisdiction and control over and within such areas.'[36] Here the United States built a naval base, which it controls to the present day. More than one hundred years after signing the lease, as part of the 'Global War on Terrorism', the United States set up an internment camp at Guantanamo that made the Spanish look like amateurs in the practices of cruelty and barbarity. Cuba may have been freed in 1898, but its territorial sovereignty was far from complete more than a century later.

A war with Spain for the independence of Cuba had promised a great deal for many segments of the American leadership. What it did not portend was a political-military empire stretching from California to the South China Sea. Fighting a war that President McKinley envisioned as limited in purpose when he signed the joint resolution of Congress on 20 April 1898 ominously transformed the United States from an influential hemispheric power into a transoceanic imperialist world power.

As a Pacific imperial power the United States joined briefly, in 1899, with other great powers in the decisive military intervention in China to repress the Boxer Rebellion. Serious tensions soon emerged with Japan, which some Americans thought was threatening American control of the Philippines and Hawaii. Closer to home, with the acquiescence of Great Britain, the United States established hegemony in the Caribbean. The war was fought to bring security and stability to the region, but the United States quickly found itself ensnared in a series of 'Banana Wars'. Fought in Cuba, the Dominican Republic, Haiti and Nicaragua, these neo-colonial police actions plagued the United States for the remainder of the twentieth century and into the twenty-first.

Finally, the Spanish-American War accelerated the US construction of the Panama Canal. Commenced in 1904 and completed ten years later, the canal permitted the US Navy to transfer its battle fleet rapidly from the Atlantic to the Pacific, depending on whether Germany or Japan was perceived to be the greater menace to American national security. The war to free the Cuban people had placed United States armed forces in the unprecedented position of seriously contemplating war with the strongest power in Asia, Japan, and with one of the strongest powers in Europe, Germany.

SIX

THE UNITED STATES IN WORLD WAR I, 1917–18

It is much easier to make war than peace.
Georges Clemenceau, Paris, 1919[1]

The course and outcome of World War I were nothing like the expectations of the participants. No-one anticipated the length, the scale of the slaughter, or the outcome of that most dreadful war the world had yet seen. Nearly ten million combatants and non-combatants lost their lives in the years between 1914 and 1918, and for much of the war no-one knew how to end the conflict. The armistices and subsequent peace treaties created a world, certainly a European world, vastly different from that envisaged by those who took up war. President Woodrow Wilson asserted that the United States entered the war to make the world 'safe for democracy' and to bring 'peace and safety to all nations', but within twenty years the world faced an even greater cataclysm.

The United States had no intention of entering the war in 1914. The nation was ill-prepared for a major war. There was no immediate military threat to the nation's security. As the war dragged on, the Wilson administration gradually convinced itself that if the United States were to function as a world power, its long-term national interest required active belligerent involvement in the war. By the end of 1916 Wilson and his advisors had reached the conclusion that if the United States did not intervene militarily on the side of the Anglo–French–Russian coalition, Germany and its allies would probably win the war. They believed a triumphant and all-powerful Germany would threaten American interests around the world, especially in the Caribbean, offering a challenge to America's hemispheric security. Germany's use of submarines to sink merchant vessels, which resulted in the loss of American lives and weapons secretly being shipped to Britain, constituted the trigger that led to a congressional declaration of war against Germany in April 1917.

In 1916, not for the first or last time, a candidate pledging to keep the United States out of war was elected president. Woodrow Wilson had campaigned for re-election promising neutrality. Yet by April 1917 he had decided that it was necessary for the New World to redeem the Old. 'Right is more precious than peace', he told a spellbound Congress.[2] Wilson led a somewhat divided country into the Great War promising to bring the conflict to a successful conclusion. He planned to play a major role in shaping the peace. The Spanish-American War had created an American empire, and World War I provided the evangelical president with the opportunity to project the idea of the United States as the world's saviour, policeman, and international leader of a new world order.

The United States reluctantly entered the war only after the president articulated his motives and goals in universal terms. In actuality, the president was motivated by considerations of national economic self-interest as well as idealism. Wilson was certainly responding to Germany's January 1917 resumption of unrestricted submarine warfare, but those provocations scarcely constituted a cause to enter the war, especially as Britain's wartime blockades represented a provocation of almost equal magnitude. In addition to implementing his personal vision for a better world, the president was motivated by the desire to protect US commercial relations with Great Britain and its allies, a desire to dismantle preferential British trade arrangements, and a steadfast determination to gain a seat at the peace conferences that would determine the future of international relations.

By January 1917 the United States had spent almost two-and-a-half years maintaining a policy of qualified neutrality toward the two warring blocs in the stalemated war in Europe: the Triple Alliance dominated by Germany and the Austro-Hungarian Empire on the one hand, and on the other, the Triple Entente of Great Britain, France and Russia. In reality, the US policy strongly favoured the Triple Entente. A highly lucrative transatlantic trade in foodstuffs and war materiel had gradually blossomed between the thriving agricultural and industrial giant of North America and Britain and France. Commercial and financial relations with Germany simultaneously withered because the Royal Navy had effectively closed German-controlled ports on the Continent. The German navy struck out against this economic warfare in the only way it could: with submarine attacks against Allied and neutral shipping.

The core of the political and diplomatic problem facing the United States and Germany was exposed on 7 May 1915, when U-20 sank the 30,000-ton British liner *Lusitania* with the loss of 1,198 people, including 128 Americans. Wilson arrogantly insisted that Americans had the right to travel into German-declared submarine operating zones on belligerent-owned liners as well as on American ones. He also advanced an archaic proposition derived from commerce-raiding practices in the age of sail: the predator must issue a warning of imminent attack for the sake of the passengers and crew aboard the targeted vessel. He refused to recognize the fact that the U-boat was a revolutionary new commerce-destroyer, highly lethal yet highly vulnerable due to its lack of armour; it could not warn its victims in advance for fear of being rammed or destroyed by armed merchant vessels. Nonetheless, to prevent the United States's entrance into the war on the side of the Anglo-French allies, Germany largely accepted Wilson's unrealistic demands until the grisly stalemate in the trenches finally drove Berlin to take 'a leap into the dark'.[3]

In January 1917 overly confident German naval officers persuaded the government of Kaiser Wilhelm II that unlimited U-boat attacks on the heavily loaded transatlantic cargo ships, which were flooding Britain with war munitions and food from the United States, could drive England out of the war within six months. On 31 January Berlin announced that starting the next day German submarines would attack without warning and sink all commercial vessels, enemy and neutral, found in or near British waters. President Wilson was incensed. He severed diplomatic relations with Germany and watched anxiously as the toll of sunken ships mounted. In late March U-boats sank three American merchantmen. He had his *casus belli*.

Wilson called for a special session of Congress to convene on 2 April. In a long speech full of high-flown rhetoric disguising highly prejudiced and often hypocritical arguments, Wilson requested that Congress declare war with Germany and permit him to do everything possible to bring the Government of the German Empire to terms and end the war. The president described the conflict in language that bore virtually no relationship to either the brutal realities of the battle-front, or to the events and issues that had led to the outbreak of war in Europe in 1914. Wilson, who had never been outside the country, emphasized the altruism of the United States and described the nation's grievances and goals in universal terms. The speech reflected the president's blend of puritanical self-righteousness and political pragmatism. He omitted any suggestion that the United States had overstepped the limits of a neutral power in the struggle, or that the United States was protecting its own national interests in the western hemisphere. Using spiritual imagery, and following what was by now a familiar formula in such presidential messages, Wilson portrayed the United States as an innocent victim of aggression faced with no choice but to retaliate against attacks by a despotic, inhuman enemy that represented a threat to humanity. Polk, Lincoln and McKinley had all successfully employed such a stratagem in calling for war, as would later presidents.

Wilson asserted that the government of Imperial Germany, in resuming unrestricted submarine warfare, had 'put aside all restraints of law or of humanity'. The German submarine warfare against commerce was, he added, 'a warfare against mankind'. The nature of submarine warfare, Wilson claimed, made neutrality impractical. The United States was not seeking revenge, but there was one choice that the United States was incapable of making:

We will not choose the path of submission and suffer the most sacred rights of our nation and our people to be ignored or violated. The wrongs against which we now array ourselves are no common wrongs; they cut to the very roots of human life.

Wilson set out the objectives of the United States in going to war:

Our object . . . is to vindicate the principles of peace and justice in the life of the world as against selfish and autocratic power and to set up amongst the really free and self-governed peoples of the world such a concert of purpose and of action as will henceforth ensure the observance of those principles.[4]

The war had been provoked and waged by autocratic governments accustomed to using their subjects as pawns and tools, Wilson said. Democratic nations did not behave in these ways. Then, in terms that described precisely how the United States had provoked war against Mexico seventy years previously, Wilson asserted that democracies 'do not, for example, set the course of intrigue to bring about some critical posture of affairs which will give them an opportunity to strike and make conquest'. Oblivious to the irony of his statement, Wilson observed: 'Cunningly contrived plans of deception or aggression . . . can be worked out and kept from the light only within the privacy of courts or behind the carefully guarded confidences of a narrow and privileged class.'

Turning to the issue of the peace, Wilson stated: 'A steadfast concert for peace can never be maintained except by a partnership of democratic nations.' Autocratic government could not be trusted. He added: 'Only free peoples can hold their purpose and their honour steady to a common end and prefer the interests of mankind to any narrow interest of their own.' The 'great, generous Russian people', who had just overthrown their monarch, were fighting for 'freedom in the world, for justice, and for peace'. They would be 'a fit partner' in such 'a league of honour'. (That is, until the Bolsheviks in 1918 won the civil war under way in that country.) Then came the passage which has become the hallmark of the speech and for which it has become famous:

> The world must be made safe for democracy. Its peace must be planted upon the tested foundations of political liberty. We have no selfish ends to serve. We desire no conquest, no dominion. We seek no indemnities for ourselves, no material compensation for the sacrifices we shall freely make. We are but one of the champions of the rights of mankind. We shall be satisfied when those rights have been made as secure as the faith and the freedom of nations can make them . . . .[5]

Wilson expressed what were perhaps his most heartfelt sentiments:

> It is a fearful thing to lead this great peaceful people into war, into the most terrible and disastrous of all wars, civilization itself seeming to be in the balance. But the right is more precious than peace, and we shall fight for the things which we have always carried nearest our hearts – for democracy, for the right of those who submit to authority to have a voice in their own governments, for the rights and liberties of small

nations, for a universal dominion of right by such a concert of free peoples as shall bring peace and safety to all nations and make the world itself at last free.[6]

His was a manifesto that paraphrased and globalized the Declaration of Independence:

To such a task we can dedicate our lives and our fortunes, everything that we are and everything that we have, with the pride of those who know that the day has come when America is privileged to spend her blood and her might for the principles that gave her birth and happiness and the peace which she has treasured. God helping her, she can do no other.[7]

Congress passed the resolution for war on 6 April. The vote was 82 to 6 in the Senate, 373 to 50 in the House of Representatives, not a unanimous action but certainly a very highly favourable empowerment for sending thousands of young Americans to their deaths. The majority of Americans had no doubts as to the wisdom of the decision to enter the war. They were convinced by Wilson that they were doing so to make the world safe for democracy.

THE WAR

World War I was 'total' for the armies and navies of Europe; for the United States it was partial and tentative. The major challenge facing the US Navy was to defeat the U-boat, a radically new weapons system. For the US Army, the task was to engage in conventional battles an ocean away from the American political and industrial base and against armies equipped with the latest weaponry. In these respects, US participation in World War I differed fundamentally from the Civil War and the Spanish-American War. The gaping disjunction existing between the US Army and Navy during World War I also contrasted sharply with those two earlier wars, and with World War II.

As Wilson was delivering his speech of 2 April requesting a Congressional declaration of war, the man who would direct the US naval campaign, Rear Admiral William S. Sims, was already en route to England. Upon Sims's arrival, the Royal Navy's first sea lord, Admiral John R. Jellicoe, told Sims that German submarines were ravaging British and neutral shipping at such a rate that the Allied Powers unquestionably would lose the war for want of food and *matériel*, possibly as early as August, certainly by October 1917. Something had to be done: the question was, what? For at least four months American naval strategy in the Great War was the subject of an acrimonious transatlantic debate. From London, Sims and Ambassador Walter Hines Page beseeched Washington to send every seaworthy destroyer to escort convoys of merchant vessels through U-boat-infested waters off the English coast.

President Wilson and Secretary of the Navy Josephus Daniels agreed that the submarine constituted the chief threat to the Allied cause, but they seriously doubted that the peril facing Great Britain was quite so extreme as portrayed by Page and Sims, both of whom radiated Anglophilia. British laggardness in prosecuting the war against the submarine irritated Wilson, and for a time he thought that direct attacks against bases on the Continent and massive mine-laying would prove more destructive to the U-boats than convoys escorted by destroyers. What finally won over Wilson and Daniels was the accumulating documentation of the steady reduction in the monthly rate of U-boat sinkings of merchant ships as the convoy system was expanded by the British Admiralty and the US Navy's man in London.

By late autumn 1917 the US naval staff in London was expanding commensurately with the growing numbers of American warships and crews under Sims's direction. At the height of the war, Sims controlled 370 ships of all classes, 5,000 officers and 70,000 enlisted men distributed among 45 bases in the British Isles and on the Continent. Together with the British commander at Queenstown, Admiral Sir Lewis Bayly, whom naval historian Sir Julian Corbett considered 'the father of destroyer tactics and organization',[8] Sims proved that in an Anglo-American naval war against German submarines the best hope for maritime victory lay in convoying to safety transports crammed with men and cargo vessels loaded with armaments.

The figures spoke for themselves. When Sims first arrived in London, Admiral Jellicoe predicted that in April 1917 the U-boats would sink 900,000 tons of merchant transports, a rate of loss that would soon starve Britain into submission. Instead, by December

1917 the Allies were losing 350,000 tons per month. In October 1918, the month before the war ended, the U-boats could sink no more than 112,427 tons. This massive reduction in losses, with the inverse monthly increase in tonnage of materiel being shipped from the United States, was accomplished between May 1917 and November 1918 by 1,500 convoys of 18,000 ships. The US Navy provided about 27 per cent of the escorting destroyers in British waters, the Royal Navy 70 per cent. Simultaneously, the United States initiated a separate category of shipments: troops and their equipment that were routed to Brest, France, on a more southerly track around the British Isles. Sims and the Admiralty protected the convoys of this morale-boosting contingent of two million American soldiers without losing a single soldier en route to Europe.

This achievement might have been expected to set the standard for US naval strategy in the post-war era, but it did not. Like the navies of most other great powers, the US Navy was fixated on large warships designed to win command of the seas in massive fleet engagements. From the end of World War I until the destruction of its battleships at Pearl Harbor on 7 December 1941, the American navy stubbornly clung to war plans and fleets that had proven irrelevant to the Great War. This was certainly not the consequence envisioned by the Anglophilic American admiral who had directed the naval war of 1917–18 for the United States.

Where Sims and the navy fought indirectly, in a war of attrition that did not meet the standard formula for massed fleet engagements, the US Army engaged the German enemy frontally, on terms prescribed by the Anglo-French high commands. As a result, the victory was less complete than it might have been, and the post-war consequences were not what the war-makers had planned.

The American Expeditionary Force (AEF) that fought in Europe in the Great War was commanded by Lieutenant General John J. 'Black Jack' Pershing, whom Theodore Roosevelt had promoted directly from captain to brigadier general in 1906. Fresh from commanding a quixotic expedition against Pancho Villa in Mexico, Pershing sailed to Europe in May 1917. A West Point graduate and veteran of the Spanish-American War, Pershing was a classical fighting general. He insisted that American soldiers should be properly trained before being despatched to Europe. This was not always possible, and much training had to be completed in Europe.

Historian Geoffrey Perret has described the American soldiers as they reached Europe: 'Half trained, gangling, awestruck, they were pitied by their British and French instructors yet cheered rapturously by British and French crowds as victory's dream.'[9]

By March 1918 Pershing commanded 500,000 American 'Doughboys' in Europe; by July of the same year there were more than one million American troops under Pershing's command. He demanded that they remain a distinct force, but often they were integrated with the British or French units under the guise of 'training'. The Battle of Le Hamel on 4 July 1918 was representative of the integration. Intended to eliminate a salient of the German army in the area east of Amiens, the battle was led by Australian Major General John Monash, arguably the war's best general. Troops of the Australian 4th Division and four companies from the US 33rd Division fought side by side in an offensive that featured massed machine guns, tanks and airplanes. The Germans were caught entirely by surprise. In 93 minutes the Australian-Americans straightened the German line, suffered 1,000 casualties and captured 1,500 Germans.

The Battle of Le Hamel was a limited tactical success, but it had no bearing on the outcome of a war in which massive infantry assaults were countered by entrenched machine guns, heavy artillery and dug-in soldiers, whose rifles could pick off their approaching enemy. It was a typical but minute example of how the Germans and the western allies fought for over four years. In such circumstances, Pershing's AEF could only contribute to allied operations. It was not until September 1918, during the Battle of Saint-Mihiel, that Pershing would command a full army, the American First, composed of 500,000 men. Saint-Mihiel was the largest offensive operation ever undertaken by US armed forces, and it resulted in a battlefield victory. It was followed by the Meuse-Argonne offensive, from 27 September to 6 October 1918, in which Pershing commanded more than one million American and French soldiers.

The Americans' two gigantic offensives recovered 200 square miles of French territory held by the German army. Pershing favoured fighting on, seeking Ulysses S. Grant's ideal of unconditional surrender. He believed that by continuing the war for a few more weeks the German army would totally collapse. It would be annihilated, as Grant would have prescribed. But it was too late. A revolution in Berlin had unseated the Kaiser, and Germany was seeking an armistice. The European people and politicians on all sides were exhausted by a war that the strategy of massed assault against trenches and machine guns had protracted for over four years. They demanded an end, and they got it. An armistice was signed, to take effect at 11.00 am on 11 November 1918. This timing was perfectly ironic symmetry for a war that had destroyed the good order of western European civilization.

Geoffrey Perret records the playful mood of those still alive in the trenches at 11.00 am on the 11th day of the 11th month of 1918: 'Men gave up a rat-like existence, emerging into the open. It was safe to stand up.' The Europeans kicked around soccer balls, drank cheap red wine, and played accordions in a macabre festival of release. The Americans, Perret contends, were relatively subdued. 'There seemed little to show for all they had suffered and done. Besides, if the Allies had won, why were the Germans celebrating as if theirs was the victory? Not every doughboy rejoiced when the firing ceased.' Their leader, John Pershing, would soon become only the fourth officer in history to be promoted to full general in the Regular Army of the United States – following Union generals Grant, Sherman and Sheridan. But because he had not been permitted to follow Grant's example of extracting an unconditional surrender, and because he had lost so many men, he 'felt no sense of triumph'.[10]

The United States had been in the war for a scant nineteen months; the Europeans for more than four years. In that relatively short period, there had been 360,000 American casualties, including 116,000 dead and 234,000 wounded. Many of the dead succumbed to disease in the primitive sanitary conditions of the trenches – but they had died all the same.

UNINTENDED CONSEQUENCES

Reflecting on World War I, historian Margaret MacMillan notes that it began with a series of mistakes and 'ended in confusion'.[11] According to David Stevenson, the settlement imposed following the war contained 'time bombs' of political instability (such as Yugoslavia) that have kept exploding until the present. 'Nothing ever seen before', Stevenson writes, 'compared with such massive concentrations of firepower and of human suffering . . . and with such meagre results.'[12] He is particularly critical of American involvement, which, he says, not only pushed Germany toward premature surrender, but was also belated, inefficient, badly led and (with respect to President Wilson) diplomatically unsophisticated in coping with European cynicism.

The consequences for the United States, at home as well as abroad, were totally unintended. The immediate goals of preventing German attacks on American shipping, and governing the conditions for the future use of new weapons such as the submarine by belligerents, were successful only in the short term; the goal of achieving a just and lasting peace was chimerical. The concept of 'freedom of the seas' continued to prove as problematic as it always had been, but more than twenty years later Germany's widespread use of submarines against US shipping did not provoke the United States into declaring war against the Axis Powers; belligerency came only after Japan's attack on Pearl Harbor. Rather than join the League of Nations, which in Wilson's view was the only guarantee against a recurrence of the tragedy of the Great War, Washington turned its back on Europe. Consumed by irrational fears of recently arrived immigrants and their imagined threatening ideologies, Americans soon embarked on a repressive policy aimed at purging the nation of potential terrorists.

The armistice of 11 November 1918, ending the war to end wars, was greeted with jubilation in the United States. Democracy had prevailed, and Americans expected that international and domestic tranquillity would follow. On 4 December 1918 Wilson, heading an American Peace Commission, sailed for Paris on the *George Washington* to translate victory on the battlefield into a peaceful world order. He felt he had to go in person as he owed it to the Americans who had lost their lives in the war. 'It is now my duty to play my full part in making good what they gave their life's blood to obtain', Wilson told Congress before departing.[13] The president was greeted in Paris by the largest crowd in French history as hundreds of thousands lined the streets delirious with joy at the sight of the man they saw as their saviour. A similar greeting awaited him in London, and in January 1919 in Rome. Despite popular adulation, after two months of meetings lasting eighteen hours a day, Wilson was unable to get his way in the peace negotiations that followed. High hopes turned to disillusionment. Part of the reason for this was that, while Wilson had laid out general principles, he had said little about the details.

On 8 January 1918, in a speech to a Joint Session of Congress, Wilson had spelled out Fourteen Points that, he said, should guide the peace process.[14] They were a visionary plan for a new world order, but they were not a blueprint for peace. They gave the world (including Germany) the hope that peace would be accompanied by renewed dignity and international cooperation, reconstruction and not revenge.

Wilson thought the United States, as an arbiter, would act with justice and generosity. The United States, the president repeatedly asserted, unlike the other participants in the conflict, neither entered the war to acquire territory, nor to seek revenge. As Wilson believed had been the case in the 1898 war with Spain, the United States once again had acted unselfishly, fighting only to provide peoples with the opportunity of freedom. He believed that American foreign policy during his own administration had been motivated by such principles. However, by the end of June 1919, when the Versailles Treaty had been signed and the Covenant of the League of Nations had been drawn up, Wilson realized the futility of seeking to remedy what he saw as generations of European hatred, fear, suspicion, greed and ambition. Despite Europe's postwar rejection of the old order, the tackling of difficult issues like Bolshevism was postponed.

World War I was the first war that the United States had fought with allies, and it insisted upon the title 'Associate' rather than agree to accept a subordinate role in which command decisions were made jointly. Yet Wilson was surprised by the unexpected opposition he faced from his peers at the Paris Peace Conference to the adoption of his Fourteen Points. Wilson thought he had set the terms for the armistice, and he expected to dictate the terms for the peace. The Allies were agreed on the need to end all wars and willing to create an international organization that would work towards this noble end. But they were irreconcilably divided on other matters and were far from unified on the post-war territorial and fiscal-economic arrangements.

Wilson was shocked by the diversity of groups and opinions in Europe, although his own ideas about national self-determination and other matters were far from clear and settled. Even his secretary of state, Robert Lansing, was unsure of what Wilson meant when he spoke of self-determination. Lansing asked himself, 'When the President talks of "self-determination" what unit has he in mind? Does he mean a race, a territorial area or a community?'[15] Lansing believed Wilson had raised hopes that could not be satisfied and would create new antagonisms that might lead to war. In Lansing's opinion, the president possessed an illusory road map to peace, filled with contradictory and vague notions.

Pre-war suspicions re-emerged among the demoralized, if victorious, allies. Anglo-French antagonisms prevented agreement on the disposition of German-occupied territories, and Anglo-American rivalry was always near the surface in negotiations concerning 'freedom of the seas' and the freeing-up of preferential trade arrangements. Securing 'freedom of the seas' was one of the pre-eminent reasons Wilson gave for entering the war. Yet at the peace conference, rather than championing the principle, Wilson relented to British demands that the right to blockade should be preserved. The president did not press for abandonment of blockade as a weapon of war, thereby ensuring that 'freedom of the seas' was unrealized. He also allowed the British and other victorious powers to retain their colonies.

Wilson and the other conferees in Paris faced extraordinary difficulties between January and July 1919. The war had created tremendous devastation in Europe. Four and a half years of slaughter had resulted in the loss of more than 3.6 million lives among the Western Allies; it had cost them more than $130 billion dollars. The war had ensured the success of Bolshevism in Russia, the unexpected collapse of the Austro-Hungarian and Ottoman empires and the emergence of long-suppressed nationalist sentiments among their subject peoples, and rising tension between China and Japan over territory and favour with the West. The war also created enormous expectations about the new world order that the allied leaders would create at the peace conference. The atmosphere was filled with uncertainty. The task of creating order out of the political chaos and territorial uncertainty was all but impossible. The scale of reconstruction required, like the destructiveness of the war itself, was unprecedented. Weighing heavily on the minds of the allied leaders was fear of the spread of revolutionary Bolshevism.

In the months following the end of hostilities, and while negotiations were proceeding in Paris, developments in Russia did not go according to Wilson's plans. The civil war between Bolsheviks and anti-Communists had been intensified by an allied (including US) military intervention, an economic blockade, and by siphoning off Russian territory to Poland, Romania and Czechoslovakia in early 1919. These hostile actions turned Vladimir Lenin against the United States and the West. Hoping to prevent a Bolshevik victory, in May 1919 the Allies recognized an anti-Bolshevik government. But by early 1920, after half-hearted and ineffectual efforts to assist the 'Whites', the United States and the Allies were reluctantly forced to recognize that they could not prevent a 'Red' Bolshevik victory.

Another outcome that was unintended and particularly troubling to the United States was the uncertain disposition and future of East Asia. As a reward for entering the war on the side of the Western Allies, Japan sought to consolidate its position in China by demanding Germany's leased territories in Shandong province and its islands in the Central Pacific. In April 1919 Wilson was forced to accept the secret wartime agreements his Allies had signed transferring Germany's rights to Japan. Wilson's acquiescence to this arrangement later became one of the reasons for the Senate's rejection of the treaty.

As a result of this compromise, the United States soon entered an arms race with an increasingly expansionistic Japan that was determined to assert its primacy in the Pacific. To defuse the rising tensions, the 1921–2 Washington Conference on the Limitation of Armaments was convened to restrict warship construction. At the conference, an existing defensive treaty between Britain and Japan was replaced by a looser arrangement that encouraged Japanese nationalist fervour, leading in turn to Japanese expansion in China. Perhaps more ominously, the acquisition by Japan of the Marshall, Mariana and Caroline Islands potentially threatened the US maritime route from Hawaii to the Philippines. The national security of the United States was greatly diminished by these developments, which were the direct but unintended result of entering a war without clearly perceived and attainable political and military goals. In World War II President Franklin D. Roosevelt would attempt to avoid similar mistakes, although he was philosophically incapable of eliminating idealism from his motivations.

Upon his return home from Paris in July 1919, Wilson faced stronger than expected opposition to his post-war arrangements, especially as they related to American participation in the newly formed League of Nations. He sent the Versailles Treaty to the Senate for ratification on 10 July, stating: 'The stage is set, the destiny disclosed. It has come about by no plan of our conceiving, but by the hand of God, who has led us into this way.'[16] But in November the irreverent Senate refused to ratify the treaty. Wilson was furious at the concerted opposition led by Republican Senator Henry Cabot Lodge. Between then and the presidential election of November 1920, Wilson sought to get the nation's support for joining the League and approving the treaty. He declared the election a referendum on his handiwork at Versailles.

Republican Warren G. Harding won the election, however, and condemned the treaty. Congress terminated the war in July 1921. In August 1921 the United States signed a treaty with Germany claiming the terms of the Treaty of Versailles valid for itself without membership in the League. Within months of the establishment of the League, the fragile peace agreements in Europe, especially in East and Southeast Europe, began unravelling. The United States, which claimed to have had entered the war to prevent the recurrence of violence, did nothing – nor indeed did it wish to, if the Senate's opposition to joining the League was any indication. Ten years after the end of the war, the United States signed the Kellogg-Briand Pact in Paris with 61 other nations, essentially renouncing war except in cases of self-defence. The Senate approved it, 85 votes to 1. Americans, sickened by the slaughter of the war, had turned inwards.

In doing so they turned on one another. Domestically, one of the most disturbing unintended outcomes of the war was the widespread restrictions on civil liberties at home. Progressivism, or bipartisan liberal reform, became the main casualty of the war. Prior to the war, political progressives – women, African-Americans and trade unionists – had been optimistic about the possibilities of redressing some of the injustices and inequalities in American life and creating greater opportunities and prosperity for the population. By war's end this optimism had been destroyed. The reasons had to do with the attacks on civil liberties undertaken by the administration to quell the voices of dissent against the war. It began with the creation of the Committee on Public Information, with George Creel as its head; loyalty oaths were introduced; and on 16 May 1918 Congress transformed the Espionage Act into the Sedition Act. In direct violation of the First Amendment of the Constitution protecting free speech, the Sedition Act made it a criminal offence to utter 'any disloyal, profane, scurrilous or abusive language' that might bring the government of the United States, the Constitution, the flag, or the uniform of the Army or Navy 'into contempt, scorn, contumely or disrepute'.[17]

While no cases involving the Sedition Act came before the Supreme Court until after the war, in 1919 Justice Oliver Wendell Holmes articulated the test of 'clear and present danger' and interpreted his own concept very narrowly.[18] He used it to imprison illegally Socialist labour leader Eugene V. Debs. President Wilson fully supported the Court's repressive approach to suspected disloyalty. So-called hyphenated Americans were particular targets of abuse. In arguing for the League of Nations, Wilson warned that those who opposed the League were allied with revolutionaries in Europe. He declared: 'Any man who carries a hyphen about with him carries a dagger that he is ready to plunge into the vitals of this Republic.'[19] George W. Bush would entirely agree with such sentiments.

Wilson's posture led to exaggerated fears of radicalism and dark visions of a communist threat. The war had encouraged socialism and radicalism. Between October 1919 and January 1920, following a number of letter bombs and threats of violence against high administration officials, Attorney General A. Mitchell Palmer initiated a series of raids on meeting halls and homes without search warrants. The assaults on personal liberties became known as the 'Red Scare'. In flagrant disregard of basic civil rights, more than 4,000 people were arrested and jailed. Palmer concentrated primarily on non-citizens, or 'aliens', as under the Alien Exclusion Act of October 1918 they could be arrested and deported using administrative procedures without indictment or trial. People were held incommunicado, were denied counsel and subjected to kangaroo courts. Many were deported. Wilson applauded these actions. Although by the spring of 1921 things had more or less returned to normal, the 'Red Scare' was to resurface even more powerfully after the next great war fought by the United States.

SEVEN

THE UNITED STATES IN WORLD WAR II, 1941–45

The world is heading toward a secret armament race of a rather desperate character.

Henry L. Stimson to Harry S. Truman, 11 September 1945[1]

World War II was the most cataclysmic war in human history. This war unleashed darker passions, killed more people, and utilized more powerful and deadly weapons than any war in human experience. It was a war almost beyond comprehension in its totality, brutality, scale and scope. It was a war that defined peoples, nations and the twentieth century. In many ways, the sheer scale of the war has discouraged, if not prevented, a detached assessment of its meaning and consequences.

If the United States held true to the idealism, utopianism and universal values espoused by Woodrow Wilson only two decades earlier, then World War II was a war that should have engaged the United States from its outbreak in Europe in 1939. If the realpolitik articulated by other American leaders had any lasting substance or significance beyond empty political rhetoric and hypocrisy, then the United States should have entered it without hesitation. If Americans believed in the efficacy of war – and they surely did – then their failure to act quickly and decisively at the onset of the European war contributed greatly to the magnitude of the war's unintended consequences.

Instead, the United States initially stayed aloof from the conflict engulfing the world, declaring itself neutral until attacked by Japan in December 1941. Or it appeared to stay aloof. In reality, President Franklin Delano Roosevelt involved the United States surreptitiously by assisting Great Britain in the European theatre. In the Far East he embargoed oil shipments to Japan, a policy he knew or believed would provoke Japan into an attack on American interests in the Pacific, necessitating an American armed response.

In so doing, Roosevelt was following the example of President Wilson during World War I, and set a precedent that would be followed by Presidents Lyndon B. Johnson and George W. Bush after him.

The similarities between the conduct of the United States in the First and Second World Wars are striking. During both wars, while the United States claimed to be officially neutral, the incumbent presidents ran a campaign for re-election pledging to keep the United States out of the war, knowing as they did so that they had taken steps leading to US participation in the war. Wilson in 1916 gained re-election with the popular slogan, 'He kept us out of war'.[2] In Boston, on 30 October 1940, Roosevelt repeated the refrain: 'I have said this before, but I shall say it again and again and again: Your boys are not going to be sent into any foreign wars.'[3] A month earlier he had completed the destroyers-for-bases deal with the United Kingdom, and in the next twelve months did a great deal to precipitate the United States' entry into war with Germany and Japan. The similarities can also be seen on the domestic front. In both wars dissent was ruthlessly stifled, and both wars were followed by an outbreak of anti-communist hysteria. Hatred shown to Americans who shared the ethnic background of foreign enemies was particularly extreme in World War II. Shortly after the attack on Pearl Harbor, Roosevelt signed an executive order in February 1942 that led to the internment of more than 120,000 Japanese-Americans, more than two-thirds of whom were American citizens.

Although he regarded fascism and nazism as a threat to the civilized world, Roosevelt was not willing to commit American troops to the war in Europe. Even when asking Congress for a declaration of war against Japan following the attack on Pearl Harbor, he did not ask Congress to declare that a state of war existed between the United States and Japan's ally in the war, Germany. He did everything he could short of deploying troops. It was the policy of minimizing American casualties taken to the level of surrealism. Writing in the 1960s, diplomatic historian Thomas A. Bailey exculpated Roosevelt, despite the fact that the president's actions basically subverted democratic and republican principles, by saying that he would have lost the election had he told the truth. Whereas Wilson entered the Great War to make the world 'safe for democracy', Roosevelt entered World War II, he said, to propagate the 'Four Freedoms': freedom from fear, freedom from want, freedom of religion and freedom from the old politics of balance of power diplomacy. Roosevelt and Churchill articulated these principles in the Atlantic Charter in mid-August 1941. The charter resurrected Wilsonian themes: no secret commitments, no territorial aggrandizement, the right to self-government for all peoples, international free trade, and the creation of an international organization to preserve the peace and prevent future wars. Like Wilson, Roosevelt almost immediately made exceptions inconsistent with these principles: Latin America, the United States' primary sphere of influence, was excluded from this declaration. Significantly, neither France nor the Soviet Union were co-authors of the statement, and this was to have tremendous long-term unintended consequences in Eastern Europe, North Africa and Southeast Asia – most conspicuously in Vietnam.

The United States was strategically ill-prepared to go to war in 1939. The reasons for this unpreparedness can be found among the unintended consequences of World War I. Following that war, recent immigrants from eastern and southern Europe had distanced themselves from their European heritage to avoid persecution and had adopted 'American' – by which they meant White Anglo-Saxon Protestant – values and patterns of behaviour. They strove to identify themselves as '100 per cent' American. More broadly, as the shock and horror of the full human and material cost of the Great War became known in the mid-1920s, and as the congressional Nye Committee of the mid-1930s revealed the enormous profits made from the war by American munitions manufacturers, the majority of Americans resolved never again to involve themselves in the intrigues and wars of empire that dogged Europe and condemned it to repeated deadly combat. Many in the United States believed the nation had been duped or dragged into the war by those institutions that profited from war – banks, financial institutions, armaments manufacturers and the military. A mood of isolationism – at least in military and diplomatic, if not in economic terms – swept the nation.

In the climate of isolationism, and in the throes of the Great Depression, the personnel, equipment and administration of the US armed forces had dramatically shrunk. Not until 1938, the year of the infamous Munich Conference between Hitler and the Anglo-French leaders, did the Congress hesitantly begin to authorize modest reconstruction of the military. Rearmament accelerated rapidly in early 1941, and in the autumn of that year American destroyers began assisting the Royal Navy in search and destroy missions against German submarines. Roosevelt characteristically deceived the American people by misrepresenting three German submarine attacks on US destroyers as unprovoked. But he capitalized on the opportunity to order the navy to 'shoot on sight' – as a purely defensive measure, of course.[4]

Roosevelt's unneutral neutrality came to an explosive end when Japanese carrier-based aircraft ravaged the American fleet at Pearl Harbor, Hawaii, on 7 December 1941. Like Presidents Polk and Wilson before him (and Lyndon B. Johnson after him) Roosevelt portrayed the attack as a complete and unprovoked surprise, while knowing that a Japanese strike had been a likely scenario for at least a year. Reinforced by an outraged American public, and armed with his stentorian eloquence, he went before Congress on 8 December. He proclaimed that Japan's sudden and deliberate attack on a nation with which it was at peace had made 7 December 1941 'a date which will live in infamy'. Roosevelt pledged that 'the American people in their righteous might will win through to absolute victory'. Looking beyond the immediate crisis to a reordering of world politics, he swore to 'make it very certain that this form of treachery shall never again endanger us'. To underscore American righteousness, the president proclaimed: 'we will gain the inevitable triumph – so help us God.'[5] The thunderous applause was still resonating throughout the halls of the Capitol Building later that day, when Congress declared that the United States was at war with Japan. There was only one dissenting vote, so completely had Pearl Harbor revolutionized the national mood. Three days later, Japan's allies, Germany and Italy, declared war on the United States, and the Congress reciprocated.

THE WAR

The Japanese Navy's surprise attack seriously damaged the moored fleet of American battleships. The attack humiliated the United

States and broke the backbone of its Pacific fleet. Pearl Harbor consequently recast the United States' strategic priorities in history's greatest war. In contravention of its pre-war agreements with the British, which gave first priority to the war in Europe, the United States ascribed new importance to the defeat of Japan. Operationally, the destruction of its battleships compelled the US Navy to adapt the aircraft carrier to the role of principal fleet combatant. American 'flattops' would relentlessly pursue Japanese forces across the Pacific. They would destroy enemy aircraft, ships and ground installations; and they would enable amphibious forces to advance systematically for the purpose of building airfields from which to bomb the Japanese mainland or to invade it.

The carrier's ascending predominance in the Pacific was demonstrated early in the war, at Pearl Harbor, and in the battles of the Coral Sea and Midway. The Battle of the Coral Sea was fought in the large body of water separating the Great Barrier Reef of Australia from the Solomon Islands. If victorious, the Japanese planned to invade Australia, but they lost. On 8 May 1942 opposing Japanese and American carriers fought a melee in which each side lost one flattop. The shaken Japanese called off the invasion. Less than a month later, on 4 June, the Americans again stopped the Japanese. In the Battle of Midway, three US aircraft carriers and several submarines defeated a Japanese armada by sinking four enemy carriers.

Following Coral Sea and Midway, the United States assumed the strategic offensive in the Southwest Pacific. On 7 August 1942 the 1st Marine Division went ashore on Guadalcanal, completely surprising the Japanese. What began with tactical surprise turned into a six-month campaign that was 'unexcelled for sustained violence on land, sea, and in the air in World War II'.[6] By the time the Japanese withdrew the last remnants of their army on 8 February 1943 they had lost 680 aircraft, 24 warships and an estimated 30,000 men. For the remaining two and a half years of the Pacific war the Japanese were on the strategic defensive. American losses also were high: 615 airplanes, 25 warships, 5,000 dead sailors, and 2,500 dead soldiers and marines. But the Americans had learned how to fight with an unbelievably complex mixture of land, sea and air power, and unlike the Japanese, possessed the seemingly unlimited capacity to replace their losses.

After the final victory in Guadalcanal the navy turned the war in the Southwest Pacific over to Army General Douglas MacArthur, who had fled from the Philippines to Australia as the Japanese army overran his garrison. He was flamboyant and given to mind-numbing rhetorical flourishes. After he departed the Philippines, he vowed, 'I shall return.'[7] This commitment governed his conduct of the war, and it determined President Roosevelt's later approval of an American invasion of the Japanese-occupied Philippines. From early 1942 until mid-1944 MacArthur master-minded the advance from the Solomons to the Philippines. His technique was to 'island-hop', that is, seize an island and build an air base for close air support of the assault on his next island target. If a Japanese island bastion was too strong to attack frontally, he simply bypassed and isolated it.

In the Central Pacific, the key to the US Navy's sweep across the ocean was the *Essex*-class aircraft carrier. The *Essex* carriers spearheaded every amphibious operation in the Central Pacific, beginning with the marines' landing on Tarawa in November, 1943. Whenever possible, Admiral Chester Nimitz emulated MacArthur and bypassed strategically less significant Japanese-held islands to capture ones that would have a measurable impact on the outcome of the war. The most notable example was the decision to ignore the Caroline Islands and span hundreds of miles of open ocean directly from the Marshall Islands to the inner ring of Japanese imperial defences in the Marianas. The primary target was Saipan: B-29 'Superfortress' bombers flying from that island could strike Japan.

On 15 June 1944, one week after the invasion of Europe at Normandy, Admiral Raymond A. Spruance sent the marines and army ashore. They were met by 30,000 Japanese, who resisted with suicidal tenacity. When the bloodshed on Saipan ended, only 1,780 Japanese surrendered; 3,426 Americans lay dead and another 13,100 were wounded. To justify this sanguinary expenditure the Army Air Force (USAAF) built a large airfield. By November B-29s were making daily bomb runs over Japan. The air war begun at Pearl Harbor had come home to the Japanese with a ferocity that would only increase in the last ten months of the conflict.

In this interval, at MacArthur's insistence, President Roosevelt ordered an invasion of the Philippines as the best route to Japan in case an invasion should be necessary. In a July 1944 conference in Hawaii, MacArthur had hinted to the president that the Democrats would face less opposition from conservative Republicans in the autumn presidential and Congressional elections if the Philippines were retaken. The presidential decision was largely political. MacArthur was the darling of conservative Republicans, and 1944 was a presidential election year.

The principal landing in the Philippines was staged on 20 October 1944, in Leyte Gulf. General MacArthur exercised authority over all aspects of the operation, including command of Vice Admiral Thomas Kinkaid's 7th Fleet. The largest and most complex sea battle in history, Leyte destroyed the major remnants of the Japanese surface fleet. But Japan would not surrender. On the contrary, the Japanese army put up a determined resistance to MacArthur at every step of the way. Retaking the capital of Manila in March 1945 cost the Americans 1,000 men, the Japanese 16,000. The Filipino people paid the highest price for their city: 100,000 dead. It was still far from over. The Americans were initiating offensive operations throughout the rest of the Philippines as late as August 1945. MacArthur's choice, endorsed by the president for political purposes, was hardly leading to an invasion of Japan.

After Leyte, the Joint Chiefs of Staff refocused on heading to Tokyo more directly, and Nimitz ordered Spruance to plan invasions of Okinawa and Iwo Jima. Okinawa lay less than 350 miles south of the southern tip of Japan. Once taken, it would serve as another base for bombers and as the launching pad of the intended amphibious invasions of Kyushu and Honshu. On 1 April 1945, after the heaviest neutralizing fire of the Pacific war, Spruance's 5th Fleet began to debouch 182,000 assault troops from 1,300 transports – 50,000 in the first day alone. The Japanese uncharacteristically allowed the Americans to move inland before counterattacking, but then they fought so stubbornly that the Americans did not consider the island secured until late June.

During the fight for Okinawa great numbers of Japanese land-based 'kamikaze' suicide bombers neutralized the US fleet air arm's supremacy and took a very heavy toll on ships and men. Spruance's flagship, the cruiser *Indianapolis*, was knocked out from under him. It took the Americans two months to devise counter-techniques, including massive B-29 bombing raids on kamikaze airfields on Kyushu. By then more than 80,000 Japanese and 24,000 Okinawan civilians had died, as had 13,000 Americans, including 4,900 sailors. The American wounded totalled 31,800. It was the bloodiest battle of the Pacific war; 368 US Navy ships were damaged, 10 per cent of which sank. The accomplishment was strategically significant. The Americans gained air bases close to Japan for intensified heavy bombing of industries and cities, and naval bases for tightening the blockade of Japan and for mounting the final invasion. The latter was a daunting proposition. The planners' estimates of prospective American dead ranged from 50,000 to 500,000.

The B-29 held the key to defeating Japan without an invasion. Since November 1944, Superfortresses flying from Saipan and Tinian in the Marianas had routinely pounded Japan from high altitude. The results were inconclusive, in part because the extreme range from the Marianas to Japan meant displacing bombs with fuel in order to make a round trip. It was to improve this situation that Spruance's 5th Fleet and three Marine Corps divisions had taken the small volcanic island of Iwo Jima between 19 February and 16 March 1945. The human cost was staggering: 20,000 of the 21,000 Japanese defending the rock died; 6,800 Americans were killed, and another 20,000 wounded. The end result was better tactical fighter protection and emergency fields for damaged bombers returning from raids. Helpful, but not decisive.

To make the B-29s more lethal, the USAAF put a brilliantly ruthless new man in charge, Major General Curtis E. LeMay. On 9 March 1945, even before Iwo Jima had completely fallen to the Americans, he unleashed 334 B-29s armed with incendiary bombs over Tokyo. In that one God-forsaken night LeMay's airmen incinerated 16 square miles of Tokyo, destroying 22 key targets and burning to death between 80,000 and 100,000 civilians. Other cities soon received the same treatment, but the emperor and the Japanese army high command ordered the people to fight on. There would have to be an invasion – or a special weapon.

In late 1942 the United States had begun development of that special weapon – an atomic bomb – in an industrially and scientifically elaborate but super-secret program called the 'Manhattan Project'. The purpose was to create an 'A-bomb' before German physicists could do so and then to extract an unconditional capitulation from whatever government survived the atomic holocaust. Very few American officials, civilian or military, knew of the project; all strategic planning was done without awareness of it. President Roosevelt could not count on a viable bomb when he went to the Yalta Conference in February 1945, for what would be his final meeting with his two major allies, Britain's Winston Churchill and Russia's Joseph Stalin. He therefore made concessions to Stalin regarding post-war Europe in order to win his assurances that the Soviet Union would enter the Pacific war within 90 days of Germany's surrender.

The war against Hitler was to have been America's primary war, but Pearl Harbor had changed all of that. Like a gigantic emotional vortex, it drew the American people, government and military to fixate on Japan. This left the early conduct of the European war to be decided largely by Churchill's dominating personality. He was deeply averse to mounting a direct attack against German-occupied France from the British Isles, the strategy preferred by US Army Chief of Staff George C. Marshall. Because Britain initially contributed more to the European war effort than the United States, Churchill carried the day with Roosevelt.

The result was a peripheral strategy beginning with the Anglo-American invasion of North Africa in November 1942, 'Operation Torch'. As soon as victory in that initial engagement was assured, Roosevelt and Churchill met at Casablanca, in Morocco, to map out the next move. The biggest surprise of the January 1943 meeting was Roosevelt's announcement that the Allies would demand 'unconditional surrender by Germany, Italy, or Japan' – a conscious hint of Ulysses S. Grant's ultimatum to the Confederates at Fort Donelson in the Civil War.[8] This uncompromising stance carried with it the threat of the total destruction of the enemy. It discouraged German officers from attempting to overthrow Hitler, and it impeded Japan's capitulation. In the same month, January 1943, Allied commanders in Europe announced the beginning of 'Operation Pointblank', a campaign that authorized large-scale US bombing of civilian population centres in Europe.

At Casablanca it was agreed to initiate attacks on Sicily and then strike the boot of Italy. This approach was followed by the Anglo-Americans throughout 1943 and well into 1944. In the meantime, at the Battle of Stalingrad, which ended in January

1943, the Soviets stopped and then forever turned back the German army. The Soviet movement westward was irresistible, and the cost in lives astronomical: 20,000 Russians died *per day* in each of the four years the Soviet Union was at war. By the time of the too-often postponed Anglo-American landing by General Dwight D. 'Ike' Eisenhower on 6 June 1944, the Red Army was already slugging its way into Eastern Europe. It took Ike and his armies until March 1945 to cross the Rhine. Their next stop was at the Elbe River, the prearranged place for meeting with the Soviet Red Army. The first contact occurred on 25 April 1945; Hitler committed suicide on 30 April, as the Russians converged on his bunker in Berlin; remnants of his high command surrendered unconditionally on 7 May. VE (Victory in Europe) Day was proclaimed as 8 May 1945, nearly six years after the European war began in Poland. The Anglo-American route from 'Torch' to the Elbe had not been a direct one, and the decisive Soviet contribution to the victory in Europe had not been anticipated in pre-war planning.

Following the defeat of Germany, the Americans were desperate to end the Pacific war as quickly as possible. President Roosevelt did not administer the *coup de grâce*; he had died suddenly on 12 April 1945. His successor, Harry S. Truman, did not know of the Manhattan Project when he was sworn in as president. At the time of Germany's surrender, less than a month after Truman's assumption of the presidency, the bomb was untested and the original rationale for its development, to beat Germany to the punch, had disappeared. The question now arose about its use against Japan. Truman and at least two of his top advisors, Secretary of War Henry L. Stimson and General Marshall, very quickly decided in the affirmative. Iwo Jima was fresh in their minds; Okinawa was still raging; an invasion of Japan promised a blood-letting on a scale previously unknown to Americans at war.

With Soviet-occupied Berlin in embers and the rest of Europe lying prostrate beneath the boots of the occupying Allied armies, it was necessary to convene another meeting of the American, British and Soviet heads of government. Truman craftily scheduled the conference at Potsdam, Germany, to coincide with the first test of an atomic device, held in Alamogordo, New Mexico, on 16 July 1945. News of the successful detonation reached Truman immediately. According to Churchill, the president became noticeably less solicitous toward Stalin, who already knew of the bomb's development through espionage. The Soviet premier was determined to enter the Pacific war for whatever spoils he could pick up, and he was intent upon creating his own nuclear arsenal as soon as possible. Truman's bluster at Potsdam merely deepened Stalin's apprehension about America's post-war intentions. When the Japanese government rebuffed Truman's cryptic offer to end the war because it did not guarantee retention of the emperor, the president on 30 July ordered two atomic bombs dropped on Japanese cities.

The end came quickly, and it appeared to be simple. On 6 August 1945 a lone B-29, named 'Enola Gay' after the pilot's mother, dropped history's first atomic bomb on the city of Hiroshima. At least 70,000 people out of a population of 500,000 died. Three days' later, on 9 August, another lone B-29 dropped an atomic bomb on the city of Nagasaki. Half of the city's buildings were destroyed; 35,000 people died instantly; another 40,000 perished more slowly, from burns and lethal doses of radiation. On 14 August, at Truman's direction, 1,000 B-29s hit Japan with conventional heavy explosive bombs. That did it (or so it seemed). Japan sued for peace. On 2 September 1945 a surrender ceremony was held in Tokyo Bay on the battleship USS *Missouri*. Apparently the bombings had obviated the need for an invasion. For the rest of their lives, those Americans soldiers who had been scheduled to participate in the landings rejoiced at the life-saving dropping of the bombs.

The reality was considerably more complex. On 8 August, true to the promise he made at Yalta, Stalin ordered the Soviet army to attack the presumably formidable Japanese Kwantung Army in Manchuria. On 9 August – the day of the Nagasaki bombing – the Soviets opened their offensive against Manchuria along three fronts with 1.6 million men, 5,550 tanks and 28,000 artillery pieces. Most of this irresistible mass had been transferred from Europe to the Far East along the Trans-Siberian railway. The Soviets joined up with the Chinese Communist leader Mao Zedong and flooded across Manchuria. The Red Army appeared on the verge of defeating Japan's army the way it had defeated Hitler's. The United States amended its demand for unconditional surrender. It grudgingly yielded to the Japanese insistence that Emperor Hirohito remain in power.

What the Americans would not tolerate was Soviet participation in the occupation and administration of post-war Japan. What Stalin would not countenance was an American monopoly over the atomic bomb. He correctly understood that the Truman administration intended the nuclear incineration of Hiroshima and Nagasaki as an intimidation of the Soviet Union, as a guarantor of Moscow's good behaviour in post-war Europe, where the Red Army dwarfed the American occupying army. The Americans thoroughly misjudged the bomb's effect on Stalin, and the unintended result of this miscalculation was the Cold War.

UNINTENDED CONSEQUENCES

The overwhelming unintended consequence of World War II was that it produced a peace that was no peace. The war did not end, the fighting just stopped. The United States faced new questions concerning not only the future of the defeated and occupied Axis powers and their dependencies, but also future relations with its allies. The issues were handled on a case-by-case basis and in an atmosphere of growing distrust between the United States and its erstwhile ally, the Soviet Union. Unconditional surrender may have been achieved (although not entirely in the case of Japan), but the Four Freedoms outlined by Roosevelt were not. Future relations with the Soviet Union raised unexpected and deeply troubling problems. What came out of the war was the Cold War: a 45-year period of nuclear stand-off covering innumerable limited regional wars around the world in which the United States and the Soviet Union used client states to do much of the fighting and dying. If one of the purposes of dropping the atomic bomb had been to intimidate or deter the Soviet Union, it failed miserably. Stalin was determined to build his own bomb and create his own nuclear deterrent to American military adventurism.

Nothing had prepared the United States for the international and domestic trauma that followed World War II. The surrender of Germany and Japan found the two defeated nations in ruins and occupied by foreign armies. Cities and infrastructure had been reduced to rubble.[9] The US Army, along with other Allied forces, faced the difficult tasks of occupying, demilitarizing and governing their former enemies. Troops encountered complex challenges in political, economic, financial, social and cultural affairs – tasks beyond the traditional combat roles of soldiers.

Germany was being inundated by millions of refugees from eastern Europe. There was no civil government or infrastructure. On VE Day, Eisenhower had 61 US divisions (1,622,000 men) in Germany, and a total force in Europe numbering 3,077,000. On 5 June 1945 the Allies proclaimed their supreme authority over German territory and enacted plans to govern Germany through four occupation zones, one for each of the Four Powers: the United States, Britain, France and the Soviet Union. These zones had been finalized at the Yalta Conference in February 1945. A further conference of the Allies at Potsdam in July and August 1945 decided upon the payment by Germany of reparations, the demilitarization and de-Nazification of Germany, and the restructuring of the German economy.

The US Army's post-war occupation of Germany lasted until 1955. US military personnel, however, remained permanently stationed in West Berlin and West Germany as part of the North Atlantic Treaty Organization (NATO) defence force until the unification of Germany in 1990 and the end of the Cold War in 1991. In Japan, after VJ Day on 14 August 1945, General MacArthur ruled as supreme commander of the allied powers. On 2 September Japan formally surrendered in MacArthur's presence aboard the USS *Missouri*, and the occupation began. By the end of 1945 more than 350,000 US military personnel were stationed in Japan. A formal peace treaty was signed on 8 September 1951, and the US occupation ostensibly ended when the treaty came into effect in April 1952. The treaty permitted US troops to be stationed in Okinawa, which remained under US control until 1972. Just under 50,000 military personnel were stationed in Okinawa as late as 2006.

Douglas MacArthur – the 'American Caesar' – oversaw the reconstruction of Japan.[10] Conditions for the Japanese under the occupation were harsh at first, but they improved in a remarkably short time. MacArthur helped by drafting a new constitution that guaranteed basic freedoms and civil liberties, and abolished the nobility. Although the constitution retained the emperor, it denied his status as a deity and removed him from politics. MacArthur also introduced reforms to break up the existing system of land ownership. Article 9 of the new Japanese Constitution prohibited Japan from maintaining any armed forces, a provision the United States increasingly came to regret during the Cold War. Pressure from the United States in the early 1950s compelled Japan to establish a 'Self Defence Force'. As a result of mutual need, within a few years, American-Japanese relations were completely transformed from the pre-war fear and suspicion, to one of economic and military cooperation. Given the ferocity of the Pacific war of 1941–5, that was a remarkable and unexpected shift.

Many of the issues relating to the post-war occupation of both Japan and Germany had been under discussion during the war. What was unintended was the ways things turned out. Almost immediately, differences emerged between the British and United States on the one hand and the Soviet Union on the other as to how to implement the arrangements. Each side accused the other of breaking the agreements. In Europe, by 1947, Britain and the United States had merged their zones into one economic area. In that year the United States announced the Marshall Plan, a massive economic stimulus package for the two zones of Germany and all of Western Europe. The Soviet Union withdrew from the Allied Control Council, the governing body of Germany established in August 1945, and in June 1948 instituted a blockade of Berlin. It had been agreed that Berlin, which was well inside the Soviet zone, would also be divided into four zones. This interdiction prompted the Allies to initiate a highly risky airlift of supplies to the western section of Berlin. The blockade was lifted after ten months, but it had provided a major stimulus to the US-inspired creation of NATO in 1949. In Asia, tensions escalated between the United States and Soviet Union over the composition of the future governments of China and Korea, and over French and British colonies seeking independence.

Although Roosevelt intended to create a post-war world in an American image, he did not intend to make the mistakes Wilson had made following World War I. In 1943 Roosevelt had formulated a 'grand design', whereby the United States would act in concert with Great Britain, the Soviet Union and China – the Big Four – to police the world. Rather than utilizing an effete and toothless League of Nations, they would shape and dominate the world through a new international organization, the United Nations, which they would control through the device of a Security Council. By early 1944 this plan had jelled into a two-tiered United Nations: a General Assembly, comprising all nations, and a Security Council, made up of the great powers, in which each of the Big Four, and later France, held a veto power. Roosevelt also believed that the United States could and would establish its economic supremacy in Europe and throughout the world utilizing such multilateral institutions as the newly established International Monetary Fund and the World Bank, both of which were dominated by the United States. American dominance would also be guaranteed by military alliances and bases throughout Europe and the Pacific.

The agreements reached at Yalta in February 1945 did not survive the war. One reason for this was the sudden death of Roosevelt on 12 April 1945. Roosevelt's death – like that of Presidents Abraham Lincoln and John F. Kennedy – is one of those key turning points in American history. Just as Lincoln's death raises the question, 'would Reconstruction have worked out better had he lived?', and Kennedy's assassination poses the question, 'would the United States have withdrawn from Vietnam earlier?', Roosevelt's unexpected death raises the unanswerable question, 'would the United States have experienced the next half-century in the state of intensely armed preparedness and perpetual military readiness called the Cold War had he lived?' Roosevelt himself was confident that he and Stalin had worked out a satisfactory modus operandi for future cooperation.

Whether or not the Cold War was avoidable has been a vexed question for the past 60 years. There is still no consensus on when or why it began. Roosevelt in his wartime negotiations and dealings with Joseph Stalin overruled State Department officials and advisors who recommended he take a hard line against what they described as Soviet expansionism in Eastern Europe. He contrarily agreed to recognize spheres of influence, even occupation, in Europe and Asia, including Southeast Asia, following the war. In these arrangements, the Soviet sphere would encompass Eastern Europe – especially Poland – and Southeastern Europe. The British sphere would include Greece, Turkey, Iran and the Middle East. The United States would exercise hegemony over Latin America. The areas of the world that had made up the empires of Great Britain and France would be returned to their pre-war circumstances. Roosevelt was optimistic that he and Stalin could work with these realities and adjust them pragmatically after the war.

During the war Washington had not anticipated the post-war weakness of Britain, as was demonstrated by its imperial collapse in India and its inability to stem a communist revolution in Greece. Nor had Washington foreseen the strength and determination of the Soviet Union, the resilience of the communists under Mao Zedong in China, and the potency of colonial independence movements. In order to overcome these obstacles to establishing the United States as the major world power, the Truman administration implemented a series of domestic and international programmes unprecedented in us historical experience.

When Vice President Truman assumed office as president in April 1945 he was ill-prepared in the area of foreign relations. His skills and interests were primarily domestic. Truman was parochial in his outlook, and had an uncritical and simplistic belief in the superiority of American values. His bellicose personality led him to miss opportunities to negotiate, and contributed to intensifying the Cold War.[11] He was surrounded by senior officials who increasingly believed that one wartime ally, the Soviet Union, was an evil, expansionist empire that had to be dealt with harshly and, if necessary, with military force. Surprisingly, at the top level of the government, only General Marshall urged restraint. Although uncertain as to the consequences of his decisions, Truman usually took immediate and decisive action. He was determined to be tough with the Soviet Union. On his first meeting with Soviet Foreign Minister V. M. Molotov on 23 April 1945, less than two weeks after Truman first learned of the atomic bomb project, the president harshly lectured the surprised old Bolshevik that the Soviet Union must honour its agreements. Whatever trust had existed between Roosevelt and Stalin rapidly crumbled. The Cold War was under way.

To Washington, the peril of Nazi domination of the world was replaced by the even more formidable peril of Soviet domination of the world. Truman and his advisors were no longer prepared to find dictatorships simply abhorrent; they were now seen as a danger to national security. Totalitarianism replaced fascism as the great threat. The language used by administration advocates of the Cold War resembled that of the abolitionist movement against slavery. It also eerily resembles the language used by neo-conservatives supporting the war in Iraq today. Leading opponents of the Soviet Union argued that the world was divided into free and unfree zones. The United States, as the leader of the free world, was engaged in an uncompromising struggle against an evil agent determined to enslave the world.

Soviet demands on Turkey and its refusal to leave northern Iran in 1946–47, the so-called 'loss of China' in 1949, and the acquisition of nuclear weapons by the Soviets in 1949 only served to confirm the view in the United States that there could be no negotiations or agreements with such an enemy. Diplomacy was ruled out as a method of dealing with the Soviet Union. It became the 'messianic' duty of the United States to destroy the atheistic opponents of liberty and freedom around the world. The Truman administration adopted a policy of 'containment'. In today's language, Washington began to work toward regime change in the Soviet Union as early as 1946. Cold War rhetoric justified the United States maintaining a military presence around the world and eradicating domestic radicalism and dissent in the name of anti-communism.

At home, fears of communist infiltration of the Federal government led to the introduction of a 'Loyalty Program' in 1947. Its agents investigated the loyalty to the United States of the more than three million Federal government employees. An alarmed public supported the passage, over Truman's veto, of the Internal Security Act in 1950, which made it unlawful 'knowingly to combine, conspire, or agree with any other person to perform any act which would substantially contribute to the establishment within the United States of a totalitarian dictatorship.' The atmosphere of heightened suspicion led inevitably to the emergence, in 1950, of a demagogue in the person of Joseph McCarthy, Republican Senator from Wisconsin. His unsubstantiated accusations damaged the reputations of thousands of loyal Americans before he was finally condemned by the Senate in 1954.

The Cold War was not a war in the sense of it being a major armed conflict. It was an ideological standoff that became a fantasy war and a war of clichés obscuring the truth. Vastly exaggerated counterfactual notions of the dangers and capacities of the opponent were created and promulgated by both sides. The Cold

War expanded capitalism, became a pretext for the United States to occupy and invade countries, and to topple undesirable governments clandestinely. Nationalist movements were often deliberately and inaccurately described as communist movements. In the name of saving people from communists, the United States invaded and installed totalitarian regimes in 'newly emerging' nation states, and then turned a blind eye to the horrors perpetrated by the regimes as they grossly violated human rights. The United States also used interventions as a means of setting up American commercial ventures as well as sympathetic and so-called 'democratic' leaders.

Further unintended consequences that resulted from the war included the disintegration of Europe's empires, and the emergence of new independent nations in Africa, the Middle East and Asia. Following World War I, the empires of the victors had remained intact and in some cases had expanded. This did not happen after World War II. The first successful challenges to empire took place in India and in Palestine. In both cases, the outcomes involved partition and subsequent violence and hostility for the next half century. Likewise, in Southeast Asia, United States support for the return of Vietnam to French rule and the subsequent partition of that country led to the unintended involvement of American forces in the civil war that erupted there in the early 1950s. The experience in Korea was similar, with the division of that country into a Soviet satrapy in the north and an American client in the south. To their great surprise, within five years of the ending of the war against Japan in the Pacific, US troops were enmeshed in a bloody war in Korea.

EIGHT

THE WAR IN KOREA, 1950–53

*It never really ended. We are still over there face-to-face with them. The
troops came home. There were no parades. They just came home.*
Retired Marine General Ray Davis[1]

In many ways the war in Korea was an unplanned outcome of
World War II. In November 1943, at the Cairo Conference, Winston
Churchill, Franklin Delano Roosevelt and Chiang Kai-shek (Jiang
Jieshi) had declared that, after Japan was defeated, Korea would
become independent 'in due course'.[2] Ominously, the timing was
left vague.

At the Yalta Conference held fifteen months later, in February
1945, Roosevelt and the Soviet leader Joseph Stalin agreed to establish an international trusteeship for Korea. They made no decision
on the exact formula for governing the nation following the Allied
victory. On 10 August 1945, a day after the entry of Soviet troops
into Manchuria and Korea, and prior to Japan's surrender on 15
August, a fateful midnight meeting was held in Washington. War
Department officials, including the future secretary of state Dean
Rusk, decided to divide Korea into two zones. They selected the
38th parallel of latitude as the dividing line between Soviet and
US zones. The Koreans did not welcome either the trusteeship idea
or the presence of foreign troops. Consequently, when 25,000
American soldiers occupied southern Korea in early September
1945, they found themselves faced by a resentful population seeking independence and capable of self-government.

Tensions heightened between northern and southern Koreans
as factional and sectional leaders, created and propped up by their
respective foreign backers, sought to unify the peninsula under
their rule. Chaos ensued and the country descended into civil
war. In January 1950 Secretary of State Dean G. Acheson publicly
declared South Korea, Taiwan (Formosa) and Southeast Asia

beyond the 'defence perimeter' of areas vital to American national interests.[3] In doing so, he unintentionally invited aggression by the proudly nationalistic communist North Korean, Kim Il-sung. The announcement proved too tempting for Kim and his two patrons, Russia's Stalin and China's Mao. They gave him their cautious approval for an invasion of the South. Hostilities ignited on 25 June, when Kim launched a full-scale attack on the South to achieve unification. In thinking the United States would not respond militarily, Kim and his backers made one of history's great miscalculations.

More than three weeks later, on 19 July 1950, President Harry S. Truman addressed Congress. He set out his war aims and sought authorization and funding to fight a war. The purpose of his speech, he told Congress, was to explain 'the significance of these events for this Nation and the world', and to make 'certain recommendations' to Congress. It was, in effect, his declaration of war. He recounted what had happened in the past two weeks. He stated that on 25 June the Republic of Korea (ROK) had been subjected to a 'naked, deliberate, unprovoked aggression, without a shadow of justification'. The attack was 'in violation of the United Nations Charter' and 'created a real and present danger to the security of every nation'. It represented 'a clear challenge to the basic principles of the United Nations Charter'. If it had not been met squarely, the effectiveness of the UN 'would all but have ended, and the hope of mankind that the United Nations would develop into an institution of world order would have been shattered'.[4]

Truman went on to say that within 24 hours of the attack the United States had called into session the Security Council, which demanded an immediate cessation of hostilities and the withdrawal of 'the invading troops' to the 38th parallel. In addition, he ordered US air and sea cover to protect 'the immediate evacuation of American women and children from the danger zone'. As the attack continued, he had extended US air and naval protection to the retreating South Korean troops. On 27 June, Truman explained, the Security Council had passed a second resolution recommending that members of the UN furnish 'such aid as might be necessary to repel the attack and to restore international peace and security in the area'. These vigorous actions by the United States and the UN had been met with universal approval 'throughout the free world', which had fresh memories of the appeasement of the 1930s. The only major nation failing to support these actions was the Soviet Union, which understandably took the view that the attack had been provoked by the South. However, Moscow's objections were muted because the Soviets had been boycotting Security Council meetings in protest at the refusal of the United States to allow the seating of the People's Republic of China (PRC) as a permanent member of the council in place of the Guomindong regime on Taiwan. The Soviet Union was not present to cast its veto.

In his speech Truman emphasized how important it was that Americans understand the nature of the US and UN military response: 'It should be made perfectly clear that the action was taken as a matter of basic moral principle. The United States was going to the aid of a nation established and supported by the United Nations, and unjustifiably attacked by an aggressor force.' South Korea was not the only country threatened. It was 'plain beyond all doubt that the international communist movement is prepared to use armed invasion to conquer independent nations'. Similar aggression might occur in other parts of the world. Accordingly, Truman reported to Congress he had ordered that military assistance be provided to the Philippine government and to the French colonists in Indochina (Vietnam). He had also positioned the Seventh Fleet to protect Taiwan from a PRC amphibious invasion.

Truman stated that the threat was global and not simply military in nature. He wanted higher productive capacities at home to underpin the common defence of peace around the world. The United States could not act alone. It should strengthen its collective security arrangements with NATO in Europe, and with the nations of Latin America. All of this would cost money, and in the final section of his speech Truman said he had authorized an increase in the level of military manpower and preparedness beyond budgeted levels. He stated he would seek from Congress ten billion dollars in military appropriations within the next few days.

Truman concluded on a high moral tone: 'The free world has made it clear, through the United Nations, that lawless aggression will be met with force . . . This is the significance of Korea – and it is a significance that cannot be overestimated.' The United States, he argued, should be proud of its role in the UN as a guarantor of world peace. The American people must 'seek a new era in world affairs' in which 'all men may live in peace and freedom, with steadily improving living conditions, under governments of their own free choice.' For ourselves, he concluded, 'we seek no territory or dominion over others . . . [We] carry in our hearts the flame of freedom. We are fighting for liberty and for peace – and with God's blessing we shall succeed.'[5]

Truman's rationale for his actions was a tour de force. There was not a single aspect of former presidential rationales for going to war that was not addressed by him. The speech contained appeals to American patriotism, bravery, altruism and duty. It played on the American sense of divine destiny and exceptionalism. It portrayed the president as sensible to the nation's needs for self-defence, preparedness, prudence and determination. It was a blend of the specific and the universal, reflecting the idea of both America's uniqueness and its international citizenship as a nation among nations. The speech raised fears and calmed them; it praised Americans and demanded more of them. And it did so in language that was simple, direct and homespun.

Truman depicted the events in Korea and his reaction to them not as a limited response to a skirmish in a remote country of marginal interest to the United States, but as an epic struggle of civilizations. The speech was to become the model for future presidential appeals to arms in the next half-century. In future conflicts every president would cover the new element Truman introduced: acknowledgment of the existence and importance (and malleability) of the newly established United Nations as a vehicle for legitimizing us foreign and military policy. That was perhaps the first unintended consequence of the war in Korea.

The speech was notable as much for what it omitted as what it had to say. Truman did not mention by name the Democratic People's Republic of (North) Korea – the so-called aggressor. Nor was there any mention of the background that had led to the creation of the two Koreas, the us occupation of South Korea since September 1945, and the role of the United States in sustaining with economic and military aid the dictatorial regime of South Korea's President Syngman Rhee, who desired to unify Korea under his rule.

THE WAR

Early on the morning of Sunday 25 June 1950, with no warning whatsoever, 75,000 troops and dozens of T-34 tanks of the North Korean army crossed the 38th parallel of north latitude in a massive invasion of South Korea. Armed with the Security Council's endorsement of 27 June, President Truman swung into action. In less than four weeks of frenetic activity he radically transformed US foreign and military policy. He ordered the US Army to fight in Korea, commanded the navy to shell North Korean targets ashore, and authorized air strikes north of the 38th parallel, the dividing line between North and South Korea. He reactivated the draft of men into the armed services on 7 July. That same day the Security Council passed a third resolution, one placing UN forces under US command. Truman immediately appointed General Douglas MacArthur the commander-in-chief of the United Nations Command, a coalition that would soon embrace 53 nations, dominated by the United States, the Republic of Korea, Britain, Australia, New Zealand and Canada. Without pausing for breath, Truman stationed ships of the Seventh Fleet in the Taiwan Strait to prevent Mao Zedong from launching an invasion of the Guomindang sanctuary, promised anti-guerrilla aid to the Philippines, and underwrote the French colonial war against Ho Chi Minh in Indochina.

As Truman was formulating his policy for Korea, the embattled American and South Korean troops continued to retreat before the advancing North Korean army. MacArthur correctly identified the port city of Pusan as the critical geographical point that must not be allowed to fall. In American hands, Pusan would be the strategic funnel through which the allied build-up of men and materiel would flow from shipment points in nearby Japan. If the allies lost Pusan they would be driven into the sea; return would be extremely difficult, if not impossible. MacArthur placed the US Eighth Army in a cordon north and west of the city with orders to hold at all costs. The so-called 'Pusan Perimeter' encircled an area 50 miles wide and 80 miles in length. It became a magnet attracting North Korea's military attention. It launched one fruitless attack after another against resupplied and reinforced American and South Korean defenders. In failing to pierce the perimeter the North Koreans failed to win the war.

MacArthur meanwhile planned for an American victory through one of history's most imaginative and decisive amphibious operations. He would land on Korea's west coast, cutting off and entrapping the North Koreans besieging Pusan. His point of assault was Inchon, a harbour on the west coast of Korea characterized by an extreme tidal range. He knew what he was doing, but there were doubters in high places. A meeting with the US Joint Chiefs of Staff was held on 23–24 August, at MacArthur's headquarters in Tokyo, not in the Pentagon – a graphic demonstration of his Augustan prestige and of Washington's determination to exercise direct oversight of the war. With flourishes of neoclassical eloquence MacArthur overcame their doubts. The invasion was on.

Air strikes and naval bombardment began on 10 September. By 20 September seventy thousand soldiers and marines had landed, along with 250 tanks and about 6,000 other vehicles. The 7th US Infantry Division and the 1st Marine Division recaptured the South Korean capital of Seoul on 28 September. The next day MacArthur escorted the dictatorial president, Syngman Rhee, in a triumphal return to Seoul and to power as an American surrogate. The shocked North Koreans reeled from the Pusan perimeter with the Eighth Army on their tail. Kim Il-sung's men fled across the 38th parallel. The Americans followed with presidential approval.

Truman made the initial decision to pursue the North Korean army beyond the 38th parallel on 11 September, four days before the Inchon landing, when he signed NSC-81. The US National Security Council directive authorized MacArthur to cross the line for the military purpose of destroying the North Korean army. The limiting provision was that 'there has been no entry into North Korea by major Soviet or Chinese forces, no announcement of intended entry, nor a threat to counter our operations militarily in North Korea.'[6] In that case, the Americans would stop, and the United States would negotiate its way out of the war. If China and Russia remained passive, MacArthur's troops were to proceed no farther north than the 40th degree of latitude, where the Korean peninsula narrows into a militarily defensible waist. Only South Korean forces were to be permitted north of the 40th: everyone else was to rigorously respect the Soviet and Chinese borders with North Korea. Exercising caution in military operations was a fundamental aspect of the Truman administration's global challenge to perceived Soviet expansionism, at least until the United States rearmed itself and its allies. The day after signing NSC-81 the Truman administration announced German rearmament, unified the NATO command, and enlarged the size of the US military in Europe. It did not, and it would not, extend the Korean War beyond the peninsula, regardless of MacArthur's recommendations to do so.

The American obsession with containing Soviet Russia and the elation generated by MacArthur's triumph at Inchon combined to undercut caution at the operational level. On 27 September the Joint Chiefs of Staff formally directed MacArthur to cross the 38th parallel in order to complete 'the destruction of the North Korean armed forces'. MacArthur replied, 'Unless and until the enemy capitulates, I regard all of Korea open for our military operations.'[7]

The fat was in the fire. MacArthur and Rhee both sought a reunified Korea under their control, and the American general by now had been authorized by the United Nations to conduct the war with precisely this goal in mind. The political objective and the military strategy of the war were completely new. What had begun as a desperate defensive war had metamorphosed into an offensive crusade designed to chastise the Soviets for what the Americans believed was their incitement of Kim Il-sung. Truman and his advisors had not intended such extreme consequences from combat in Korea when they made their first commitment to use force in the closing days of June.

In early October MacArthur manoeuvred his Eighth Army up the western flank of Korea to capture the north's capital of Pyongyang. He pointed the Republic of Korea's army and the US Marines at Wonsan, a seaport almost directly east across the peninsula from Pyongyang. As his men advanced, the general resentfully flew to Wake Island for an extraordinary meeting with Truman. The president was choreographing an intricate political ballet and was suspicious of MacArthur's political ambitions. November would see the first congressional election to be held since the 1949 communist seizure of power in China and the Soviet detonation of an atomic bomb. MacArthur was a darling of the ultra right-wing Republicans who blamed the Democrats for the 'loss' of China. He had to be kept at least nominally subordinate to the civilian commander-in-chief until after the election.

On 15 October the two adversaries and their assistants met for five hours. Truman raised the possibility, based on Central Intelligence Agency estimates, of Chinese intervention, but MacArthur brushed it off as unlikely. He glibly added that if Mao's army came in it would be summarily routed. Referring to current operations, MacArthur predicted that Pyongyang and Wonsan would soon be taken, after which his forces would head for the Manchurian border, that is, the Yalu River. The war would end; some of the American troops would be out of Korea by Thanksgiving; all except a small garrison force would be removed by Christmas. None of the Washington men at the meeting reminded the general of the stipulation that US troops were not to go beyond the 40th parallel. When MacArthur and the president parted the general felt entirely justified in ordering American combat forces north to the Yalu. They began their march to infamy soon after Pyongyang fell on 19 October.

The Chinese communists were thoroughly alarmed and determined to repel an American military presence on their border. Beijing used an Indian diplomat as an intermediary to warn the Americans, but Washington dismissed him as a communist lackey. Pressured by Stalin to save Korea from the Americans and from Syngman Rhee, Mao chose the military option. On 24 November 1950, the Chinese struck at South Korean units attached to the US Eighth Army in the west. By dawn the next day three South Korean divisions were in full retreat. The US Second Division joined them soon. By 27 November eight full corps of Chinese troops – perhaps 300,000 men – were attacking along the entire front. The US Eighth Army scrambled south in disarray. In the words of Geoffrey Perret, 'Bug-out fever ran through Eighth Army'.[8] On 28 November MacArthur notified Washington of the obvious: 'We face an entirely new war.'[9] The United States was now matched directly against the military might of communist China. Korea became a war of words about the war in the field.

The protagonists in the debate were MacArthur on one side, President Truman on the other, with the Joint Chiefs of Staff somewhere in the middle. Truman used Korea as a vehicle for extending military aid to the French in Indochina and to the Philippine government, both of which were battling communist-backed nationalist insurgencies. He deployed the navy to shelter the pro-western nationalist Chinese on Taiwan from an attack by the communist regime in Beijing. On 19 December he went to the extent of declaring a state of national emergency, beefed up NATO with more American troops, and asked for an annual defence appropriation of $50 billion, a quantum increase from the $15 billion prevailing since 1945. Truman was militarizing the Cold War, but he was not prepared to expand the actual fighting beyond Korea. He feared sparking an unstoppable escalation to a major, probably nuclear, war with the Soviet Union. He was determined to maintain control of the situation – and of his headstrong general.

MacArthur would countenance no substitute for an American victory in Korea, even if it meant enlarging the war geographically and militarily. Early in December he met with army chief of staff General J. Lawton Collins in Tokyo. MacArthur demanded reinforcements from the United States, an attack on mainland China by the Guomindong troops on Taiwan, US air attacks on Manchuria, and a US naval blockade of the entire Chinese coast. He later said, 'I would have dropped between 30 and 50 atomic bombs' and spread across the peninsula 'a belt of radioactive cobalt'.[10] He was not alone in this draconian advocacy, but he was its most visible proponent.

In the first four months of 1951 US forces gradually and painfully stabilized the front along an east-by-northeast line crossing the peninsula slightly above the 38th parallel. This hard-fought achievement met the initial US war aims of June 1950. MacArthur stubbornly interpreted it as operational stalemate and political appeasement of communist China. He publicly expressed his disdain for limited war. He endorsed statements made by leaders of veterans' advocacy groups, such as the American Legion. Then he crossed the constitutional Rubicon forbidding serving military officers from criticizing their commander-in-chief, the president of the United States. In early April he sent a letter denouncing the administration's Eurocentric policy to the Republican speaker of the House of Representatives, Joseph Martin.

With MacArthur's tacit acquiescence, Martin read the letter on the floor of the House. The general laid out the case for the congressman and other 'Asia-firsters' in the Republican party: 'if we lose this war to Communism in Asia the fall of Europe is inevitable; win it and Europe most probably would avoid war and yet preserve freedom . . . There is no substitute for victory.'[11]

Truman confided to his diary, 'This looks like the last straw. Rank insubordination.' This president was the wrong man to cross: '*I want him fired.*' At 1.03 am on Tuesday 10 April 1951 the president announced on the radio that he had 'relieved General MacArthur of his commands and . . . designated Lieutenant General Matthew B. Ridgeway as his successor'.[12]

The dismissal of MacArthur did not end the Korean War, but it did incontrovertibly limit it. For two more years the Americans, their UN allies and their communist adversaries slaughtered one another without advancing or retreating. Casualties relentlessly mounted in what resembled the horrifically pointless bloodshed in the trenches of the Western Front of World War I, until the combat dead numbered perhaps two million Chinese and North Korean soldiers. More than 33,000 Americans died and another 100,000 were wounded. Over a million Korean civilians perished as their countryside was bombed incessantly. While the murder and devastation proceeded, negotiators haggled over the fate of prisoners of war, especially those held by the allies who did not want repatriation to China or North Korea.

The newly inaugurated Republican president, Dwight D. Eisenhower, put a stop to the tragedy by indirectly threatening to use nuclear weapons if China did not sign an armistice. Beijing complied on 27 July 1953. By then Stalin had died, the United States had detonated a hydrogen bomb, the annual American defence budget had levelled out at what was then a staggering $50 billion, and the United States was committed to the strategy of 'massive retaliation'. The Cold War was fully militarized; Korea soon would be relegated to the attic of the national memory as an embarrassing deviation from the American military preference for fighting massive wars of annihilation. In truth, however, Truman's assertion of direct control over his field commander had the significant unintended consequence of setting a limiting precedent for the wars in Vietnam and Iraq.

UNINTENDED CONSEQUENCES

The Korean War was very different from the one the United States had finished fighting only five years earlier. It was an undeclared 'police action' rather than a total war. The war in Korea was also the first war fought by the United States with UN authorization. The Americans were happy to be part of a coalition in which they called the shots throughout the war. However, it was also a war that, like most of the previous wars fought by the United States, began with what appeared modest or limited aims (in this case to drive North Korean troops out of the South and to restore law and order) and ended up as a universal war against evil forces (in this case the spectre of communism). During the conflict the gap between the political goals and military means became so blurred that the original limited aims of the war were lost. The war was transformed into a global crusade against communism.

The most dramatic unintended consequence of the war was that the United States did not achieve a decisive victory. The war ended with an armistice – not a peace treaty – and thus early in the twenty-first century the peninsula is technically still at war. The war left the peninsula permanently divided, with a garrisoned pro-Soviet and pro-Chinese totalitarian communist state in North Korea and a pro-American dictatorial republic (democratized in the late 1980s) in the South. Korea is still politically divided at the 38th parallel, and the Demilitarized Zone (DMZ) remains the most heavily defended border in the world. A total of 35,000 American troops remain stationed in Korea more than fifty years after the war's so-called end as part of the still-functioning UN Command, which directs all allied military forces in South Korea.

This is a long way from the total victory sought and prophesized by MacArthur and expected in Washington in October 1950. With breathtaking arrogance, MacArthur had told Truman in mid-October, when they met on Wake Island in what was essentially a political campaign trip for Truman, that, even if China entered the war, US troops would be victorious and the war would be over by Thanksgiving. Truman, with wilful gullibility, agreed. Following the ceasefire both sides withdrew nearly to the positions they had occupied prior to the conflict.

The war's unintended consequences began during the fighting itself. The war's military commander, the popular and powerful Douglas MacArthur, was relieved of duty in April 1951 after publicly disagreeing with his commander-in-chief by calling for a widening of the conflict. That decision exerted a significant influence upon the American military-political landscape for the next half-century. It transformed the relationship between the civilian policy-makers and the uniformed executors of that policy. More so than in all previous American wars, with perhaps the exception of the Civil War, Korea was characterized by very direct presidential control over the operational commander. This was an especially remarkable phenomenon given the prestige of the commander, Douglas MacArthur, and the limited popularity of the president, Harry S. Truman. The general preferred a strategy of unlimited warfare; the president rejected unlimited warfare – as experienced in World War II – in favour of a model harking back to limited conflicts such as the Mexican and Spanish-American wars. Ever since Truman fired MacArthur, politicians have dominated American strategy-making and war-fighting. The US military has never quite adjusted to this functional change in the hierarchy of war-makers.

The tension between military and civilian leadership was muted somewhat during the presidency of Dwight D. Eisenhower (1953–61) because the civilian chief executive officer and commander-in-chief of the United States was also the most revered American military leader in living memory. In Eisenhower's administrations the military contented itself with the development of new offensive (and defensive) weapons systems built with the fourfold increase in military appropriations approved during the Truman years and sustained by post-Korean fears of Soviet communism.

The tranquillity did not survive Eisenhower. During the Cuban missile crisis of 1962, President John F. Kennedy's civilian advisors asserted themselves and overruled military advice urging a military strike against Cuba because such an attack carried inherent risks of a Soviet – possibly nuclear – response. In the Vietnam War President Lyndon B. Johnson was so fearful of insubordination by his field commander, General William C. Westmoreland, that he pleaded with him not to become another MacArthur. It is true that the decision to end the first war against Iraq was driven by the chairman of the Joint Chiefs of Staff, General Colin Powell. However, Powell had made his career as a uniformed Washington bureaucrat; he was much more of a political general in the tradition of General George C. Marshall than he was a field commander in the model of MacArthur. In the second Iraq war, the domination exerted by Secretary of Defense Donald

Rumsfeld over his military chiefs became palpable. The only avenue by which dissenting general officers could express themselves was in the public media, after they had retired and were no longer significant to the shaping of the war. It took a decisive electoral defeat of the Republicans by the Democrats in the 2006 congressional elections to force Rumsfeld from office. His successor, Robert Gates, a lifelong Cold War bureaucratic operative, was unlikely to restore the high level of independent military thinking that had prevailed in the United States prior to 1950.

The Korean War destroyed whatever slim chance may have existed to normalize relations with the People's Republic of China and the Soviet Union. China's entry into the war was initially unforeseen by the United States; the consequences were long-lasting. To China, and to the Soviet Union, Washington's military response to events in Korea demonstrated the determination of the United States to expand its influence and presence aggressively throughout East Asia. The Soviet response was to supply China with military aid, enabling it to become a major military power. To the United States, the war confirmed its fears of an expansionistic communist China backed by a single-minded Soviet Russia resolved to spread communism globally. These conflicting mirror images would cause another regional civil war to escalate into a major US military confrontation with a small Asian nation. The Vietnam War was an unintended consequence of Korea.

NINE

THE WAR IN VIETNAM, 1964–75

. . . how many times must the cannon balls fly
Before they're forever banned?
Bob Dylan, 'Blowin' in the Wind', 1962

The war in Vietnam was, in many ways, an unintended consequence of World War II and of Korea. The decision by the victorious allies to return the government of Vietnam to the French
immediately after the departure of Japanese forces led inevitably
to the commencement of a war of liberation by nationalist
Vietnamese against their former colonial rulers. The Korean War
added urgency to the idea in Washington that the French represented a bulwark against the spread of communism in Southeast Asia,
a region rich in resources such as rubber and oil.

Presidents Harry S. Truman and Dwight D. Eisenhower were
persuaded by their hawkish advisors that the United States should
provide limited military assistance to the French to resist the establishment of a regime they believed was supported by the Chinese
communists. Truman extended some aid to the French as part of
his area-wide early response to the North Korean invasion of
South Korea in 1950. Eisenhower rejected a French plea for direct
US military intervention, but he did authorize the insertion of
American military 'advisors' into Vietnam to assist the French. In
the early 1950s, almost by stealth, the United States became
involved in the struggle between the colonial power, France, and
the national liberation movement taking place in Vietnam.

Despite being supplied with US weapons diverted from NATO,
the French were forced to withdraw from Vietnam after a humiliating
defeat at Dien Bien Phu in 1954. At peace negotiations conducted
in Geneva, the country was divided into two autonomous sections
along the 17th parallel of north latitude, in much the same way as
Korea had been following World War II. Elections were scheduled

for the following year, but they never took place – in large part because of US opposition. Like Korea, two competing regimes emerged: one in the North, which was communist; the other in the South, which proclaimed its adherence to the West. Again like Korea, they fought one another to unify the nation. A colonial rebellion had morphed into a civil war. The United States chose to see this struggle as one between the forces of good and evil.

In 1961 the young, inexperienced and testosterone-driven new American president, John F. Kennedy, enthusiastically embraced the opportunity to prove that the United States would not allow a so-called 'democratic' and 'friendly' regime to be overrun by a dictatorial communist regime, with all the implied consequences for other allies around the world, especially those in Europe and the oil-rich Middle East. Kennedy, also relying upon hawkish civilian advisors, sent his newly created 'special forces' to support the troops of the patently corrupt and brutal southern regime against the insurgent National Liberation Front (NLF) and the army of North Vietnam. At the time of Kennedy's assassination in November 1963, the United States military was irretrievably involved in the civil war taking place in Vietnam. Kennedy's successor, President Lyndon B. Johnson, saw no alternative but to continue and deepen America's military commitment. Johnson felt trapped by an inherited war, by politics, by military doctrine and Cold War containment assumptions, and by his own Texas-style 'never-run-from-a-fight' mentality.

Johnson was always mindful of the American political firestorm attendant upon the 1949 communist victory in China. He would not risk even a small-scale repetition by abandoning South Vietnam to aggression from the North and ultimately to Chinese expansionism. He told Ambassador Henry Cabot Lodge to 'go back and tell those [Vietnamese] generals that Lyndon Johnson intends to stand by our word'.[1] Of equal importance to Johnson was his 'Great Society' legislative programme of civil liberties and social welfare. He knew that to have both guns and butter, he must win the support of politically conservative and militarily hawkish southern legislators. In the first nine months of his presidency he took several steps to achieve his incompatible goals. First, he increased the number of American military advisors in South Vietnam from 16,300 to 23,000. To command them he selected a southerner, General William C. Westmoreland. Next, in the spring of 1964, he substantially increased the volume and nature of covert operations aimed directly at North Vietnam. These included intelligence-gathering flights over the North and commando raids along North Vietnam's coast, the latter staged from US Navy vessels. Hanoi was infuriated by the coastal raids and retaliated in a manner that provoked direct American military intervention in Vietnam. Once again an American war would begin with a dramatic episode intentionally provoked by the US Government.

On 2 August 1964 North Vietnamese patrol craft launched a torpedo attack against the USS *Maddox*, a destroyer conducting clandestine operations along North Vietnam's coast in the Gulf of Tonkin. Two days later the *Maddox*'s commanding officer erroneously reported another attack against his ship and against another destroyer, the USS *Turner Joy*. President Johnson's reaction was instantaneous and decisive. With the full backing of Secretary of Defense Robert Strange McNamara, the president ordered punitive air strikes against North Vietnam. He went to the people and Congress pleading for a resolution empowering him to protect US armed forces and the nations covered by the Southeast Asia Treaty Organization (SEATO), established in 1955.

Johnson's address to the American people on 4 August 1964 reprised the high moral tone of American innocence to be found in the war messages of all presidents since James K. Polk. Without mentioning the purposes for which the US destroyers were operating off the North Vietnamese coast, he reported: 'renewed hostile actions against the United States on the high seas have required me to order the military forces of the United States to take action in reply.' He had ordered air strikes 'against gunboats and certain supporting facilities in North Vietnam'. The gunboats' attack on the destroyers had renewed the 'determination of all Americans to carry out our full commitment to the people and government of South Vietnam'. He, of course, sought 'no wider war'. But he did want a Congressional 'resolution making it clear that our government is united in its determination to take all necessary measures in support of freedom and peace in Southeast Asia'.[2] Johnson was running for re-election to the presidency as an advocate of a peaceful solution to the Vietnam imbroglio, and the resolution he sought would enable him to show that he was prepared to use limited force to save America's friend. Truman had tried a similar gambit in 1950, and his war had escalated from one of defence to one of offence. Johnson's war would do the same.

On 7 August 1964 a submissive Congress passed the 'Gulf of Tonkin Resolution' authorizing the president to 'take all necessary measures to repel armed attack against the forces of the United States and to prevent further aggression'.[3] The affirmative vote was absolutely overwhelming: 416 to 0 in the House; 88 to 2 in the Senate. Johnson now had all the authority he needed to wage war, but he did not use it immediately. He waited until after he was safely re-elected for a full four-year term as president in November, and inaugurated on 20 January 1965. At this point his top advisors were recommending that to stave off South Vietnam's collapse Johnson must take 'positive action now'.[4] Secretary of Defense McNamara, Assistant Secretary of Defense John McNaughton, and the new ambassador to Saigon, retired four-star Army General Maxwell D. Taylor, all urged him to seize the first excuse to launch air strikes and gradually shape a sustained air war over North Vietnam.

THE WAR

The desired event came two weeks after the presidential inauguration. On 7 February 1965 the National Liberation Front, a country-wide body of supposedly independent guerrillas sustained and supported by Hanoi, attacked a US Army barracks and nearby helicopter base at Pleiku, killing nine Americans. Johnson responded with massive air strikes, as advised, and the war in Vietnam commenced. Between 1965 and 1968 the United States embarked upon large-scale military operations in Vietnam, and in the following years, until 1973, launched increasingly intensive air attacks upon North Vietnam and Cambodia. Towards the end of American involvement, the United States reduced its forces, replacing them with South Vietnamese troops in what President Richard M. Nixon called 'Vietnamization' of the war. There was no consistent, clearly articulated, American strategy or policy throughout the Vietnam War. It ended in 1975, with the total defeat of South

Vietnam, and the unification of Vietnam under the control of the North.

Johnson did not predict that failure when he authorized the sustained bombing of the North in 1965, dubbed 'Rolling Thunder'. In one month alone, in April 1965, US bombardiers flew 3,500 sorties against North Vietnam. To increase their lethality the aircraft used napalm fire-bombs. The evaluations of the bombing varied widely. General Taylor dismissed the air strikes as a 'few isolated thunderclaps', not heavy or intensive enough to break Hanoi's will.[5] At the same time, General Westmoreland expressed fears of retaliatory raids in the South by the NLF or North Vietnamese Army (NVA) regulars. Westmoreland asked for protective American ground forces, but Taylor paradoxically warned that US troops were ill-prepared for anti-guerrilla operations. He predicted that their presence would simply encourage the South Vietnamese Army (ARVN) to let the Americans do most of the fighting.

The contradictory advice was typical of what Johnson received throughout the war. In this case he deferred to Westmoreland. On 8 March 1965 two battalions of US Marines went ashore at Da Nang. The inexorable escalation to an eventual total of 543,000 fighting men and women had begun, not because the raid on Pleiku was significant but because the men surrounding Johnson feared the disgrace of withdrawal more than they did an open-ended war with an uncertain purpose. They believed that by fighting in Vietnam the United States somehow could contain Soviet expansionism. William Colby, the chief of the Central Intelligence Agency's (CIA) Far Eastern Division from 1963 to 1968, later said the alternative would have been 'a communist Mexico allied to a still-vibrant Soviet Union'.[6]

In November 1965 the Americans fought and won the kind of battle they prefer: a direct encounter between well-armed regular units that the US forces can defeat by employing overwhelming firepower. The brutal contest took place in the Ia Drang Valley, in the Central Highlands of South Vietnam, between 14 and 16 November. It began when the US Army's helicopter-borne 1st Cavalry Division (Airmobile) intentionally dropped into the middle of a major staging area of the North Vietnamese Army. Surrounded and outnumbered, the Americans threw everything conceivable at the NVA, including rockets and machine-gun fire from helicopter gun ships and bombs dropped by B-52s flying from Guam. When it was over, the NVA had lost 2,000 men, the Americans 79 killed and 121 wounded. The NVA concluded that by committing combat forces the United States had guaranteed a prolonged war with great loss of life, but the end result would be the same: a communist South Vietnam. The American high command, specifically General Westmoreland and Secretary of Defense McNamara, interpreted the victory as justification for an infusion of several thousand more American troops.[7]

For the next two and a half years, with an ever-expanding force at his command, Westmoreland pursued his chimerical, so-called strategy of 'search and destroy'.[8] He hoped to bleed the enemy to death through frontal encounters such as that at the Ia Drang Valley, but rarely did the NVA comply by coming out in force. Instead, it relied on the NLF guerrillas – called the Viet Cong or 'VC' – to wear down the Americans and sap the South Vietnamese of loyalty to the United States by terrorizing rural villagers. The great asset of the North was its ability to infiltrate the South with men and materiel. At first, much of the resupplying was done from the sea, with junks and small boats. Fairly soon, however, in 'Operation Market Time', the US Navy interdicted the sea lanes by aggressively boarding and searching coastal vessels.[9] The North then turned almost entirely to resupply by land, along a rough-hewn road called the 'Ho Chi Minh Trail' running from North Vietnam through Laos and Cambodia into South Vietnam.

The jungle highway was virtually invisible from the air, and in any case the United States generally, but not always, felt constrained from bombing it out of respect for the neutrality of Laos and Cambodia. This strategic artery corresponded approximately to the American advantage in unimpeded transoceanic overseas resupply and reinforcement by airplanes and by ships. US permissiveness enabled the North to engage and evade at will, until it was ready to try for the decisive victory. That moment came in January 1968, with the battle the Americans named 'Tet' because it occurred during the lunar new year holiday. On the eve of the battle many in the administration were expressing doubts about the possibility of winning in Vietnam, but President Johnson, in his State of the Union address on 17 January, described most of South Vietnam as secure from enemy attacks. Two weeks later, on

31 January, the NVA and VC unleashed a highly coordinated and widespread attack against 36 of South Vietnam's 44 provisional capitals and another 100 villages, many of which they captured and held until driven out with great losses.

Conceived by the legendary General Vo Nguyen Giap, architect of the 1954 victory over the French at Dien Bien Phu, Tet was intended to provoke a nationwide popular uprising against the government of South Vietnam and its American sponsors. It began at about 2.45 am with an assault on the American embassy in Saigon; VC soldiers penetrated the compound before the marine guards killed them. It embraced Hue, the old and sacred national capital, where the US soldiers and marines killed 5,000 communist troops before they recaptured the city on 2 March. It included a siege of the hill fortress of Khe Sanh, near North Vietnam. The Americans successfully held out for 77 days; they dropped 100,000 tons of bombs and shells, and killed an estimated 10,000 enemy attackers. Of Khe Sanh, a desperate Johnson allegedly said, 'I don't want any damn Dienbienfoo.'

General Westmoreland declared Tet an overwhelming American victory by about 9.00 am on 31 January. As if to somehow solidify his 'victory', Westmoreland asked for 206,000 more American troops, in addition to the 500,000 already 'in country'. Washington denied his request because complying would involve calling up the National Guard and reserves, an impossibility given the spreading anti-war sentiment within the population. Nonetheless, despite the surreal nature of Westmoreland's evaluation of Tet, US military writers ever since have claimed that the American defence during Tet and the subsequent counteroffensive constituted an American triumph. They cite the alleged destruction of the Viet Cong as an effective fighting force, and they note that there was no national anti-American uprising in South Vietnam.[10] They also entirely misconstrue the significance of military operations. Battles are fought for political purposes, and Tet was arguably the most politically decisive engagement in American history.

As President Johnson had feared, Tet became the American Dien Bien Phu. The graphic, if temporary, occupation of the American embassy grounds by the VC gave the lie to all claims that there was a 'light at the end of the tunnel' in this war. Secretary of Defense Robert McNamara, who had begun to doubt his own formulas and predictions for victory, was dismissed by Johnson and moved to the presidency of the World Bank. In his stead, on 1 March 1968, Johnson appointed an old Democratic political insider, Clark Clifford, who had enough clarity of vision and integrity of character to advise Johnson the war was unwinnable. A few days later, on 12 March, the staunchly anti-war senator from Minnesota, Eugene McCarthy, captured 42 per cent of the votes in the New Hampshire Democratic electoral primary. This was an unheard-of setback for a sitting Democratic president, and it stung Johnson into making one of the most painful decisions any American president has ever made. On 31 March, in a nationally televised speech, he recapitulated his ongoing attempts to end the war. He hoped some-how to negotiate an end to the North's military penetration of the South, and as an inducement to Hanoi he announced the suspension of much of the bombing of North Vietnam. In the last passages of his speech, and completely without forewarning his staff, he sig-nalled his dispassionate statesmanship and hope for conclusive negotiations with Hanoi. He said he would neither seek nor accept the Democratic nomination for the presidency of the United States. Tet had brought down an American president; a second would fall to Vietnam as surely as the night follows the day.

The *annus horribilis* of 1968 rolled on as relentlessly as the Mississippi River. In April the mesmerizing African-American civil rights leader Martin Luther King was assassinated. Before his death he had broken with Johnson over the Vietnam War, an unanticipated rift in the Great Society directly attributable to the conflict. On 5 June a second great reformer fell to an assassin's bullet: Robert F. Kennedy, the leading contender for the Democratic presidential nomination, was gunned down in Los Angeles after winning the California electoral primary. The Democratic Convention that met in Chicago in August was the scene of unprecedented violence; its nominee, Hubert H. Humphrey, was Johnson's vice president. He could not convincingly disassociate himself from the war. As a result, Richard M. Nixon, the Republican candidate, won the November presidential election by assuring the electorate that he had a plan to end the war in Vietnam.

Nixon had no plan, other than to be elected president of the United States. During his first year in office he floundered about, looking for some solution to Vietnam. By July he had proclaimed a policy of 'Vietnamization', which meant gradually turning the fighting of the war over to the South Vietnamese. The writer and army colonel Harry G. Summers, Jr, recognized the policy as one of withdrawal and he contrasted it with Korea where, he said, the Americans had built up the South Korean army before drawing down their own forces. Marine Lieutenant Colonel (later General) Bernard E. Trainor, who would write compelling books on the American wars against Iraq, said with bitter resignation, 'We're no longer here to win, we're merely "campaigning" to keep the [American] casualties down.'[11] Summers's and Trainor's views were representative of the US military's feeling about Vietnamization, but they were impotent in the face of growing Congressional discontent with the war. The legislative body was steadily forcing the reduction of troops by cutting appropriations. The level plummeted to 334,000 in 1970; 156,800 by the end of 1971; and 69,000 in mid-1972.

Throughout these three years Nixon reacted spasmodically, brilliantly and unscrupulously. He bombed and briefly invaded Cambodia in order to neutralize NVA sanctuaries. By these actions he helped destabilize the hapless neutral nation, contributing to a prolonged civil war and years of genocide by an unspeakably ruthless new regime. He undercut the rules of war by releasing Army First Lieutenant William Calley from prison. The lieutenant had been convicted by a court martial for allowing his men to murder intentionally at least 22 civilians in a village called My Lai during a fire-fight in 1968. Senior army officers loathed Calley for desecrating the venerable distinction between military combatants and civilians, and they deplored his early release from prison.

Astoundingly, American civilians fell before US rifles during Nixon's presidency. In May 1970 four students gently protesting the war at Kent State University in Ohio were shot to death by National Guardsmen. Anti-war protest intensified sharply in June 1971, when a former Marine Corps officer and high official in the Pentagon, Daniel Ellsberg, convinced the *New York Times* to publish a highly critical, secret, official history of the early years of the Vietnam War. The so-called 'Pentagon Papers' revealed to a shocked nation that the government frequently lied to the American people about the war. Nixon was enraged. He secretly approved formation of a clandestine squad of political burglars, called 'the plumbers', to break into buildings and search for incriminating evidence to use against Ellsberg in particular and Democrats in general.[12]

In the midst of this domestic turmoil and social breakdown, Nixon and his national security advisor, Henry A. Kissinger, managed to concoct a ruthless but sophisticated policy by which to extricate the United States from Vietnam without sacrificing what the president described as America's 'honour'. The Nixon–Kissinger plan was simple yet complex. Its simplicity lay in the concept: to persuade China and the Soviet Union to tolerate unlimited bombing of North Vietnam and the mining of the port of Haiphong. The complexity lay in negotiating such tacit complicity in a war against a fellow communist state. Kissinger, a brilliant but unscrupulous geopolitician, was ideally suited for the job. In 1970 and 1971 he arranged the groundbreaking visits by Nixon to Beijing and Moscow. The trip to China in February 1972 was a historic break in the American-imposed isolation of China, and it began the long process of full normalization of relations between Washington and Beijing. In Vietnam it bore fruit within a month. The North Vietnamese Army chose late March 1972 to launch a massive conventional military assault. On 4 April Nixon said to a senior aide, 'The bastards have never been bombed like they're going to be bombed this time.'[13] After proving true to his word, he went to a 'summit' meeting in Moscow. In late May he signed formal agreements with the Soviets to limit the proliferation of intercontinental ballistic missiles.

Returning home with tacit authorization to act in Vietnam as he pleased, Nixon ordered the mining of North Vietnam's ports and a ferocious bombing of the North. There were two phases of the airborne bloodbath. In 'Linebacker I', which lasted until October, more than 125,000 tons of bombs were dropped on storage facilities, air bases, power plants, bridges and hospitals in the North. The American people did not object. Running for re-election against George McGovern, a peace candidate who had been a B-24 bomber pilot in World War II, Nixon impressively won 60 per cent of the popular vote and 49 states in the Electoral College. Politically reinforced at home, Nixon faced South Vietnamese resistance to a negotiated sell-out and the North's suspicion that he was insincere about negotiating an American withdrawal. He told the

Joint Chiefs of Staff they had one 'last chance to use military power to win this war' and then approved 'Linebacker II'.[14] The 'Christmas bombing' was conducted from 18 to 28 December. B-52s flew 742 sorties; fighter-bombers flew another 640; at least 1,600 North Vietnamese civilians died. Fifteen B-52s and eleven other aircraft were shot down by the North; 93 airmen went missing, and 31 others were added to the long list of prisoners of war. This aerial bloodletting was a bit much even for some Air Force officers. Mark Clodfelter, a USAF historian, denounced Nixon as 'the Mad Bomber'.[15]

The bombing served the diplomatic purpose of inducing the North to agree to terms of American withdrawal from Vietnam that somehow satisfied Nixon's sense of a 'peace with honour'. On 23 January, in Paris, Henry Kissinger and his North Vietnamese counterpart, Le Duc Tho, signed a treaty stipulating that the United States would withdraw its military forces from Vietnam within sixty days and the two sides would release their prisoners of war. It was understood that Hanoi would pause for a decent interval before trying seriously to overrun the South, which was promised a large amount of US military aid. A recalcitrant Congress, however, slashed in half Nixon's request for $1.5 billion in 1974. The government of South Vietnam was demoralized to the extent of paralysis; its army disintegrated as a fighting force; and on 30 April the Viet Cong and NVA poured into Saigon. Humiliated US diplomats and other fortunate refugees evacuated the American embassy from the roof, by helicopter. In the nearly eleven years since the disingenuously contrived Gulf of Tonkin Resolution flew through the Congress, the United States had lost 58,219 men and women. At least three million Vietnamese had perished. Civilian deaths in neighbouring Laos and Cambodia numbered in the millions. The dollar cost of the war to the United States has been set at $170 billion. Senator Mike Mansfield of Montana, a learned man, pithily asked, 'for what?'[16] The answer was: 'blowin' in the wind.'

UNINTENDED CONSEQUENCES

The first and most obvious unintended consequence of the war in Vietnam was a humiliating defeat for the United States. America took years to recover from the domestic trauma created by the war and by the military defeat. It is important to distinguish between the unintended consequences of the war itself, however, and the unintended consequences of the fact of defeat. The ultimate tragedy, or irony, for the United States, is that the administration bypassed or sabotaged several peace initiatives during the course of the war. 'Operation Marigold', one such initiative in late 1966, ended when the bombing of Hanoi was resumed. Another, the British sponsored 'Sunflower' initiative in February 1967, came to nought. There were, in other words, missed opportunities to negotiate peace and there were alternatives to continued war – and humiliating defeat.

Internationally, rather than winning friends for the United States and democracy, the war was counter-productive. Through their arrogance, their ignorance of the peoples and cultures of the region, and their brutal conduct of the war, successive US administrations alienated many countries. The unconscionable atrocities, deliberate killing, and imprisonment and torture of civilians by US forces during the so-called 'search and destroy' missions shocked the world when they became known. Democracy was damaged both at home and abroad. The United States had not learned the lessons of previous wars: that once persuasion is replaced by coercion and the use of military force, the battle for hearts and minds is lost. Although they stated confidently that they were 'nation building', US leaders woefully misread the region's nationalist movements. The majority of US senators, for example, had never been outside the country, and the view from within the Washington 'beltway' was a highly provincial one.

As was the case in the two World Wars, US motives were mixed. In addition to an idealistic desire to extend democratic institutions, the United States sought to extend its economic interest and project its power in Southeast Asia. Washington claimed that communist China was manipulating insurgencies in Vietnam, Laos and Cambodia. But Vietnamese nationalism was as ardently anti-Chinese as it had been anti-French and anti-American. The United States also claimed it was fighting in Southeast Asia to prevent the 'dominoes' from falling to communism. But they didn't 'fall': some of the countries in the region ended up fighting one another. Vietnam and Cambodia still have to resolve their differences. Finally, the war prolonged the Cold War by setting back negotiations with China and the Soviet Union.

Domestically, the war in Vietnam was the defining moment for a whole generation of young Americans. Presidents Truman, Eisenhower, Kennedy, Johnson and Nixon had no idea that their military interventions in Vietnam would shape the political and social consciousness of the United States for the next half-century or more, just as the two World Wars had for previous generations. Frustrations building up over the previous two decades were released in a burst of reformist movements that included the fight against poverty, the civil rights movement, the women's rights movement and the counterculture movements embracing gay rights, free speech and sexual liberation. To the dismay of many Southerners, and despite often violent opposition, the civil rights movement made significant progress during the war years, a largely unintended consequence of the high proportion of African-Americans who became politicized while serving in the front lines of Vietnam. As the war progressed, however, and as US resources were increasingly diverted to prosecuting the war, these democratic movements slowed. Many were corrupted in the public mind by a malicious campaign to identify them with the allegedly unpatriotic anti-war movement.

The war in Vietnam unexpectedly destroyed two presidents and put an end to President Johnson's 'War on Poverty' and dream of the Great Society. The cost of the war and the resulting inflation, the abuse of executive power that took place during the war and the violations of civil liberties led to divisiveness, violent protest and unrest across the country in the late 1960s and early '70s. The savagery of the war made it increasingly unpopular at home, and as early as 1965 a student-led anti-war protest movement had powerfully emerged.

Outrage at the war mounted steadily. Defoliation by 'Agent Orange' sprayed from US aircraft to uncover a hidden 'enemy' violated international prohibitions against the use of chemical warfare. Its legacy was a generation of malformed Vietnamese children and cancer-related deaths for American troops. Writing in 1965, the journalist Bernard Fall extrapolated from officially admitted Vietnamese deaths to project 400,000 casualties by the end of that year. He dripped bitter sarcasm: 'Since the entire Viet

Cong force is estimated at between 150,000 to 160,000 it means that we have "overkilled" the Viet Cong by two and a half times. Obviously this isn't true.'[17] The official lies meant that the war could not indefinitely be fought with professionals, or volunteers, so in December 1969 a military draft was introduced. Many young men – mostly white and eligible for enrolment in colleges and universities – who outwardly believed in war as a reasonable instrument of policy found ways to avoid serving. One of the armchair warriors was future Vice President Richard B. Cheney.

The war also produced a major realignment of American politics. Because of the anti-war and civil rights protests, demonstrations and riots, the Democratic Party became deeply divided (witness the Chicago nominating convention in 1968) and thus weakened. At the same time, the Republicans launched their 'Southern Strategy' based on a law-and-order theme to win the once 'Solid South' for their party. They succeeded, as evidenced in the 1972 election. The Republicans, and conservatives in general, have increasingly dominated national politics since.

As a result of being defeated in this war, Americans remained deeply divided over the political and military conduct of the war, and the animosity, verging on downright hostility, that developed between civilian and military elites over who was to determine and control foreign policy lingers to this day. Despite pressures to respond militarily to overseas crises, future presidents acted with greater caution and prudence. President James E. 'Jimmy' Carter preferred diplomacy to military intervention and was widely praised for his role in facilitating a peace treaty between Israel and Egypt in March 1979. However, he was seen by a majority of Americans as being weak when he refused to authorize large-scale military action when 66 us diplomats were captured in Iran in November 1979 and held hostage for 444 days. Although the hostages were released after lengthy negotiations in January 1981, virtually at the moment of the inauguration of Ronald W. Reagan as president, the crisis greatly contributed to Carter's defeat. President Reagan also, despite his jingoist rhetoric and willingness to intervene militarily in the Caribbean, was circumspect at times. In February 1984 he withdrew American peacekeeping forces from Lebanon following the death of 241 servicemen, including 220 marines, in a suicide bombing attack on their barracks in Beirut the previous October, rather than risk further inflaming a volatile Middle East.

In narrow military and strategic terms, defeat in Vietnam forced an unintended reassessment of accepted doctrines governing war. The military blamed the senior American political leadership for the loss in Vietnam and also for the debacle experienced in Korea two decades earlier. Many felt that President Truman had denied the United States its victory in Korea when he dismissed General MacArthur, the US Far Eastern commander, in April 1951 because MacArthur publicly advocated expansion of the war into China, to include the use of nuclear weapons. In Vietnam senior US military officers chafed under the close operational and tactical oversight of President Johnson and Secretary of Defense McNamara. They also resented the refusal of the American political leaders to expand the war with ground attacks against North Vietnam or to erect a Maginot Line-like defensive barrier along the 17th parallel from the Gulf of Tonkin westward through Laos to Thailand.

These complaints conveniently overlooked conditions on the ground in Vietnam, including the re-emergence of 'fragging', a practice originating with the Mexican War. This consisted of placing an explosive device (in Vietnam, a fragmentation grenade) in the tent or under the cot of an officer who was too aggressive to suit his troops. Nearly 100 US officers were killed in this manner in Vietnam; another 500 officers and non-commissioned officers (NCOs) survived attempted fragging by enlisted men who were often draftees from minority groups. Racial grievances were a powerful motivating factor: Geoffrey Perret notes, 'Nearly all the victims were white.'[18] This internecine warfare constituted an entirely unintended consequence of the war. Other unintended casualties of the war included the innumerable veterans who suffered debilitating post-traumatic stress disorder, thousands of whom committed suicide.

American military leaders wanted a predominant role in determining the strategy, if not always the political objectives, of the wars their nation fought. To military professionals, World War II was the ideal war: the United States had been fully mobilized, had no hesitation in applying every kind of deadly power, and had resoundingly defeated its enemies. But their complaints about the limitations imposed on them in the conduct of the Vietnam War overlooked the dangers their alternative policies presented. Had the United States expanded the war as the generals wanted, there existed the danger of a wider war with China and possibly even one with Soviet Russia, prolonged occupation of the North, and a stepped-up guerrilla war in the South. Given the level of domestic US opposition the war had generated by the mid-1970s, it is unlikely that the American people would have accepted a war without end.

In searching for answers as to how to fight future wars, strategic planners found the solutions they sought in nostalgia for the American past and in the nineteenth-century Prussian military theorist Carl von Clausewitz. According to one influential strategist, former colonel of infantry, Harry G. Summers, Jr, if the United States had followed the doctrines of Clausewitz in Vietnam, its proper mission would have been to attack and destroy the political-military heart of North Vietnam through invasion and conquest. In saying that this was what Clausewitz prescribed, Summers was draping a hallowed gown of historic and intellectual respectability over the US Army's preferred way to fight. Summers's prescription guided army strategists for at least two decades after the Vietnam War.[19]

One of the principal architects of the new Clausewitzian strategy was General Colin Powell. In the last years of the Cold War, during the administration of Ronald Reagan, Powell served in several high governmental positions. As an assistant to Secretary of Defense Caspar W. Weinberger, Powell developed what became known as the Powell–Weinberger Doctrine. This formulation held that the United States should not go to war unless its vital national interests were at stake. If it went to war, the doctrine held, the United States should apply overwhelming firepower in order to terminate the war as quickly as possible. The Powell–Weinberger formula for victory was clearly derived from Clausewitz's concept of war as a suitable instrument of national policy and the Prussian's belief in applying massed firepower to critical centres of gravity. It represented the theoretical death knell to limited war *à la* Vietnam and Korea. It became the operative principle of American war-making when Powell was appointed chairman of the Joint Chiefs of Staff by President George H. W. Bush in 1989.

The new doctrine set the stage for an evanescent military triumph in the 1991 Gulf War against Iraq, but the impermanence of the US victory soon caused the concept to unravel. In 2003 it would be replaced by Secretary of Defense Donald Rumsfeld's dreamy belief that the United States can win wars without committing large numbers of troops, without sustaining substantial military casualties, and without inflicting heavy casualties on the civilian population of the country the United States has chosen to fight.

TEN

THE WARS AGAINST IRAQ, 1991–2007

The whole last century is littered with failures of prediction.
Paul Wolfowitz, June 2001[1]

The war launched against Iraq in February 2003 was billed as a war of necessity, an effort to make the United States safer following shocking attacks by suicide bombers flying commercial aircraft into the New York World Trade Center and the Pentagon building in Washington, DC, on 11 September 2001, which killed more than 3,000 people. In reality, the war was an extension of – or the completion of – the first Gulf War, 'Operation Desert Storm', launched against Iraq by George H. W. Bush on 17 January 1991 to force Iraq's ruler, Saddam Hussein, to withdraw from his five-month occupation of neighbouring Kuwait.

The Gulf War of 1991 was the first war fought by the United States after the collapse of the Soviet Union and the end of the Cold War. The war itself was unexpected, in that the United States was drawn into a situation it had indirectly, inadvertently, helped create. In ways reminiscent of its actions in relation to Korea in 1950, the United States in mid-1990 had conveyed ambiguous messages to the Iraqi regime, which it had formerly supported against Iran, concerning Iraq's increasingly menacing dispute with neighbouring Kuwait. Confident that the United States would not forcefully respond, 140,000 Iraqi troops and 1,800 tanks invaded an unprepared Kuwait on 2 August 1990 and overran the small Gulf state within two days. Iraq was seeking redress for real and imagined grievances concerning massive Iraqi debts owed to Kuwait accrued during the Iraq–Iran war between 1980 and 1988, Kuwait's overproduction of oil, and disputes between the two states about sovereignty over local islands. Arab states, the United States, the Soviet Union and many other nations immediately condemned the invasion.

Later the same day, 2 August, the UN Security Council voted 14 to 0 to demand Iraq's 'immediate and unconditional withdrawal' from Kuwait.[2] The Bush administration needed a pretext to strengthen its military capacity in the region in response to the crisis and encouraged Saudi Arabia to call upon the United States for military support in case it, too, was invaded. The president immediately deployed land, sea and air forces to the Kingdom. By October a US-led, UN coalition had built up its military strength in the area to 400,000 troops, augmented by extensive air and naval forces; by early November coalition forces totalled 700,000. The US military and civilian leadership agreed that it was unlikely Hussein would relinquish Kuwait, which he had declared a province of Iraq, unless forced out by military means. On 29 November the United States secured UN Security Council Resolution 678 authorizing the UN coalition 'to use all necessary means' if Iraq had not withdrawn from Kuwait by 15 January 1991.[3]

Just seven days before the 15 January deadline for Iraqi withdrawal, President Bush sent a letter to Congressional leaders requesting their support for UN Resolution 678 and approval to wage war in the Persian Gulf. 'The current situation in the Persian Gulf,' he wrote, 'brought about by Iraq's unprovoked invasion and subsequent brutal occupation of Kuwait, threatens vital US interests.' He did not spell out just what those vital interests were but he added, 'the situation also threatens the peace'. On 12 January a divided Congress gave Bush the authority he requested. The Senate vote was 52 to 47; the House followed suit with a vote of 250 to 183. Of 55 Democratic senators, 45 voted against the Congressional resolution authorizing the use of force. With more than 500,000 American troops already deployed to the Gulf, and US national prestige and credibility on the line, many members of Congress felt they had little choice but to approve the president's request. On 14 January Bush signed House Joint Resolution 77, authorizing the 'Use of Military Force Against Iraq'.

THE FIRST WAR AGAINST IRAQ

Two days later, on 16 January (17 January in Iraq), allied air forces launched an attack on military targets in Iraq and Kuwait from

Saudi Arabia and from US and British aircraft carriers in the Persian Gulf. President Bush announced the start of 'Operation Desert Storm' in a nationally broadcast address: 'The battle has been joined . . . Saddam Hussein's forces will leave Kuwait . . . our goal is not the conquest of Iraq, it is the liberation of Kuwait.' Bush pronounced this, the first Persian Gulf War, 'The right war, at the right place, at the right time and against the right enemy.'[4] A defiant Iraqi president, Saddam Hussein, declared that the 'mother of all battles' had begun and launched the first of a number of Iraqi Scud missile attacks against Israel. For a few tense hours it looked as though Israel would retaliate against Iraq, causing the Arabs to leave the coalition. Months of preparation and diplomacy were threatened by a few, poorly aimed, 1950s-vintage ballistic missiles. Later that evening, US Patriot surface-to-air missiles were launched against the incoming Scud ballistic missiles. The use of Patriot missiles in Israel's defence helped to keep that country out of the Gulf War, thereby preserving the American-European-Arab alliance.

Operation Desert Storm provided a spectacular demonstration of US high technology, leading to stunning military success. The United States used an impressive array of stealth and precision weaponry to eliminate Iraq's communications, command and control systems. On 23 January, after some 12,000 sorties, General Colin Powell, chairman of the Joint Chiefs of Staff, said that allied forces had achieved air superiority and would focus air attacks on Iraqi ground forces around Kuwait.

An unrelenting and intensive allied air campaign crippled the Iraqi army and prevented it from mounting an effective defence. Nevertheless, despite the use of so-called smart weapons, on 13 February US bombs killed up to 500 Iraqi civilians in an air raid shelter in Baghdad. The largely conscript Iraqi army offered virtually no resistance, fleeing Kuwait after only 100 hours of ground fighting. On 15 February Iraq began a series of heavily qualified offers of peace, all of which were rejected by the UN. On 22 February Bush and his allies gave Iraq 24 hours to begin withdrawing unconditionally from Kuwait, or face a final all-out attack that would for the first time include coalition ground forces. Hussein rejected the offer. The following day General H. Norman Schwarzkopf, commander of the coalition armies, launched a large-scale ground assault involving 100,000 US and 50,000 allied troops against Iraqi soldiers, many of whom surrendered to the advancing forces. On 27 February, an astonishingly short four days later, Bush declared: 'Kuwait is liberated, Iraq's army is defeated.' He announced that the allies would suspend combat operations at midnight. A ceasefire was announced the next day. Allied and Iraqi forces suspended their attacks as Iraq pledged to accept all United Nations resolutions concerning Kuwait. Iraq agreed to a formal truce on 3 March, and a permanent ceasefire on 6 April. A total of 147 US military personnel died in combat, and another 236 died as a result of accidents or other causes.

UNINTENDED CONSEQUENCES OF THE FIRST WAR

The Arab world breathed a sigh of relief at the end of the war, having feared even greater devastation and loss of life in Iraq. Approximately 60,000 Iraqis were killed in the war (around 56,000 military and 3,500 civilians), and the destruction of infrastructure was widespread. The American leadership was exultant. The war was the first 'live' televised war, and it was described as a textbook military campaign by the allies. The American military believed it had fashioned a winning strategy based on the use of overwhelming force. Generals had made the decisions and chosen the targets, not civilians in Washington, which many believed had hindered the military in the Vietnam War. Journalist Michael R. Gordon and Lieutenant General Bernard E. Trainor described the war as one 'without precedent in the annals of warfare. It was the dawn of a new era in which high technology supplanted the bayonet, a war in which one side had a clear picture of events while the other floundered deaf, dumb, and blind.' The same authors stated that 'equally important, it was a test of [Colin] Powell's doctrine of decisive force, of joint warfare, and of Congress's attempt to reform and reorganize the military to avoid the pitfalls of the Vietnam War. Once the political objectives were set, this had been the generals' war to win or lose.' But, Gordon and Trainor conclude, despite meticulous planning and brilliant execution the war had been 'an incomplete success'.[5]

The war achieved its goal of liberating Kuwait. However, US-backed military power was not the answer to the political challenges facing the region, or facing US interests in the region. Much of Iraq's army was destroyed, but Saddam Hussein, the person with whom above all the United States was quarrelling, remained in power with his political and security apparatus intact.

In the aftermath of the war, on 6 March 1991, President Bush announced to Congress the advent of a 'New World Order'. He was dreaming. The unintended consequences that flowed from the first war against Iraq soon revealed that the 'new world order' was an empty slogan. Among the first casualties was Bush himself, defeated by William Jefferson Clinton in the 1992 US presidential elections for his neglect of domestic issues. Under Clinton the United States proved itself incapable of resolving local ethnic wars erupting in Central and Eastern Europe and Africa. Nor was it able to produce peace in the Arab–Israeli conflict.

Announcing the liberation of Kuwait, President Bush had told the American people:

> we must now look beyond victory and war. We must meet the challenge of securing the peace. In the future, as before, we will consult with our coalition partners. We've already done a good deal of thinking and planning for the post-war period. And Secretary [of State James A.] Baker has already begun to consult with our coalition partners on the region's challenges.

A day after the war, Bush optimistically predicted that future adversaries who studied the Gulf War would think twice before challenging the United States. He boasted:

> I think because of what has happened we won't have to use US forces around the world. I think when we say something that is objectively correct, like don't take over a neighbour, or you're going to bear some responsibility, people are going to listen. Because I think out of all this will be a new-found – put it this way, a re-established – credibility for the United States of America.[6]

Bush may well have thought so. His wishful statement shows how out of touch he was with the reality of the world – especially the Middle Eastern world. It also reveals the hubris that military power engenders, and the dangers that flow from such arrogance. Within weeks of the liberation of Kuwait, the Kurdish and Shi'ite populations of Iraq discovered the meaning of the 're-established credibility' of the United States. Encouraged by the United States and its allies, Kurds in the north and Shi'ites in the south sought to overthrow Saddam Hussein, only to be mercilessly crushed by his regime. Approximately 35,000 died in the post-war violence. The United States stood by and did nothing to assist those it had promised to protect. Nor did the re-established credibility of the United States prevent aggression against Americans and their interests.

In the next decade American interests in Africa and the Middle East repeatedly came under attack. The attacks were fuelled to some extent by hatreds engendered by the US war against Iraq. In October 1993 eighteen US soldiers were killed in Mogadishu, Somalia, when Americans came under fire in a UN operation against Somali guerrilla fighters. On 7 August 1998 more than 220 people were killed (including 12 Americans) and over 4,000 wounded in simultaneous car bomb explosions at US embassies in the East African capital cities of Dar es Salaam (Tanzania) and Nairobi (Kenya). On 12 October 2000 the destroyer USS *Cole* was attacked and severely damaged in Yemen; seventeen sailors were killed. These were not the kind of consequences George H. W. Bush had intended at the conclusion of Desert Storm.

The American public learned later that the attacks on US overseas facilities were carried out by local members of a terrorist network, al-Qaeda, led by a wealthy, Saudi-born, radical Islamist, Osama bin Laden. Al-Qaeda was an organization of loosely coordinated radical Islamic groups, many of whom had fought as *mujahideen* to expel the Soviet Union from Afghanistan in the 1980s. Bin Laden and his followers opposed America's presence and operations in the Middle East. Their opposition increased following US participation in the 1991 Gulf War. Al-Qaeda may not have agreed with Saddam Hussein's secular regime and his brutal treatment of Shi'ites at home, but it preferred an Arab, Muslim ruler to a foreign presence. They especially resented American military bases in the region, particularly in Saudi Arabia, which they saw as an insult to Islam. Bin Laden believed that the Americans were infidels propping up a corrupt, insufficiently Islamic, Saudi elite. He resented American military operations in Somalia and military involvement in Yemen. As the United States continued to expand its presence in the Middle East during the 1990s, al-Qaeda began targeting US interests abroad. And as Americans discovered to their shock and horror on 11 September 2001, al-Qaeda was clearly not intimidated by America's newly found military power or impressed by its re-established credibility.

THE SECOND WAR AGAINST IRAQ

11 September 2001 – soon known as 9/11 – appeared to change everything. In a hastily prepared and disjointed address to the nation that evening, a clearly shaken and agitated President George W. Bush, told the American people they had been attacked because they were 'the brightest beacon for freedom and opportunity in the world'. He added:

> the search is underway for those who are behind these evil acts. I've directed the full resources of our intelligence and law enforcement communities to find those responsible and to bring them to justice. We will make no distinction between the terrorists who committed these acts and those who harbour them.[7]

By 20 September the Bush administration had resolved on a plan of action. In those crucial nine days that shaped the response of the United States to 9/11, the administration had determined that it would characterize the attacks as coming from a foreign foe rather than from a domestic one. The president told a joint session of Congress, in a speech televised nationally, that on 11 September, 'the enemies of freedom committed an act of war against our country'. The attacks had been perpetrated, Bush stated, by 'a collection of loosely affiliated terrorist organizations known as al-Qaeda. They are the same murderers indicted for bombing American embassies in Tanzania and Kenya, and responsible for bombing the USS *Cole*.'[8] He deliberately misled the American public and Congress by comparing the attack to that on Pearl Harbor, harking back to that infamous moment, ignoring the fact that the attack on Pearl Harbor was launched from foreign warships against military personnel, whereas the attacks of 9/11 were launched from domestic airports and the victims included large numbers of civilians. However closely associated with al-Qaeda the suicide bombers may have been, if there were US failures in preventing the attacks, they were failures of domestic law enforcement and airport security, not ones of foreign intelligence-gathering.

Until 9/11, Washington had regarded attacks by terrorists as random acts of violence by unconnected, disorganized and state-sponsored groups of extremists. The president explained to Congress that the leaders of al-Qaeda were located in Afghanistan, and supported the Taliban regime which ruled that country. Bush made a number of demands on the Taliban, including that they deliver to the US authorities all the leaders of al-Qaeda in Afghanistan, close immediately and permanently all the terrorist training camps in Afghanistan, and hand over every terrorist – and every person in their support structure – to appropriate authorities. He added: 'These demands are not open to negotiation or discussion. [Applause] The Taliban must act, and act immediately. They will hand over the terrorists, or they will share in their fate.'

Bush was not content with identifying al-Qaeda as the enemy: 'Our war on terror begins with al-Qaeda, but it does not end there. It will not end until every terrorist group of global reach has been found, stopped and defeated.' [Applause] He went on in terms that make Wilson and Truman seem timid:

This war will not be like the war against Iraq a decade ago, with a decisive liberation of territory and a swift conclusion. It will not look like the air war above Kosovo two years ago, where no ground troops were used and not a single American was lost in combat.

Our response involves far more than instant retaliation and isolated strikes. Americans should not expect one battle, but a lengthy campaign, unlike any other we have ever seen. It may include dramatic strikes, visible on TV, and covert operations, secret even in success. We will starve terrorists of funding, turn them one against another, drive them from place to place, until there is no refuge or no rest. And we will pursue nations that provide aid or safe haven to terrorism. Every nation, in every region, now has a decision to make. Either you are with us, or you are with the terrorists. [Applause] From this day forward, any nation that continues to harbour or support terrorism will be regarded by the United States as a hostile regime.

The fight was not just America's fight, it was not just America's freedom that was at stake, the president asserted. It was 'the world's fight. This is civilization's fight. This is the fight of all who believe in progress and pluralism, tolerance and freedom.'[9]

In addition to overseas military actions, Bush stated that steps would be taken domestically to protect American citizens against terrorism. He announced that dozens of Federal departments and agencies, as well as state and local governments, would be coordinated at the highest tier by the new Office of Homeland Security, whose director held cabinet-level status and reported directly to the president. In creating the Office of Homeland Security, President Bush increased the power of the executive to unparalleled levels, threatening the constitutional protections of individuals to a degree never before envisioned. He and his advisors devised a radical theory of a strong 'unitary executive', a presidency not co-equal with the Congress and the Federal Judiciary, but superior to them both.[10]

Bush concluded his address with the confident assertion that, although the course of the conflict was not known, 'its outcome is certain. Freedom and fear, justice and cruelty, have always been at war, and we know that God is not neutral between them.' What Bush did not tell the American people or Congress was that US policies and actions had contributed in part to the events leading to 9/11. As noted above, Osama bin Laden had made his opposition to American policy in the Middle East well known prior to 9/11. To that extent, the attacks of 9/11 were an unintended consequence of the first war against Iraq.

The Taliban and the Bush administration were never going to agree on what action to take concerning the al-Qaeda leader. Just three weeks later, on 7 October 2001, the United States and NATO launched bombing raids on Afghanistan, targeting Kabul, Jalalabad and Kandahar using Tomahawk cruise missiles launched from US and British submarines, ships and aircraft. The Taliban's air defences were weakened, although they remained a danger to coalition helicopters operating in the area. By mid-November, ground forces of the Northern Alliance, with whom the Taliban had been engaged in a bitter civil war for years, had forced the Taliban to retreat from the capital, Kabul, leaving it in the hands of the Northern Alliance and their US and NATO allies. The Taliban and their Pashtun and al-Qaeda fighters were devastated by US and NATO aerial attacks, especially those from AC-130 'Spooky' gunships that mounted chainguns and howitzers. Despite the hurricane of firepower directed against them, Osama bin Laden and Taliban leader Mullah Omar escaped capture.

The high technology weaponry, carpet bombing and even so-called pinpoint bombing utilized by the US and its allies were massively disproportionate and totally inappropriate to seeking out and capturing Osama bin Laden in Afghanistan. Whatever other outcome eventuated from the Afghanistan campaign, the televised images of the wealthiest nation on earth using the most sophisticated and destructive weapons against one of the poorest nations in the world, causing widespread misery to innocent Afghanis, caused inestimable harm to the cause of the United States. Incidents like that in which members of an Afghan wedding party were gunned down from the air because the groom was tall and looked like Osama bin Laden distressed and outraged moderate Muslims around the world, and they acted as potent recruiting material for the radical Islamic cause. The first Gulf War and the Afghanistan War may have extirpated Vietnam from the consciousness of the American military, but the central lesson of Vietnam – that you cannot win the hearts and minds of a people by bombing them – had clearly not been learned. Furthermore, despite the number of bombs dropped, the United States remains just as vulnerable to attacks from al-Qaeda, which has been transformed under Bush's watch from a regional organization into a worldwide movement.

It soon became clear, however, that Osama bin Laden and the war in Afghanistan were not the main targets of the neoconservative policy-makers surrounding President George W. Bush. They had another agenda, and 11 September provided them with the perfect opportunity to pursue it. Vice President Richard Cheney and Secretary of Defense Donald Rumsfeld had unfinished business in the Middle East: the overthrow of their nemesis, President Saddam Hussein in Iraq.

As Secretary of Defense from March 1989 to January 1993 under President George Bush Sr, Cheney had supported General Powell's decision to discontinue the attack on Iraq and overthrow the Iraqi dictator. However, during the 1990s Cheney and Rumsfeld, who had worked together when the former was White House chief of staff in the Gerald Ford administration and Rumsfeld was Ford's Secretary of Defense, changed their minds about the wisdom of the decision not to continue into Baghdad. Together with other conservative colleagues and old friends, Paul D. Wolfowitz and Richard N. Perle, they decided that Saddam Hussein was a threat to American oil and strategic interests in the region and had to go.

Almost from the end of the 1991 war, the United States and the United Kingdom had declared much of Iraq to be 'no fly' zones for Iraqi military aircraft as a means of limiting Saddam Hussein's military capacity and to help protect the Shi'ite and Kurdish populations. Sorties were flown almost daily by allied aircraft, and a deadly one-sided cat-and-mouse game intensified between Saddam's anti-aircraft missile launchers and American and British aircraft. No allied aircraft were shot down and thousands of Iraqi 'targets' were hit. Saddam Hussein remained in power because the popular revolution against him – of which Americans dreamed – never materialized.

By the turn of the twenty-first century, thanks to a huge and carefully orchestrated propaganda campaign by the Bush administration, there was a widespread perception in the United States and in the West that Saddam Hussein had built up a large arsenal of biological and chemical weapons, and that he even possessed a nuclear capability despite economic sanctions that had been imposed by the UN as an additional means of preventing the Iraqi regime from developing 'weapons of mass destruction' (WMD). Within weeks of 9/11, the campaign was intensified, and by early 2002 Saddam Hussein was being described as the greatest evil facing mankind, representing a real and immediate threat to the United States. The administration set out to convince Americans that Iraq was not only directly involved in 9/11, and that removing Saddam Hussein was a part of the effort to vanquish the terrorists who attacked the United States, but also that Baghdad possessed WMD that it intended to use without warning.

The public campaign began with Bush's State of the Union speech on 29 January 2002. Bush identified Iraq, together with Iran and North Korea, as constituting an 'axis of evil'. He vowed that the US 'will not permit the world's most dangerous regimes to threaten us with the world's most destructive weapons.'[11] As an indication of how serious he was, Bush introduced a new defence doctrine on 2 June 2002, in a speech to the graduating class of the US Military Academy at West Point: the doctrine of pre-emption. In some instances, the president asserted, the United States must strike first against another state to prevent a potential threat from growing into an actual one: 'Our security will require all Americans . . . [to] be ready for preemptive action when necessary to defend our liberty and to defend our lives.'[12] The doctrine probably had its origins in what has been identified as Cheney's 'One Percent Rule'. That rule states that if the evidence suggests there is even only a 1 per cent chance of an attack being planned, the US response should be to act as if it is a certainty.[13]

On 12 September 2002, one year after the attacks on New York City and Washington, DC, Bush addressed the UN, challenging the delegates to enforce their own resolutions against Iraq. If they did not do so, Bush stated, the United States would have no choice but to act unilaterally against Iraq. A month later, on 11 October, Congress authorized an attack on Iraq. In an effort to head off the now seemingly inevitable US assault, the UN Security Council on 8 November unanimously approved Resolution 1441. It imposed tough new arms inspections procedures on Iraq and formulated precise, unambiguous definitions of what constituted a 'material breach' of the resolution. Should Iraq violate the resolution, it faced 'serious consequences', the punitive nature of which the Security Council would then determine.[14]

In mid-November, for the first time in almost four years, UN weapons inspectors returned to Iraq. In early December, in the vain hope of stalling American military action, Iraq submitted a 12,000-page declaration on its chemical, biological and nuclear activities, claiming it possessed no banned weapons. Undeterred, on 21 December 2002 President Bush approved the deployment of US troops to the Gulf region, predicting a build-up to around 200,000 troops on location by March.

People around the world reacted to these fast-moving events with alarm. Massive peace demonstrations of between 6 to 10 million people in over 60 countries took place on 15 February 2003. A week later, UN arms inspector Hans Blix ordered Iraq to destroy its al-Samoud 2 missiles by 1 March. The UN inspectors stated that the missiles, whose range enabled them to reach Israel, were illegal. Iraq began to destroy the prohibited missiles on 1 March. On 24 February the United States, the United Kingdom and Spain submitted a proposed resolution to the UN Security Council stating that Baghdad had failed to take the final opportunity afforded to it in Resolution 1441; it was now time to authorize the use of military force against Iraq. France, Germany and Russia countered with a resolution stating that inspections should be intensified and extended to see if there existed 'a real chance to the peaceful settlement of this crisis'. The tripartite alternative to the bellicose 24 February proposal asserted that 'the military option should only be a last resort'.

Despite three weeks of intense lobbying efforts, including a saturation media campaign and an extraordinarily dramatic performance by Secretary of State Colin Powell before the UN Security Council on 5 February 2003, the United States could not muster sufficient support among council members to secure passage of its resolution. As a result, the United States did not call for a vote. Washington would act unilaterally. On 17 March Bush delivered an ultimatum to Saddam Hussein that he knew would be dismissed: the Iraqi leader must leave the country within 48 hours or else face an attack. Two days later, on 19 March 2003 (20 March in Iraq), Bush declared war on Iraq; Operation 'Iraqi Freedom' was launched.

THE WAR

An initial air strike, called a 'decapitation attack', targeted Saddam Hussein and other Iraqi leaders in Baghdad. A second round of air strikes was launched and ground troops entered the country, crossing into southern Iraq from Kuwait. Secretary of Defense Donald Rumsfeld declared that the initial phase of the war was mild compared to what was to come: 'What will follow will not be a repeat of any other conflict. It will be of a force and a scope and a scale that has been beyond what we have seen before.'[15] It was termed 'shock and awe'. Rumsfeld was proven right during the first five days of the war. Then the war became exactly what it had been in Vietnam: a war of conventional forces fighting against ideologically driven guerrillas – a type of asymmetrical war the Americans could not win.

Approximately 100,000 American soldiers and marines, supported by 26,000 British as well as smaller forces from other nations, collectively called the 'coalition of the willing', were deployed in staging areas primarily in Kuwait prior to the war. The number of Iraqi military personnel prior to the war was estimated at around 389,000 with 44,000 Fedayeen Saddam paramilitaries and approximately 650,000 reserves. Most Iraqi troops were equipped with outdated weapons; they were ill-trained, and had low morale.

The invasion was swift. The Iraqi government and the military collapsed in about three weeks. Coalition forces quickly secured oil wells and the oil infrastructure of Iraq, although about 44 wells were set ablaze and destroyed by the dissolving Iraqi army or by accidental fire. The wells were quickly capped, however, preventing the ecological damage and loss of oil that had occurred at the end of the first Iraq war.

Three weeks into the invasion, us forces moved into Baghdad. Initial engagements with armoured units south of the city destroyed most of the Republican Guard's armour, and the southern outskirts of the city were occupied. On 5 April us tanks and armoured vehicles reached Baghdad airport in Operation 'Thunder Run'. Two days later they reached the palace of Saddam Hussein, where they established a base. Following the palace seizure, and television coverage of this event throughout Iraq, Iraqi forces and government officials conceded defeat. On 9 April Baghdad was formally occupied by us forces and the power of Saddam Hussein was declared ended. Much of Baghdad remained unsecured, however, and fighting continued within the metropolitan area. Saddam had disappeared; his whereabouts were unknown. In a widely publicized and staged event televised worldwide, a large statue of the dictator in central Baghdad was toppled by a us M88 tank retriever, as a crowd of Iraqis cheered. Coalition troops promptly began searching for the key members of Saddam Hussein's government.

On 1 May 2003, aboard the aircraft carrier uss *Abraham Lincoln*, President George W. Bush announced that 'combat operations in Iraq have ended', although he did add there was still 'difficult work to do in Iraq'.[16] That difficult work looked to the uninitiated eye very much like combat operations. On 6 May Paul Bremer, a former State Department head of the US counter-terrorism efforts, was appointed as civil administrator of post-war Iraq. The 1.5 million-strong Ba'ath Party was dissolved on 10 May, and the Iraqi army of the old regime was abolished on 23 May. A new army was to be created. The UN Security Council, on 22 May, passed resolution 1483, which recognized the US and the UK (the Coalition Provisional Authority) as occupying powers, approved the formation of an Iraqi Interim Authority, and ended UN sanctions against Iraq. US Army General Tommy Ray Franks assumed control of Iraq as the supreme commander of occupation forces. It was impossible to determine whether this was the beginning of the end, or the end of the beginning.

UNINTENDED CONSEQUENCES OF THE SECOND WAR

As with the Spanish-American War, almost immediately after the so-called cessation of hostilities, the United States found itself facing an insurgency. Violence throughout the country followed the fall of Baghdad as Iraqi religious and regional groups began to fight each other, redressing old grievances. Coalition forces quickly found themselves embroiled in a potential civil war as sectarian tensions between Sunnis, Shi'ites and Kurds erupted into violence the occupiers could not control. US planners had been oblivious to the chasms dividing the groups, and they were unprepared for the upheaval. This chaos was an unintended consequence of Donald Rumsfeld's refusal at the war's outset to countenance 'nation building' by the United States.

During May 2003 thousands of Shi'ite Muslims and militias returned to Iraq from Iran, where they had spent years in exile. In the following twelve months their opposition to the allied occupation hardened, and they formed a potent armed resistance movement. The most well organized were the followers of a young and charismatic Shi'ite cleric, Muqtada al-Sadr, in the Shi'ite holy city of Najaf. In the north, toward the end of May, Kurds resumed control of the ethnically Kurdish city of Kirkuk. On 28 May they elected

Abdul Rahman Mustafa as mayor/governor and a 30-member governing council to work with him.

In June US Deputy Secretary of Defense Paul Wolfowitz told Congress that the widespread opposition facing allied forces in northern, central and southern Iraq could be termed a 'guerrilla war'. On 22 July the two sons of Saddam Hussein, Qusai and Udai Hussein, were killed by US forces in a fierce gun battle in Mosul, in northern Iraq. Armed opposition to the US occupation increased, however, especially from Sunni Muslims encouraged by a tape purportedly from their deposed leader calling for revenge. Although the Sunni Muslims were a minority in Iraq, Saddam Hussein was a Sunni. The Sunnis were terrified that the Shi'ite majority would extract a terrible revenge upon them for the years of persecution they had suffered under the dictator.

On 13 August 2003 Iraq began pumping crude oil through a 190-mile long pipeline from Kirkuk to Ceyhan on Turkey's Mediterranean coast. The line was immediately attacked by saboteurs. The Governing Council of Iraq announced a new Cabinet, which was sworn in on 3 September. Paul Bremer was to remain as civil administrator in overall authority until a new government was elected. Iraqi guerrillas continued daily attacks on US and allied soldiers as well as upon Iraqis supporting the occupying powers.

Coalition forces failed to locate the weapons of mass destruction (WMD) in Iraq that had served as the prime justification for the pre-emptive allied invasion. The non-existence of WMD was further confirmed by the US-led Iraq Survey Group of scientists and military personnel, who reported early in October that they had found no weapons. They unearthed evidence, however, of 'intent' to build them. A conflict that would destabilize the Middle East had been justified by ghosts in the imaginations of the inhabitants of Donald Rumsfeld's 'house of war'.[17]

On 13 December 2003 a 'shabby and weak' Saddam Hussein was captured without a fight by US soldiers in a 'spider hole' in the ground near his hometown of Tikrit. Saddam was tried and convicted of mass murder and executed on 30 December 2006. Despite Saddam's capture, Iraqi insurgents intensified their attacks on coalition forces. In January 2004 thousands of Shi'ites demonstrated in Basra and Baghdad in support of the demand by top Shi'ite cleric Grand Ayatollah Ali Sistani that any planned transitional government should be directly elected by Iraqi parties, threatening the Coalition Provisional Authority's plans to transfer power to the Governing Council.

Shocking images of torture, cruelty and sadistic abuse of Iraqi prisoners held by US soldiers in Abu Ghraib prison, about 20 miles west of Baghdad and once the infamous home of Saddam Hussein's torture chambers, were carried by the world's media in late April 2004. The pictures sparked worldwide outrage and fury. Despite attempts by Bush and the administration to apologize for the atrocities, the revelations caused inestimable damage to the coalition – especially to the moral authority of the United States. Around 6,000 prisoners were held at Abu Ghraib when the abuses occurred. Some days later, Americans were horrified by a videotape posted by an al-Qaeda linked website showing the execution of an American captive, an act of revenge for the Abu Ghraib torture of Iraqis.

More than three years after Bush had declared an end to combat operations, Iraqi civilian anger and frustration continued to be directed toward the occupying forces because of the inability of the coalition to provide public works services, law and order, and safety and stability. The coalition's occupation in Iraq, like that in Afghanistan, had degenerated into counter-insurgency operations involving the use of torture, prolonged detention without trial, and the killing of tens of thousands of civilians. In the summer of 2006 the Iraqi insurgency continued, despite intensive efforts by the coalition to prevent it. Nonetheless, the military operation in Iraq has been described by the faithful as astonishingly successful: 'probably the most successful war ever fought between a democracy and a dictatorship.'[18]

* * *

However one regards the second war against Iraq, there can be no denying that its consequences are not what its planners in Washington had in mind. The list of unanticipated consequences of this war – in addition to the insurgency described above – is almost endless. Not for a moment did Washington's planners think that US casualties after the 'military phase' would be more than ten times the number of US forces killed during the war. Nor did they dream that oil prices would reach more than $70 a barrel three years after the downfall of Saddam Hussein. Never in their wildest fantasies could they have imagined that US Secretary of State Colin Powell would be forced to cancel a visit to the Olympic City in Athens, Greece, in summer 2004 because of promised demonstrations against him by Europeans who regarded him as a war criminal as a result of the war in Iraq. Nor did they believe that in November 2006 large parts of Iraq would remain out of the control of the US and Iraqi security forces. The official view was that the Iraqi elections at the end of January 2005 would lessen the insurgency, improving the overall security situation in Iraq. The post-election violence throughout much of Iraq dramatically refuted the accuracy of the expectation.

By November 2006 Powell and Rumsfeld had been forced out of office. That month the Pentagon reported that more than 2,800 American servicemen and servicewomen had died in Iraq. Of this total, nearly 2,700 died in the 'post-combat' phase of operations that began on 1 May 2003. Of the 21,400 Americans wounded in Iraq, all but 1,000 were wounded in this second phase, and some 9,700 of the 21,400 were too severely disabled to return to duty. As high as these figures of American dead and wounded are, the number of Iraqi casualties is astronomical.

At one point US and US forces had some 10,000 Iraqis in detention, almost all on suspicion of involvement in the insurgency. More than 95 per cent of them were Iraqi nationals, throwing into doubt the oft-quoted official view that the insurgency was being substantially resourced from outside Iraq. The American presence, which, it was hoped, would stabilize Iraq, had become a force for destabilization.

When thinking about embarking on war in Iraq, the neoconservative Washington planners foresaw the overthrow of a sadistic dictator followed by the discovery of WMD and the embracing of democracy by a grateful, formerly repressed Iraqi population who would establish a pro-Western regime. The administration's hawks anticipated a war resulting in a substantial reduction in the threat of international terrorism, an increase and stabilization in the region's oil production, and the extension of benevolent American influence throughout the Middle East. Instead, they witnessed a highly unstable and volatile Middle East, an increased rather than a lessened danger from terrorist attacks worldwide, a more unpredictable oil supply, widespread mistrust of the United States and its motives throughout the world, and their own nation becoming more and more accustomed to terror alerts and infringements of personal liberty. The reality was that US leaders failed to look beyond their own and their country's immediate ambitions and desires; they did not plan prudently for a darkening future. Secretary of Defense Rumsfeld anticipated a short rather than a long war. Much of the military planning for Iraq did not extend beyond the next supposed turning point: the transfer of sovereignty, the election, and so on. To ensure that they did not benefit from experience gained in Iraq, the United States rotated mid-level commanders back to Washington after short stints, so that everyone could get his or her combat medals. This was repeating a mistake made in Vietnam. Frequent rotation of battlefield commanders raises the question of what would have happened if Lincoln had removed Grant from command prior to the Battle of Vicksburg.[19]

By fall 2006 Operation Iraqi Freedom was deteriorating further into chaos in Iraq, and domestic support in America was rapidly evaporating. Uncertainty reigned in government circles; frustration characterized military operations; the press and public were shocked and dazed by the intensifying ferocity of the insurgency and the disproportionate responses of US troops. The war and its 'post-combat' phase clearly were not going as planned; Americans were confused as to why not; they were looking, if not for someone to blame, at least for some explanations.

Many Americans came to believe that the principal purpose of the Bush administration – dominated by oil men – was to secure Iraq's vast oil reserves so that the United States could control production and maintain lower prices. They increasingly believed that the arguments about terrorism, weapons of mass destruction, tyranny, democracy and other public rationales were simply ruses to disguise the real motivation for the invasion. There can be no doubting that one of the major elements of American policy over the past thirty years has been the pursuit and control of oil production and resources. The United States appears to have embarked upon an imperial venture in which its military has been transformed into a global oil-protection force.[20]

Reconstruction of Iraq produced the disturbing unintended consequences of continued high levels of violence. President Bush had intended the war in Iraq to be a victory in his 'war on terror'. In fact the reverse occurred. The US presence in Iraq expanded opportunities for militant extremists to strike against both the Americans and Iraqis themselves. Iraq was opened up as a base of operations for Islamist groups and al-Qaeda, the opposite of Bush's intentions. Washington had not learned the lessons of the Philippine insurrection or of Vietnam – the presence of foreign troops in a politically and socially divided country can breed violent resistance and turmoil that cannot be subdued with arms.

Vietnam demonstrated conclusively that the United States cannot win a war like the Iraq war by utilizing 'search and destroy' missions to kill insurgents. Such raids create more enemy fighters than they destroy. Civilians, the key to success, are alienated by such heavy-handed raids. Rather than kill insurgents, it is more important to protect civilians.[21] The United States did not adopt this strategy because it violated some key Rumsfeldian notions about how the US military should operate in the twenty-first century. Rumsfeld wanted a quick, lethal visit by a light, lean force reliant upon technological superiority, mobility and firepower rather than the prolonged presence of a large body of occupying troops that had spelled success in Japan and Germany following World War II.

Addressing the graduating cadets of the US Military Academy at West Point in May 2006, President George W. Bush compared himself to President Harry Truman. Bush said Truman had acted boldly against the 'fanatic faith' of Cold War communism in the same way he had responded to the threat of terrorism since the attacks of 11 September. Bush compared the current war against Islamic radicalism to the Cold War, describing it as a fight against followers of 'a murderous ideology that despises freedom, questions all dissent, has territorial ambitions and pursues totalitarian aims.' Like Truman, Bush stated, he was 'laying the foundations for victory'. Bush promised the neophyte military officers: 'We will never back down, we will never give in, and we will never accept anything other than complete victory.'[22]

The trouble is that neither Bush nor Truman defined 'complete victory' – or indeed knew what it meant. Complete victory has come to represent the continuity of a vision that results from defining the enemy in universal terms as evil. This vision, some call it idealism, goes back in American history to Woodrow Wilson's presidency at least, if not before. One of the unintended consequences of such a distorted vision and definition of the enemy is that the goal of victory becomes elusive and is never reached. No sooner is one enemy defeated than another appears to take its place. Short-sighted political and military decisions and poor judgements inevitably follow. The war in Iraq is a perfect example.

Bush's Iraq war was and is a 'phoney war' in the worst possible sense. The case for war was proven to be a house of cards; the outcome has been the spread of violence. The president repeatedly asserted defensive and protective intentions for his nation and people. For example, on 4 July 2004 he said: 'We will engage these enemies in these countries [Iraq and Afghanistan] and around the world so we do not have to face them here at home.' In reality, the large portion of the human and financial capital resources that the United States is recklessly expending to fight against culturally and ethnically divided nation-states racked by civil turmoil is not making America safer.[23] The war in Iraq could not address America's biggest vulnerability – its openness to unconventional attacks by hostile groups that do not respect borders. Events such as the commuter train bombings in Madrid in March 2004, and the London Underground bombings in July 2005, illustrate that terrorists live and operate within jurisdictions comparable to the United States; they cannot be safely isolated and attacked in 'rogue states'.

Military action against Saddam Hussein and the subsequent occupation of Iraq elevated the terrorist risk. Since Iraq, no US adversaries will attempt to fight against conventional US military forces. They will utilize the tactics of a David seeking to topple Goliath. Nonetheless, the Bush administration remains wedded to conventional notions of US warfare, believing that the overwhelming application of military force against terrorist organizations and their sponsors is the best deterrent to new attacks like 9/11.[24] In the face of mounting evidence to the contrary, the Department of Defense has boldly proclaimed that the 'Global War on Terrorism' has killed or captured two-thirds of known al-Qaeda leaders. The US government claims that it has liberated 25 million Afghanis and 27 million Iraqis, and guaranteed free elections in both nations. This kind of thinking ignores the fact that the influence of al-Qaeda is directly proportional to the degree to which young Muslims sense that they and their religion are oppressed and under attack by the West.

There are other unintended consequences arising from the massive projection of US military force throughout the Muslim world from North Africa to Southeast Asia, and the persistent warnings of devastating air strikes against Iran. They include the increasing influence of al-Qaeda and other forms of Islamist radicalism. US military technological supremacy has fostered anti-Western sentiment, undermined secular reformist trends and destabilized states throughout the region.[25] It has renewed the self-confidence of Iran's leaders. George W. Bush's 'long war' on terror, which initially worried the policy-makers in Tehran, especially the mullahs, has turned to their strategic advantage. Enemies on either side – the Baathists in Baghdad and the Taliban in Kabul – are now gone. The expulsion of Syria from Lebanon under US pressure has left Iran as the major foreign influence in that country, at least until the Israeli invasion of July 2006. Iran has always played a leading role in Islamic history. It was never colonized by the Western empires. It occupies a central position in the 'Islamic arc' stretching from the Atlantic to the Indian Ocean. It has the largest economy and the strongest military in the Muslim world; it has vast quantities of rapidly appreciating oil wealth. Its alienation by the United States is an irredeemable tragedy for both nations.

Perhaps the most disturbing unintended consequence of the first and second wars against Iraq has been the emergence within the US administration of the belief that the world could not be managed within a legal framework, by negotiation or conciliation. Bush and the neoconservatives concluded that what was required to secure the safety of the United States was the use of overwhelming American military force against 'terror'. If the unintended consequences of previous wars are any guide, then there is no saying where such a course of action will lead. By late 2006, after three years of refusing to face the issue, there appeared some national willingness to confront the disastrous unintended consequences of the Iraq war. On 6 December, in the Senate hearings to confirm Robert Gates as Rumsfeld's successor as Secretary of Defense, the very senior Senator Robert C. Byrd (Democrat, West Virginia) pointedly asked the candidate about the 'unexpected consequences' of the continued American occupation. Gates replied: 'I think that we have seen, in Iraq, that once war is unleashed, it becomes unpredictable.' The question and answer at least mark a first step.

CONCLUSION

. . . from where the sun now stands, I will fight no more forever.
Chief Joseph of the Nez Perce[1]

Our study has, we hope, demonstrated that the wars fought by the United States produced unintended consequences that outweighed the intended consequences in shaping subsequent events. The wars also produced sharp and significant shifts in US policy. When the unintended consequences of the major wars of the United States are closely examined, Carl von Clausewitz's maxim that 'war is a continuation of policy by other means' is invalidated. Going to war did not solve problems, it created new ones.

But if, as we have suggested in this book, war has produced such unwanted and undesirable unintended consequences, it might be asked why has the United States so frequently resorted to military force to resolve international crises adversely affecting its interests, or as a method of imposing its will? Are there alternatives to war as an instrument of policy?

As we have demonstrated, US leaders gave many reasons for going to war. Most of these wars lived on in the history and memory of the nation as successes, and those who fought them were, and are, revered as heroes. The unintended consequences were overlooked or forgotten. US leaders, and the people, refused to face the realities of the outcomes of the wars fought. Those who advocated and planned the wars the United States embarked upon were frequently driven by base and exaggerated fear. They were also motivated by ambition, nationalistic jingoism, a messianic religious zeal that led them to see their nation as the self-appointed saviour of the world. Their aims were confused, and their knowledge of the enemy lacking. They optimistically, and invariably wrongly, believed the wars would be short and that the United

States would emerge victorious. Administrations discounted the costs in human life – both American lives and those of the enemy – and the social and political repercussions at home and abroad that resulted from the resort to arms. War was romanticized and idealized, made into a sanitized abstraction that ignored the consequences for its practitioners.

In 2006 Eliot A. Cohen and John Gooch, two influential analysts who do not shy away from espousing war as a suitable instrument of national policy, described the misreading of history in different terms:

> The story of the Iraq war is not over, of course. But it is, already, a reminder that the most powerful and competent military the world has ever known can still stumble, and stumble badly. It can make large mistakes not because of stupidity or incompetence, but because it has chosen to embrace a comfortable version of history rather than an accurate one.[2]

Our book has offered an extremely uncomfortable version of history for all of those who would like to believe that wars can ever go right.

As we have shown, the wars fought by the United States lasted longer than expected, and they ended in ways very different from those imagined at the outset by the leaders. The results were at best inconclusive. Today, the United States has power without wisdom.[3] The nation does not recognize the limits of arms despite repeated experiences confirming their deficiencies. American military power is irrelevant in solving the problems of poverty, illiteracy and human rights abuses that encourage war. The use of military force against terrorism has produced political failures and created enduring enmities. In the past, terrorism was somewhat restrained. It is no longer restrained today, and with the possibility of more states and even non-state groups obtaining nuclear weapons there is an even greater danger of unpredictable anarchy. Furthermore, as we have seen, war has weakened and endangered secular democratic institutions at home. Wars have invariably led to the militarization and unlawful extension of executive power, and if the present trend continues the outcome is more likely to be slavery than peace and security. The nation has lost faith in an administration

controlled by religious fanatics who have wire-tapped citizens without warrants, tortured military prisoners and violated the principles
of due process and the rule of law.

In the twenty-first century there is a blurring between peace
and war. The conclusions of war may not bring, or may not mean,
a state of peace. The traditional dichotomies – war and peace,
armies and civilians, war and post-war, victims and perpetrators –
may no longer be helpful. Modern technologies, modern ways of
fighting wars, especially by urban-based insurgencies, mean that
these diverse issues are no longer watertight compartments that
can be narrowly defined – if indeed they ever were, or could be.
Clausewitz would have good reason to rethink his observations
about war and policy if he were to make them today.

One obvious alternative to war when unilateral diplomatic
efforts have failed the United States is collective diplomacy utilizing the United Nations and relying on its peacekeeping units (the
'blue helmets') to calm tensions and separate factions on the verge
of war. Other international agencies, such as the World Bank,
International Monetary Fund and International Court are institutions where talking and investing can blunt war-making. Non-gov-
ernmental organizations (NGOs), such as Amnesty International,
Greenpeace and the International Red Cross, can also provide
research data on human rights violations, publicize examples of
environmental ruin, and extend humanitarian aid – all to remind
governmental leaders that the costs of war are great, and to stim-
ulate public discussion of those costs. War crimes tribunals such as
the UN International Criminal Tribunal for the former Yugoslavia,
based in The Hague, are a potential deterrent to war as they caution leaders that they may be held accountable for the slaughter of
civilians. Leaders might, as a result, be less eager to unleash brute
military forces.

In recent years US leaders have described the United Nations
as ineffectual, and they have also argued that it has not always
acted in accordance with US wishes or interests. The real difficulty
these organizations present as alternatives to war, however, is that
they are inherently inadequate because they are dominated to such
a large extent by the United States. Many countries rightly perceive
them as extensions of, or proxies for, the United States. They lose
their effectiveness as detached arbiters in disputes or negotiations

nations may have with the United States. Presidents of the World Bank, for example, have included former Secretary of Defense Robert McNamara and former Deputy Secretary of Defense Paul Wolfowitz. Many countries feel they are being bullied or intimidated by the United States when dealing with these international agencies, and they resent it. Such reactions make achieving desirable outcomes through negotiations much more difficult.

We acknowledge that international NGOs have a role to play in reducing the reasons for war. One of the largest problems for the majority of the world's poorest nations, and one that often leads to internal division and civil war and to external aggression, is that their governments are unable to provide basic human services such as health care, clean water and food. Their peoples are all too frequently wracked by disease, their lands ravaged by drought and erosion. If NGOs like the Gates Foundation, for example, can reduce the problems that create misery for people and that have produced civil strife and war, then governments are going to be more stable and the chances for peaceful solutions will be improved.

However, so long as the world's most militarized country, the United States, remains committed to massively reflexive resorts to force and has a controlling influence over these international bodies, worthy though they may be, they cannot be seen as an alternative to war. The threat of war is always present should countries refuse to comply with the demands of such bodies. They too often become additional instruments of US policy and, if they fail, they are replaced by military action.

It is essential that the United States finds alternatives to war, for its own sake and for the future survival of democracy as a political system at home and abroad. George W. Bush has repeatedly told the American people that the United States is waging a worldwide war on terrorism 'over there' so that it does not have to be fought 'over here'. In the next decade and beyond, the United States, in its efforts to win the so-called 'war on terrorism' will attempt militarily to increase its power further and further beyond its borders. This is a futile course of action. Military actions – especially in the Middle East – have generated greater antagonism toward the United States, and increased the likelihood of an attack on US soil, by giving life, even legitimacy, to radical Islam. This revitalized hostility, combined with technological innovations in weapons in the hands of its enemies, makes US military action self-defeating. The massive, unfolding, hostile response to the presence of United States armed forces in Iraq and Afghanistan hopefully presages the last example of the 'old thinking' in the United States. Rather than calling for an expanded and greater use of military force, as was the call in Vietnam when faced with a similar failure to change a culture it did not understand, in these theatres of conflict the United States should be looking for ways to encourage democratic change through restraint and patience. The word 'negotiation' should become synonymous with the concept of power, rather than the word 'war'.

A change of thinking will come eventually. Contemporary Europe may offer a model. After 500 years of fighting for a few thousand square miles in northern Europe, Europeans have opted for peace and virtual disarmament. The European Union and its institutions have democratized Europe in new and innovative ways that have significantly reduced the likelihood of war. There is less opportunity for the folly, hubris and concentration of power that has led to wars in the past. Wars may have been used to build a sense of national identity and patriotism, but they have no place in the twenty-first century. Every alternative is a palliative, nothing can be fundamental until the United States massively reduces its armaments, and then undertakes serious work with international NGOs by pouring in billions of dollars. The United States needs to rebuild its deteriorating, neglected and underfunded educational system, and tottering domestic transportation infrastructure. It must assiduously and uncompromisingly address energy conservation and global warming.

This may be a utopian viewpoint; this book, however, shows that war has never worked out as expected and has invariably raised as many problems as it solved; so why not suggest visionary alternatives? This book has shown repeatedly how the United States did not really benefit from its wars: instead it had to deal with unintended consequences. It is time to try radical reductions of military spending, a genuine commitment to negotiation rather than the use of armed force, and the rebuilding of a dilapidated socio-economic infrastructure. We realize that some doubters will scoff at this suggestion, finding it too visionary: Martin Luther King, Mahatma Gandhi and Nelson Mandela are among those who faced such criticisms. Yet even conservative diplomats like George F. Kennan appealed for the use of quiet, patient diplomacy over the rattling of nuclear weapons. Our view is simply that a survey of the unintended consequences of the United States at war demonstrates that war is folly, and it is futile. Once this is admitted other possibilities become legion.

REFERENCES

PREFACE

1 Carl von Clausewitz remains the most comprehensive, percep-
tive contributor to political/military and strategic thought. In
whole or in part, he is required reading in America's intermedi-
ate level and senior military schools, as well as in many civilian
strategic studies programmes. The quotation can be found in
Book One, 'On The Nature of War', of Clausewitz's *On War*,
ed. Michael Howard and Peter Paret (Princeton, NJ, 1984).

INTRODUCTION

1 Hannah Arendt, *The Human Condition* (Chicago, 1958). See
especially discussion in Chapter 5.
2 Richard Stengel, 'Why History Matters', *Time* (3 July 2006), p. 4.
3 Max Boot, *The Savage Wars of Peace* (New York, 2002). For a
devastating critique of Boot's perspective, see Chalmers
Johnson, *The Sorrows of Empire: Militarism, Secrecy, and the
End of the Republic* (New York, 2004), p. 70.
4 Russell F. Weigley, *The American Way of War: A History of
United States Military Strategy and Policy* (Bloomington, IN,
1973), p. xix.
5 Weigley, *The American Way of War*, p. xxii.
6 Rumsfeld, quoted in Eliot Weinberger, 'What I Heard about
Iraq in 2005', *London Review of Books*, XXVIII/1 (5 January
2006), p. 8.
7 Stephen Kinzer, *Overthrow: America's Century of Regime
Change from Hawaii to Iraq* (New York, 2006).

1 John Adams to Abigail Adams, in *The Book of Abigail and John: Selected Letters of the Adams Family, 1762–1874*, ed. L. H. Butterfield, et al. (Cambridge, MA, 1975), pp. 122–3.

2 'The Unanimous Declaration of the Thirteen United States of America, In Congress, 4 July 1776'; available at www.ushistory.org/Declaration/document, accessed 25 July 2006.

3 Colin Kidd, 'Damnable Deficient', review of David McCullough, *1776: America and Britain at War* (New York, 2005), in *London Review of Books*, XXVII/22 (17 November 2005), pp. 30–31.

4 Ibid.

5 Geoffrey Perret, *A Country Made by War: From the Revolution to Vietnam: The Story of America's Rise to Power* (New York, 1989), p. 15.

6 Howe, quoted in J.F.C. Fuller, *Decisive Battles of the USA* (New York, 1942), p. 37 [italics in original].

7 Quotation from one of his soldiers, quoted in ibid., p. 44.

8 J. W. Fortescue, quoted in ibid., p. 92.

9 Vergennes, quoted in Thomas G. Paterson, et al., *American Foreign Relations: A History* (Boston, MA, 2005), I, p. 13.

10 Fuller, *Decisive Battles*, p. 63.

11 Ibid., p. 69.

12 Washington, quoted in Russell F. Weigley, *The American Way of War: A History of United States Military Strategy and Policy* (Bloomington, IN, 1973), p. 14.

13 *The American Heritage Pictorial Atlas of United States History* (New York, 1966), p. 103.

14 Greene, quoted in Weigley, *American Way of War*, p. 36.

15 Washington, quoted in Fuller, *Decisive Battles*, p. 72.

16 Cornwallis to George Washington, quoted in ibid., p. 89.

17 Vergennes, quoted in Paterson, et al., *American Foreign Policy* (Lexington, MA, 1983), I, p. 22.

18 John Adams to Abigail Adams, quoted in *The Book of Abigail and John*, ed. Butterfield et al., pp. 122–3.

19 Gordon S. Wood, *The Creation of the American Republic, 1776–1787* (Chapel Hill, NC, 1969), pp. 567–74.

20 William T. Hagan, *American Indians* (Chicago, 1961), p. 38.

21 Michael Paul Rogin, *Fathers and Children: Andrew Jackson and the Subjugation of the American Indian* (New York, 1975), pp. 127–8.

1 Obadiah German, US Senator from New York, 13 June 1812, *Annals of Congress*, 12th Congress, 1st Sess., Columns 272, 275–82. Quoted in Norman A. Graebner, ed., *Ideas and Diplomacy: Readings in the Intellectual Tradition of American Foreign Policy* (New York, 1964), p. 116.

2 Madison, 'War Message to Congress', 1 June 1812, in James D. Richardson, ed., *Messages and Papers of the Presidents, 1789–1898* (Washington, DC, 1896–8), I, pp. 499–505.

3 J.F.C. Fuller, *Decisive Battles of the USA* (New York, 1942), p. 125.

4 Bradford Perkins, *The Creation of a Republican Empire, 1776–1865* (Cambridge, 1993), p. 145.

5 Richard Mentor Johnson, 11 December 1811, quoted in Graebner, ed., *Ideas and Diplomacy*, p. 106.

6 Hull, quoted in Geoffrey Perret, *A Country Made by War: From the Revolution to Vietnam: The Story of America's Rise to Power* (New York, 1989), p. 109.

7 Perret, *A Country Made by War*, p. 109.

8 Jefferson, quoted in Fuller, *Decisive Battles*, p. 106.

9 Madison, quoted in ibid., p. 107.

10 Perry, quoted in ibid., p. 114.

11 Fuller, ibid., p. 116.

12 Mahan, quoted in ibid., p. 122.

13 Wellington, quoted in ibid., pp. 122–3.

14 Donald R. Hickey, *The War of 1812: A Short History* (Urbana, IL, 1990), pp. 114–15.

15 'Report and Resolutions of the Hartford Convention, 4 January 1815', in Henry Steel Commager, ed., *Documents of American History* (New York, 1963), pp. 209–11.

16 Madison, 'Proclamation for a Day of Thanksgiving and Prayer', 4 March 1815, Washington, DC, in Richardson, ed., *Messages and Papers of the Presidents*, pp. 560–61.

17 Hickey, *The War of 1812*, p. 109.

18 Perkins, *The Creation of a Republican Empire*, p. 146. See also Reginald Horsman, *The War of 1812* (New York, 1969), p. 268.

19 Treaty of Ghent, 1814, Article X, The Avalon Project at Yale Law School, available at www.yale.edu/lawweb/avalon/diplomacy/britain/ghent.htm#art10, accessed 25 July 2006.

20 Perret, *A Country Made by War*, p. 133.

21 See Russell Thornton, *American Indian Holocaust and Survival: A Population History since 1492* (Oklahoma City, OK, 1987).

22 See 'Andrew Jackson's Actions and Deeds against Southeastern

Indians', *American Indian Nations*, University of California at Riverside, available at www.americanindian.ucr.edu/ discussions/jackson/deeds.html, accessed 25 July 2006.
23 Robert Remini, *Andrew Jackson and his Indian Wars* (New York, 2001), pp. 143–62.

3 THE WAR AGAINST MEXICO, 1846–48

1 James L. O'Sullivan, 'The Great Nation of Futurity', *The United States Democratic Review*, VI/23 (1839), pp. 426–30.
2 John S. D. Eisenhower, 'Polk and his Generals', in *Essays on the Mexican War*, ed. Douglas W. Richmond (Arlington, VA, 1986), p. 35.
3 Ampudia, quoted in Richard B. Morris, ed., *Encyclopedia of American History* (New York, 1976), p. 231.
4 James K. Polk, Message to Congress, 11 May 1846, in James D. Richardson, ed., *A Compilation of the Messages and Papers of the Presidents, 1789–1898* (Washington, DC, 1896–98), IV, pp. 437–43.
5 Ibid.
6 Morris, ed., *Encyclopedia of American History*, p. 234.
7 Allan R. Millett and Peter Maslowski, *For the Common Defense: A Military History of the United States of America* (New York, 1984), p. 148.
8 Ibid., p. 149.
9 Treaty transmitted to Senate 22 February 1848, in Richardson, ed., *Messages and Papers of the Presidents*, pp. 573–4.
10 Polk, quoted in Thomas G. Paterson, et al., *American Foreign Relations: A History* (Boston, MA, 2005), I, p. 115.
11 K. Jack Bauer, *The Mexican War, 1846–1848* (Lincoln, NE, 1974), p. 361.
12 Ibid., p. 364.
13 Ibid., p. 369.
14 J.F.C. Fuller, *Decisive Battles of the USA*, p. 146.
15 Webster, quoted in Robert Kelley, *The Shaping of the American Past*, (Englewood Cliffs, NJ, 1975), I, p. 345.

4 THE CIVIL WAR, 1861–65

1 Sherman, quoted in Lloyd Lewis, *Sherman: Fighting Prophet* (New York, 1932), p. 637.
2 For discussion of the legacy of the Civil War in the American

consciousness see David W. Blight, *Race and Reunion: The Civil War in American Memory* (Cambridge, MA, 2001).

3 James M. McPherson, *Drawn with the Sword: Reflections on the American Civil War* (New York, 1996), p. 57.

4 Lincoln, Second Inaugural Address, 4 March 1865, in James D. Richardson, ed., *Messages and Papers of the Presidents, 1789–1898*, VI, pp. 276–7.

5 McPherson, *Drawn with the Sword*, p. 71.

6 Lincoln, Message to Special Session of Congress, 4 July 1861, in Richardson, ed., *Messages and Papers of the Presidents*, VI, pp. 20–31.

7 Ibid.

8 Lincoln, Second Inaugural Address, 4 March 1865, in ibid., pp. 276–7.

9 Weigley, *The American Way of War*, p. xxii.

10 Perret, *A Country Made by War*, p. 210.

11 Alexander, quoted in ibid., p. 210.

12 Ibid., p. 211.

13 Grant, quoted in ibid., p. 219.

14 Ibid., p. 224.

15 Ulysses S. Grant, *Personal Memoirs of U. S. Grant* (New York, 1885–6), I, pp. 480–81, quoted in J.F.C. Fuller, *Decisive Battles of the USA*, p. 261.

16 Lincoln, quoted in Perret, *A Country Made by War*, p. 225.

17 Weigley, *The American Way of War*, p. 117.

18 Lincoln to Welles, quoted in Perret, *A Country Made by War*, p. 229.

19 Grant to Sherman, April 4, 1864, quoted in Fuller, *Decisive Battles of the USA* (New York, 1942), p. 294.

20 Grant, quoted in Weigley, *The American Way of War*, p. 147.

21 Grant, quoted in ibid., p. 148.

22 Halleck, quoted in ibid., p. 148.

23 Sherman, quoted in ibid., p. 149.

24 Grant, *Personal Memoirs*, II, pp. 177–8, quoted in Weigley, *The American Way of War*, p. 142.

25 Benjamin Schwarz, 'Lee and Sherman', *The Atlantic* (April 2006), pp. 95–8.

26 US Constitution, Article 1, Section 8, Clause 15, provides Congress the power: 'To provide for calling forth the Militia to execute the Laws of the Union, suppress Insurrections and repel Invasions.' See Richard B. Morris, ed., *Encyclopedia of American History*, p. 570.

27 Lincoln, Executive Order No. 1, Relating to Political Prisoners,

14 February 1862, in Richardson, ed., *Messages and Papers of the Presidents*, VI, pp. 102–4.
28 Lincoln, First Inaugural Address, 4 March 1861, in ibid., pp. 5–12.
29 Fuller, *Decisive Battles of the USA*, p. 320.
30 Weigley, *The American Way of War*, p. xxii. See also Chapter 7.

5 THE WAR AGAINST SPAIN, 1898

1 Henry Cabot Lodge, *The War against Spain* (New York, 1899), preface.
2 John A. S. Grenville and George Berkeley Young, *Politics, Strategy and American Diplomacy: Studies in Foreign Policy* (New Haven, CT, 1966), p. 229.
3 William McKinley, First Inaugural Address, 4 March 1897, The Avalon Project at Yale Law School, available at www.yale.edu/lawweb/avalon/presiden/inaug/mckin1.htm, accessed 28 July 2006.
4 McKinley, quoted in Thomas Paterson, et al., *American Foreign Relations: A History* (Boston, MA, 2005), II, p. 16.
5 Hearst, quoted in 'The Spanish-American War', Small Planet Communications, available at www.smplanet.com/imperialism/remember.html, accessed 28 July 2006.
6 Naval court of inquiry, quoted in Kenneth J. Hagan, *This People's Navy: The Making of American Sea Power* (New York, 1992), p. 213.
7 'The Spanish-American War', Small Planet Communications.
8 McKinley, Message to Congress, 11 April, 1898, in James D. Richardson, ed., *Messages and Papers of the Presidents, 1789–1898* (Washington, DC, 1896–8), X, p. 139ff.
9 Warren Zimmermann, *The First Great Triumph: How Five Americans Made their Country a World Power* (New York, 2002), p. 261.
10 John L. Offner, *An Unwanted War: The Diplomacy of the United States and Spain over Cuba* (Chapel Hill, NC, 1992); Zimmermann, *The First Great Triumph*, p. 264.
11 Roosevelt, quoted in Perret, *A Country Made by War*, p. 278.
12 Long, quoted in Hagan, *This People's Navy*, p. 219.
13 Dewey, quoted in ibid., p. 219.
14 Anonymous poet, quoted in ibid., p. 221.
15 Long, quoted in ibid., p. 215.
16 Cervera, quoted in J.F.C. Fuller, *Decisive Battles of the USA*, p. 341.

17 Roosevelt, quoted in Ivan Musicant, *Empire by Default: The Spanish-American War and the Dawn of the American Century* (New York, 1998), p. 422.

18 Alger, quoted in Fuller, *Decisive Battles of the USA*, p. 354.

19 Shafter, quoted in ibid., p. 353.

20 Sampson, quoted in Jack Sweetman, *American Naval History: An Illustrated Chronology of the US Navy and Marine Corps, 1775–Present* (Annapolis, MD, 2002), p. 99.

21 McKinley, quoted in Zimmermann, *The First Great Triumph*, p. 300.

22 Merritt, quoted in Allan R. Millett and Peter Maslowski, *For the Common Defense* (New York, 1994), p. 282.

23 Dewey, quoted in Zimmermann, *The First Great Triumph*, p. 305.

24 Dewey, quoted in ibid., p. 305.

25 Long, quoted in ibid., p. 305.

26 Quotation from ibid., p. 307.

27 Hay, quoted in ibid., p. 310.

28 Carl Russell Fish, *The Path of Empire: A Chronicle of the United States as a World Power* (Washington, DC, 2003), available at mirror.pacific.net.au/gutenberg/etext02/tpemp10.txt, accessed 28 July 2006.

29 Ibid.

30 See 'The Philippine–American War: McKinley's Benevolent Assimilation Proclamation', Washington, DC, 21 December 1898. Quoted in James A. Blount, *American Occupation of the Philippines, 1898–1912* (New York, 1973), available at www.msc.edu.ph/centennial/benevolent.html, accessed 28 July 2006.

31 See Veltisezar B. Bautista, *The Filipino-Americans: From 1763 to the Present: Their History, Culture, and Traditions* (Farmington Hills, MI, 2002), available at www.msc.edu.ph/centennial/filam1.html, accessed 28 July 2006.

32 See 'Philippine–American War (1899–1913): History of the Philippines (1898–1946)', available at en.wikipedia.org/wiki/History_of_the_Philippines_(1898-1946), accessed 28 July 2006.

33 Aguinaldo, quoted in Fish, *The Path of Empire*.

34 Waller, quoted in Geoffrey Perret, *A Country Made by War: From the Revolution to Vietnam: The Story of America's Rise to Power* (New York, 1989), p. 297.

35 Roosevelt, State of Union Message, 7 December 1903, available at www.theodore-roosevelt.com/sotu3.html, accessed 28 July 2006.

REFERENCES

36 See M. E. Murphy, 'The History of Guantanamo Bay, Cuba, 1494–1964, US Naval Base Guantanamo Bay, Cuba', available at www.nsgtmo.navy.mil/history/gtmohistorymurphyvol1ch3.htm, accessed 28 July 2006.

6 THE UNITED STATES IN WORLD WAR I, 1917–18

1 Georges Clemenceau, Speech at Verdun, France, 20 July 1919, quoted in Margaret MacMillan, *Paris 1919* (New York, 2003), p. xxx.
2 Gene Smith, *When the Cheering Stopped: the Last Years of Woodrow Wilson* (New York, 1964), p. 33. See also Ellis W. Hawley, *The Great War and the Search for a Modern Order* (New York, 1979), chapters 1–3.
3 German Chancellor Theobald von Bethmann-Hollweg, quoted in Thomas G. Paterson, et al., *American Foreign Relations: A History* (Lexington, MA, 1995), II, p. 96.
4 Woodrow Wilson, War Message, 2 April 1917, The World War I Document Archive, Brigham Young University Library, available at www.lib.byu.edu/~rdh/wwi/1917/wilswarm.html, accessed 28 July 2006.
5 Ibid.
6 Ibid.
7 Ibid.
8 Corbett, quoted in Elting E. Morison, *Admiral Sims and the Modern American Navy* (Boston, MA, 1942), p. 378.
9 Perret, *A Country Made by War*, p. 320.
10 Perret, *A Country Made by War*, pp. 336–7.
11 MacMillan, *Paris 1919*, p. 19.
12 David Stevenson, *Cataclysm: The First World War as Political Tragedy* (New York, 2004), p. 477. See also pp. 409–31.
13 MacMillan, *Paris 1919*, p. 3.
14 Woodrow Wilson, Fourteen Points Speech, 8 January 1918, quoted in *The Papers of Woodrow Wilson,* ed. Arthur S. Link, et al. (Princeton, NJ, 1984), p. 536. United States Department of State, available at usinfo.state.gov/usa/infousa/facts/democrac/51.htm, accessed 28 July 2006.
15 MacMillan, *Paris 1919*, p. 11.
16 Paterson, et al., *American Foreign Relations* (Boston, MA, 2005), II, p. 91.
17 United States. Sedition Act, 16 May 1918. A Portion of the Amendment to Section 3 of the Espionage Act of 15 June 1917.

The World War I Document Archive, Brigham Young University
Library, available at www.lib.byu.edu/~rdh/wwi/1918/usspy.
html, 28 July 2006. The act was subsequently repealed in 1921.

18 Supreme Court of the United States, *Debs v. United States*, 249
US 211, 10 March 1919. Justice Oliver Wendell Holmes delivered
the opinion of the court. University of Missouri-Kansas City,
School of Law, available at www.law.umkc.edu/faculty/projects/
ftrials/conlaw/debs.html, accessed 28 July 2006.

19 Woodrow Wilson, Final Address in Support of the League of
Nations, Pueblo, CO, 25 September 1919, quoted in James
Andrews and David Zarefsky, eds, *American Voices: Significant
Speeches in American History, 1640–1945* (New York, 1989),
available at American Rhetoric, www.americanrhetoric.com/
speeches/wilsonleagueofnations.htm, accessed 28 July 2006.

7 THE UNITED STATES IN WORLD WAR II, 1941–45

1 Stimson, quoted in Michael Tomasky, 'His Father's House',
review of James Carroll, *House of War: The Pentagon and the
Disastrous Rise of American Power* (New York, 2006), *New
York Times Book Review*, 2 July 2006.

2 Wilson, quoted in Paterson, et al., *American Foreign Relations*,
II, p. 80.

3 Roosevelt, quoted in James MacGregor Burns, *Roosevelt: The
Lion and the Fox* (New York, 1956), p. 449.

4 Roosevelt, quoted in Kenneth J. Hagan, *This People's Navy: The
Making of American Sea Power* (New York, 1991), p. 295.

5 Roosevelt, quoted in Burns, *Roosevelt*, pp. 165–6.

6 Richard B. Frank, 'Battle of Guadalcanal', in *The Oxford
Companion to American Military History*, ed. John W.
Chambers, II (Oxford, 1999), p. 304.

7 MacArthur, quoted in Geoffrey Perret, *Old Soldiers Never Die:
The Life of Douglas MacArthur* (New York, 1996), p. 282.

8 Roosevelt, quoted in Jon Meacham, *Franklin and Winston: A
Portrait of a Friendship* (London, 2004), p. 209.

9 See Thomas G. Paterson, *On Every Front: the Making and
Unmaking of the Cold War* (New York, 1992), Chapter 1, for
eyewitness descriptions of Europe and Japan at the end of the
war.

10 See William Manchester, *American Caesar* (Boston, MA, 1978).

11 See Arnold A. Offner, *Another Such Victory: President Truman
and the Cold War, 1945–1953* (Palo Alto, CA, 2002).

1 Ray Davis, speaking at dedication of Korean War Memorial in Washington, DC, 27 July 1995, available at gtalumni.org/news/topics/fall95/davis.html, accessed 29 July 2006.
2 Conference proceedings, quoted in Callum A. MacDonald, *Korea: The War before Vietnam* (New York, 1986), p. 7.
3 Acheson, quoted in Perret, *A Country Made by War*, p. 449.
4 Harry S. Truman, 'Special Message to the Congress Reporting on the Situation in Korea', in *Harry S. Truman, Public Papers of the Presidents of the United States, 1950* (Washington, DC, 1965), pp. 527–37.
5 Ibid.
6 NSC-81, quoted in MacDonald, *Korea: The War before Vietnam*, p. 48.
7 Orders to MacArthur and his reply quoted in ibid., pp. 47–8.
8 Perret, *A Country Made by War*, p. 461.
9 MacArthur, quoted in Perret, *Old Soldiers Never Die*, p. 564.
10 MacArthur, quoted in Stanley Weintraub, *MacArthur's War: Korea and the Undoing of an American Hero* (New York, 2000), pp. 263–4.
11 MacArthur, quoted in ibid., p. 330.
12 Truman, quoted in ibid., pp. 330–31, 338–9.

1 Johnson, quoted in George C. Herring, *America's Longest War: The United States and Vietnam, 1950–1975* (New York, 1996), p. 122.
2 'Excerpts from President Johnson's Address to the American Public, 4 August 1964, 11:37 p.m.', available at www.congresslink.org, accessed 22 July 2006.
3 *Congressional Record*, CX (7 August 1964), 18471, quoted in Thomas G. Paterson, et al., *American Foreign Relations: A History* (Boston, MA, 2005), II, p. 350.
4 Taylor, quoted in Herring, *America's Longest War*, p. 142.
5 Taylor, quoted in ibid., p. 144.
6 Colby, quoted in Kenneth J. Hagan, 'Early Vietnam: Could We Have Won?', *Naval History* (March–April 1997), p. 35.
7 Harold G. Moore and Joseph Galloway, *We Were Soldiers Once. . . and Young: Ia Drang – The Battle that Changed Vietnam* (New York, 2002).
8 The concept is succinctly explained in Perret, *A Country Made*

by War, p. 513.

9 The operation is well described and illustrated in Craig L. Symonds, *The Naval Institute Historical Atlas of the US Navy* (Annapolis, MD, 1995), pp. 210–11.

10 See especially Harry G. Summers, Jr, *On Strategy: A Critical Analysis of the Vietnam War* (Novato, CA, 1995), p. 134.

11 Trainor, quoted in Harry G. Summers, Jr, *Historical Atlas of the Vietnam War* (New York, 1995), p. 165.

12 For the whole story, see Daniel Ellsberg, *Secrets: A Memoir of Vietnam and the Pentagon Papers* (New York, 2002).

13 Nixon, quoted by Mark Clodfelter, 'Nixon and the Air Weapon', in *An American Dilemma: Vietnam, 1964–1963*, ed. Dennis E. Showalter and John G. Albert (Chicago, IL, 1993), p. 169.

14 Nixon, quoted in Dale Andrade, *America's Last Vietnam Battle* (Lawrence, KS, 2001), p. 480.

15 See Mark Clodfelter, *The Limits of Air Power: The American Bombing of North Vietnam* (New York, 1989).

16 Mansfield, quoted in Paterson, et al., *American Foreign Relations*, II, p. 397.

17 Bernard Fall, 'This Isn't Munich, It's Spain', *Ramparts Vietnam Primer* (San Francisco, n.d.), pp. 60–61.

18 Perret, *A Country Made by War*, pp. 527, 533.

19 For disagreement over Summers's views see Andrew F. Krepinevich, Jr, *The Army and Vietnam* (Baltimore, MD, 1986).

10 THE WARS AGAINST IRAQ, 1991–2007

1 Wolfowitz, quoted in Gabriel Kolko, *Another Century of War?* (New York, 2002), p. 108.

2 UN Security Council Resolution, 660, 2 August 1990 (Condemning the Invasion of Kuwait by Iraq), UN Doc. S/RES/660 (1990).

3 UN Security Council Resolution, 678, 29 November 1990, UN Doc. S/RES/678 (1990).

4 Ian Bickerton, et al., *43 Days: the Gulf War* (Melbourne, 1991), p. 64. Statements by Presidents Bush and Hussein during the war are taken from this book.

5 Michael R. Gordon and Bernard E. Trainor, *The Generals' War* (Boston, MA, 1995), p. x.

6 Ibid., p. 467.

7 George W. Bush, Address to Nation, 11 September 2001.

8 George W. Bush, Address to Joint Session of Congress, 20 September 2001.

9 Ibid.

10 For the unitary executive by its two principal proponents, see Christopher S. Yoo and Steven G. Calabresi, *A History of the Unitary Executive: Executive Branch Practice from 1789 to 2005* (New Haven, CT, 2003).

11 George W. Bush, State of the Union Address, 29 January 2002.

12 George W. Bush, Address to US Military Academy graduating class, 2 June 2002.

13 Ron Suskind, *The One Percent Doctrine: Deep Inside America's Pursuit of its Enemies* (New York, 2006).

14 UN Security Council Resolution, 1441, 8 November 2002.

15 Rumsfeld, Press Briefing, Pentagon, 20 March 2003.

16 George W. Bush, The White House, Office of the Press Secretary, 1 May 2003.

17 The phrase is from James Carroll, *House of War: The Pentagon and the Disastrous Rise of American Power* (Boston, MA, 2006).

18 John Keegan, in a number of articles in the *Daily Telegraph* between April and June 2003, wrote extensively about the success of the war.

19 David Brooks, 'Winning in Iraq', *New York Times*, 28 August 2005.

20 See Kevin Phillips, *American Theocracy* (New York, 2006).

21 Andrew F. Krepinevich, Jr, 'How to Win in Iraq', *Foreign Affairs* (September–October 2005). Tom Donnelly and Gary Schmitt advocated the same approach in a *Washington Post* essay on 26 October 2003; and so did dozens of mid-level Army and Marine Corps officers in Iraq.

22 George W. Bush, The White House, Office of the Press Secretary, 27 May 2006.

23 George W. Bush, quoted in David E. Sanger 'In Courting West Virginians, Bush Speaks of Military's Might', *New York Times*, 5 July 2004.

24 See Stephen E. Flynn, 'America the Vulnerable,' *Foreign Affairs* (January–February 2002). See also Flynn, 'The Neglected Home Front,' *Foreign Affairs* (September–October 2004); *Foreign Affairs* (February 2003).

25 Tom Porteous, *The Caliphate Myth*, 13 February 2006, available at www.TomPaine.com, accessed 23 August 2006.

CONCLUSION

1 Chief Joseph, as remembered by Ohiyesa (Charles A. Eastman), available at www.indians.org/welker/joseph.htm, accessed 23 August 2006.
2 Eliot A. Cohen and John Gooch, *Military Misfortunes: The Anatomy of Failure in War* (New York, 2006), p. 251.
3 Gabriel Kolko, *Another Century of War?* (New York, 2002), p. 146.

BIBLIOGRAPHY

OVERVIEWS AND REFERENCES

Ambrose, Stephen E., and Douglas G. Brinkley, *Rise to Globalism: American Foreign Policy since 1938* (New York, 1997)

Anderson, Fred, and Andrew Cayton, *The Dominion of War: Empire and Liberty in North America, 1500–2000* (New York, 2005)

Arendt, Hannah, *The Human Condition* (New York, 1959)

Bassford, Christopher, *Clausewitz in English: The Reception of Clausewitz in Britain and America, 1815–1945* (New York, 1994)

Boot, Max, *The Savage Wars of Peace: Small Wars and the Rise of American Power* (New York, 2002)

Bradford, James C., *Oxford Atlas of American Military History* (New York, 2003)

Chambers, John Whiteclay, ed., *Oxford Companion to American Military History* (Oxford, 1999)

Cohen, Eliot A., and John Gooch, *Military Misfortunes: The Anatomy of Failure in War* (New York, 2006)

Collins, John M., *Military Strategy: Principles, Practices, and Historical Perspectives* (Washington, DC, 2002)

Dallek, Robert, *The American Style of Foreign Policy: Cultural Politics and Foreign Affairs* (New York, 1983)

Fuller, J.F.C., *Decisive Battles of the USA* (New York, 1942)

Graebner, Norman, ed., *Ideas and Diplomacy: Readings in the Intellectual Tradition of American Foreign Policy* (New York, 1964)

Griffith, Robert, and Paula Baker, eds, *Major Problems in American History since 1945* (Boston, MA, 2007)

Hagan, Kenneth J., *This People's Navy: The Making of American Sea Power* (New York, 1992)

Hanson, Victor Davis, *Ripples of Battle: How the Wars of the Past Still Determine How we Fight, How we Live, and How we Think*

(New York, 2003)

Hunt, Michael H., *Ideology and US Foreign Policy* (New York, 1988)

Kelley, Robert L., *The Shaping of the American Past* (Englewood Cliffs, NJ, 1975)

Kinzer, Stephen, *Overthrow: America's Century of Regime Change from Hawaii to Iraq* (New York, 2006)

LaFeber, Walter, *The New Empire: An Interpretation of American Expansion, 1860–1898* (Ithaca, NY, 1998)

Merrill, Dennis, and Thomas G. Paterson, eds, *Major Problems in American Foreign Relations*, 2 vols (Boston, MA, 2005)

Millett, Allan R., and Peter Maslowski, *For the Common Defense: A Military History of the United States of America* (New York, 1984, rev. 1994)

Murray, Williamson, MacGregor Knox and Alvin Bernstein, eds, *The Making of Strategy: Rulers, States, and War* (Cambridge, 1994)

Paret, Peter, ed., *Makers of Modern Strategy: From Machiavelli to the Nuclear Age* (Princeton, NJ, 1986)

Paterson, Thomas G., et al., *American Foreign Relations*, 2 vols (Boston, MA, 2005)

Paterson, Thomas, et al., eds, *Encyclopedia of US Foreign Relations* (New York, 1997)

Perret, Geoffrey, *A Country Made by War: From the Revolution to Vietnam* (New York, 1989)

Steele, Ian K., *Warpaths: Invasions of North America* (Oxford, 1994)

Stephanson, Anders, *Manifest Destiny: American Expansionism and the Empire of Right* (New York, 1995)

Sweetman, Jack, *American Naval History: An Illustrated Chronology of the US Navy and Marine Corps, 1775–Present* (Annapolis, MD, 2002)

Symonds, Craig L., *Historical Atlas of the US Navy* (Annapolis, MD, 1995)

Van Alstyne, Richard W., *The Rising American Empire* (New York, 1960)

Von Clausewitz, Carl, *On War* (Princeton, NJ, 1984)

Walzer, Michael, *Arguing about War* (New Haven, CT, 2004)

Weigley, Russell F., *The American Way of War: A History of United States Military Strategy and Policy* (Bloomington, IN, 1973)

Williams, William A., *The Tragedy of American Diplomacy* (New York, 1988)

Zinn, Howard, *A People's History of the United States* (New York, 2003)

Butterfield, L. H., et al., *The Book of Abigail and John: Selected Letters of the Adams Family, 1762–1874* (Cambridge, MA, 1975)

Calloway, Colin, *The American Revolution in Indian Country* (Cambridge, 1995)

DeConde, Alexander, *The Quasi-War: The Politics and Diplomacy of the Undeclared War with France, 1797–1781* (New York, 1966)

Gilbert, Felix, *To the Farewell Address: Ideas of Early American Foreign Policy* (Princeton, NJ, 1961)

Gross, Robert A., *The Minutemen and their World* (New York, 2001)

Lepore, Jill, *The Name of War: King Phillip's War and the Origins of American Identity* (New York, 1998)

Martin, James Kirby, and Mark Edward Lender, *A Respectable Army: The Military Origins of the Republic, 1763–1789* (Arlington Heights, IL, 2006)

Middlekauff, Robert, *The Glorious Cause: The American Revolution, 1763–1789* (New York, 2005)

Perkins, Bradford, *The Creation of a Republican Empire, 1776–1865* (Cambridge, 1993)

Shy, John, *A People Numerous and Armed: Reflections on the Military Struggle for Independence* (Ann Arbor, MI, 1990)

Wood, Gordon S., *The Creation of the American Republic* (Chapel Hill, NC, 1969)

THE SECOND WAR AGAINST GREAT BRITAIN

Coles, Harry L., *The War of 1812* (Chicago, 1965)

Cusick, James G., *The Other War of 1812: The Patriot War and the American Invasion of Spanish East Florida* (Gainesville, FL, 2003)

Heidler, David S., and Jeanne T. Heidler, eds, *Encyclopedia of the War of 1812* (Santa Barbara, CA, 1997)

Hickey, Donald R., *The War of 1812: A Forgotten Conflict* (Urbana, IL, 1990)

Horsman, Reginald, *The War of 1812* (London and New York, 1969)

Pratt, Julius W., *The Expansionists of 1812* (New York, 1949)

Roosevelt, Theodore, *The Naval War of 1812* (New York, 1999)

Saunt, Claudio, *A New Order of Things: Property, Power, and the Transformation of the Creek Indians, 1733–1816* (Cambridge, 1999)

THE WAR AGAINST MEXICO

Bauer, K. Jack, *The Mexican War, 1846–1848* (Lincoln, NE, 1974)

Eisenhower, John S. D., *So Far From God: The US War with Mexico, 1846–1848* (New York, 1989)

Graebner, Norman, *Empire on the Pacific: A Study in American Continental Expansion* (New York, 1955)

Horsman, Reginald, *Race and Manifest Destiny: The Origins of American Racial Anglo-Saxonism* (Cambridge, MA, 1981)

Johannsen, Robert W., *To the Halls of the Montezumas: The Mexican War in the American Imagination* (Oxford, 1985)

May, Robert E., *Manifest Destiny's Underworld: Filibustering in Antebellum America* (Chapel Hill, NC, 2002)

Richmond, Douglas W., *Essays on the Mexican War* (Arlington, VA, 1986)

Singletary, Otis A., *The Mexican War* (Chicago, 1962)

THE CIVIL WAR

Blight, David W., *Race and Reunion: The Civil War in American Memory* (Cambridge, MA, 2002)

Catton, Bruce, *U. S. Grant and the American Military Tradition* (New York, 1954)

Fellman, Michael, *Citizen Sherman: A Life of William Tecumseh Sherman* (New York, 1995)

——, *Inside War: The Guerrilla Conflict in Missouri during the American Civil War* (Oxford, 1989)

Foner, Eric, *A Short History of Reconstruction, 1863–1877* (New York, 1990)

Luvaas, Jay, *The Military Legacy of the Civil War: The European Inheritance* (Chicago, 1959)

McPherson, James M., *Drawn with the Sword: Reflections on the Civil War* (New York, 1996)

Mindell, David A., *War, Technology, and Experience aboard the USS Monitor* (Baltimore, MD, 2000)

Utley, Robert, *Frontier Regulars: The United States Army and the Indian, 1866–1891* (Lincoln, NE, 1973)

THE WAR AGAINST SPAIN

Cosmas, Graham A., *An Army for Empire: The United States Army in the Spanish-American War* (College Station, TX, 1971)

Foner, Philip S., *The Spanish-Cuban-American War and the Birth of American Imperialism, 1895–1902* (New York, 1972)

Hill, Richard, *War at Sea in the Ironclad Age* (London, 2000)

Linn, Brian McAlister, *Guardians of Empire: The US Army and the Pacific, 1902–1940* (Chapel Hill, NC, 1997)

Mahan, Alfred T., *The Influence of Sea Power upon History, 1660–1783* (New York, 1987)

Morgan, H. Wayne, *America's Road to Empire* (New York, 1965)

Morison, Elting E., *Admiral Sims and the Modern American Navy* (Boston, MA, 1942)

Musicant, Ivan, *Empire by Default: The Spanish-American War and the Dawn of the American Century* (New York, 1998)

Offner, John L., *An Unwanted War: The Diplomacy of the United States and Spain over Cuba, 1895–1898* (Chapel Hill, NC, 1992)

Perez, Louis A., *The War of 1898: The United States and Cuba in History and Historiography* (Chapel Hill, NC, 1998)

Porch, Douglas, *Wars of Empire* (London, 2000)

Shulman, Mark R., *Navalism and the Emergence of American Sea Power, 1882–1893* (Annapolis, MD, 1995)

Tompkins, E. Berkeley, *Anti-Imperialism in the United States* (Philadelphia, PA, 1970)

Widenor, William C., *Henry Cabot Lodge and the Search for an American Foreign Policy* (Berkeley, CA, 1980)

Zimmermann, Warren, *The First Great Triumph: How Five Americans Made their Country a World Power* (New York, 2002)

THE UNITED STATES IN WORLD WAR I

Audoin-Rouzeau, Stéphane, and Annette Becker, *14–18: Understanding the Great War* (New York, 2002)

Daniels, Josephus, *Our Navy at War* (New York, 1922)

Ferguson, Niall, *The Pity of War, 1914–1918* (New York, 1999)

Fleming, Thomas, *The Illusion of Victory: America in World War I* (New York, 2003)

Fussell, Paul, *The Great War and Modern Memory* (Oxford, 2000)

Gamble, Richard M., *The War for Righteousness: Progressive Christianity, the Great War, and the Rise of the Messianic Nation* (Wilmington, DE, 2003)

Gardner, Lloyd C., *Safe for Democracy: The Anglo-American Response to Revolution, 1913–1923* (New York, 1984)

Goldstein, Erik, and John Maurer, eds, *The Washington Conference,*

1921–22 (London, 1994)

Harries, Meirion, and Susie Harries, *The Last Days of Innocence: America At War, 1917–1918* (New York, 1997)

Hawley, Ellis W., *The Great War and the Search for a Modern Order* (New York, 1979)

Joll, James, *The Origins of the First World War* (London, 1992)

Kennedy, David M., *Over Here: The First World War and American Society* (Oxford, 2004)

Kittredge, Tracy Barrett, *Naval Lessons of the Great War* (Garden City, NY, 1921)

Klachko, Mary, and David F. Trask, *Admiral William Shepherd Benson: First Chief of Naval Operations* (Annapolis, MD, 1987)

MacMillan, Margaret, *Paris 1919: Six Months that Changed the World* (New York, 2001)

Marder, Arthur J., *From the Dreadnought to Scapa Flow*, IV (London, 1969)

May, Ernest R., *The World War and American Isolation, 1914–1917* (Cambridge, MA, 1959)

Morison, Elting E., *Admiral Sims and the Modern American Navy* (Boston, MA, 1942)

Patenaude, Bertrand M., *Big Show in Bololand: The American Relief Expedition to Soviet Russia in the Famine of 1921* (Stanford, CA, 2002)

Sims, William S., *Victory at Sea* (London, 1920)

Smith, Gene, *When the Cheering Stopped: the Last Years of Woodrow Wilson* (New York, 1964)

Strachan, Hew, *The First World War* (Oxford, 2003)

Zieger, Robert H., *America's Great War: World War I and the American Experience* (Lanham, MD, 2001)

THE UNITED STATES IN WORLD WAR II

Bergerud, Eric, *Touched with Fire: The Land War in the South Pacific* (New York, 1996)

Bickel, Keith, *Mars Learning: The Marine Corps' Development of Small Wars Doctrine, 1915–1940* (Boulder, CO, 2001)

Blum, John Martin, V *was for Victory: Politics and American Culture during World War II* (New York, 1976)

Burns, James MacGregor, *Roosevelt: The Lion and the Fox* (New York, 1956)

Crozier, Andrew, *The Causes of the Second World War* (Oxford, 1997)

Davidson, Joel R., *The Unsinkable Fleet: The Politics of US Navy Expansion in World War II* (Annapolis, MD, 1996)

Dower, John W., *Embracing Defeat: Japan in the Wake of World War II* (New York, 1999)

——, *War without Mercy: Race and Power in the Pacific War* (New York, 1986)

Eiler, Keith E., *Mobilizing America: Robert P. Patterson and the War Effort, 1940–1945* (Ithaca, NY, 1997)

Frank, Richard B., *Guadalcanal* (New York, 1990)

Frieser, Karl-Heinz, *The Blitzkrieg Legend* (Annapolis, MD, 2005)

Greenfield, Kent Roberts, *American Strategy in World War II: A Reconsideration* (Malabar, FL, 1982)

Hart, B. H. Liddell, *History of the Second World War* (New York, 1970)

Hasegawa, Tsuyoshi, *Racing the Enemy: Stalin, Truman, and the Surrender of Japan* (Cambridge, MA, 2005)

Hogan, Michael J., ed., *Hiroshima in History and Memory* (Cambridge, 1996)

Hone, Thomas C., Norman Friedman and Mark D. Mandeles, *American and British Carrier Development, 1919–1941* (Annapolis, MD, 1999)

Johnson, Marilynn, *The Second Gold Rush: Oakland and the East Bay in World War II* (Berkeley, CA, 1996)

Linn, Brian McAlister, *Guardians of Empire: The US Army and the Pacific, 1902–1940* (Chapel Hill, NC, 1997)

Manchester, William, *American Caesar* (Boston, MA, 1978)

May, Ernest, *Knowing One's Enemies: Intelligence Assessment before the Two World Wars* (Princeton, NJ, 1984)

McKercher, B.J.C., and Roch Legault, eds, *Military Planning and the Origins of the Second World War in Europe* (Westport, CT, 2000)

Meacham, Jon, *Franklin and Winston: A Portrait of a Friendship* (London, 2004)

Miller, Edward S., *War Plan Orange: The US Strategy to Defeat Japan, 1897–1945* (Annapolis, MD, 1991)

Millett, Allan R., and Williamson Murray, *A War to Be Won* (Cambridge, MA, 2000)

——, eds, *Calculations: Net Assessment and the Coming of World War II* (New York, 1992)

——, *Military Innovation in the Interwar Period* (Cambridge, 1996)

Murray, Williamson, *War in the Air, 1914–45* (London, 1999)

Overy, Richard, *Why the Allies Won* (New York, 1995)

Porch, Douglas, *The Path to Victory: The Mediterranean Theater in World War II* (New York, 2004)

Reynolds, David, Warren F. Kimball and A. O. Chubarian, eds, *Allies at War: The Soviet, American and British Experience, 1939–45* (New York, 1994)

Spector, Ronald H., *Eagle against the Sun* (New York, 1985)

Stoler, Mark A., *Allies and Adversaries: The Joint Chiefs of Staff, the Grand Alliance, and US Strategy in World War II* (Chapel Hill, NC, 2003)

Stoler, Mark A., and Melanie S. Gustafson, eds, *Major Problems in the History of World War II* (Boston, MA, 2003)

Strahan, Jerry, *Andrew Jackson Higgins and the Boats that Won World War II* (Baton Rouge, LA, 1994)

Trachtenberg, Marc, *A Constructed Peace: The Making of the European Settlement, 1945–1963* (Princeton, NJ, 1999)

Weinberg, Gerhard L., *A World at Arms: A Global History of World War II* (Cambridge, 1994)

THE WAR IN KOREA

Cagle, Malcolm W., and Frank A. Manson, *The Sea War in Korea* (Annapolis, MD, 1957)

Hanley, Charles J., Sang-Hun Choe and Martha Mendoza, *The Bridge at No Gun Ri: A Hidden Nightmare from the Korean War* (New York, 2001)

James, D. Clayton, *Refighting the Last War: Command and Crisis in Korea, 1950–1953* (New York, 1993)

Kaufman, Burton I., *The Korean War: Challenges in Crisis, Credibility, and Command* (New York, 1986)

MacDonald, Callum A., *Korea: The War before Vietnam* (New York, 1986)

Offner, Arnold A., *Another Such Victory: President Truman and the Cold War, 1945–1953* (Palo Alto, CA, 2002)

Stueck, William, *Rethinking the Korean War: A New Diplomatic and Strategic History* (Princeton, NJ, 2002)

——, *The Korean War: An International History* (Princeton, NJ, 1995)

Weintraub, Stanley, *MacArthur's War: Korea and the Undoing of an American Hero* (New York, 2000)

THE WAR IN VIETNAM

Appy, Christian G., *The Vietnam War Remembered from All Sides* (New York, 2003)

Buzzanco, Robert, *Masters of War: Military Dissent and Politics in the Vietnam Era* (Cambridge, 1997)

Cable, Larry E., *Conflict of Myths: The Development of American Counterinsurgency Doctrine and the Vietnam War* (New York, 1986)

Daum, Andreas W., Lloyd C. Gardner and Wilfried Mausbach, eds, *America, the Vietnam War, and the World: Comparative International Perspectives* (Cambridge, 2003)

DeBenedetti, Charles, with Charles Chatfield, *An American Ordeal: The Antiwar Movement of the Vietnam War* (Syracuse, NY, 1990)

Ellsberg, Daniel, *Secrets: A Memoir of Vietnam and the Pentagon Papers* (New York, 2002)

Herring, George C., *America's Longest War: The United States and Vietnam, 1950–1975* (New York, 1996)

Kaiser, David, *American Tragedy: Kennedy, Johnson, and the Origins of the Vietnam War* (Cambridge, 2000)

Krepinevich, Andrew F., *The Army and Vietnam* (Baltimore, MD, 1986)

Logevall, Fredrick, *Choosing War: The Lost Chance for Peace and the Escalation of War in Vietnam* (Berkeley, CA, 1999)

Mann, Robert, *A Grand Delusion: America's Descent into Vietnam* (New York, 2001)

McMahon, Robert J., ed., *Major Problems in the History of the Vietnam War* (Boston, MA, 2003)

McMaster, H. R., *Dereliction of Duty: Lyndon Johnson, Robert McNamara, the Joint Chiefs of Staff, and the Lies that Led to Vietnam* (New York, 1997)

Moore, Harold G., and Joseph Galloway, *We Were Soldiers Once . . . and Young: Ia Drang –The Battle that Changed Vietnam* (New York, 1992)

Sorely, Lewis, *A Better War: The Unexamined Victories and Final Tragedy of America's Last Years in Vietnam* (New York, 1999)

Summers, Harry G., *Historical Atlas of the Vietnam War* (Boston, MA, 1995)

——, *On Strategy: A Critical Analysis of the Vietnam War* (Novato, CA, 1982)

Young, Marilyn B., *The Vietnam Wars, 1945–1990* (New York, 1991)

Zumwalt, Elmo R., *On Watch* (New York, 1976)

THE WARS AGAINST IRAQ

Anderson, Jon Lee, *The Fall of Baghdad* (New York, 2004)

Arnove, Anthony, *Iraq: The Logic of Withdrawal* (New York, 2006)

Bamford, James, *A Pretext for War: 9/11, Iraq, and the Abuse of America's Intelligence Agencies* (New York, 2004)

Bickerton, Ian, et al., *43 Days: the Gulf War* (Melbourne, 1991)

Blix, Hans, *Disarming Iraq* (New York, 2004)

Bodansky, Yossef, *The Secret History of the Iraq War* (New York, 2004)

Franks, Tommy, *American Soldier* (New York, 2004)

Garrels, Anne, *Naked in Baghdad: The Iraq War as Seen by* NPR's *Correspondent* (New York, 2003)

Glantz, Aaron, *How America Lost Iraq* (New York, 2005)

Gordon, Michael R., and Bernard E. Trainor, *Cobra 11: The Inside Story of the Invasion and Occupation of Iraq* (New York, 2006)

——, *The Generals' War: The Inside Story of the Conflict in the Gulf* (Boston, MA, 1995)

Hersh, Seymour M., *Chain of Command: The Road from 9/11 to Abu Ghraib* (New York, 2004)

Keegan, John, *The Iraq War* (New York, 2004)

Kitfield, James, *Prodigal Soldiers: How the Generation of Officers Born of Vietnam Revolutionized the American Style of War* (Washington, DC, 1995)

Marolda, Edward, and Robert Schneller, *Sword and Shield: The* US *Navy and the Persian Gulf War* (Washington, DC, 1998)

McGeough, Paul, *In Baghdad: A Reporter's War* (Crow's Nest, NSW, 2003)

Murray, Williamson, and Robert H. Scales, *The Iraq War: A Military History* (Cambridge, MA, 2003)

Purdum, Todd S., *A Time of Our Choosing: America's War in Iraq* (New York, 2003)

Ricks, Thomas E., *Fiasco: The American Military Adventure in Iraq* (New York, 2006)

Suskind, Ron, *The One Percent Doctrine: Deep Inside America's Pursuit of its Enemies since 9/11* (New York, 2006)

Woodward, Bob, *Bush at War* (New York, 2002)

——, *Plan of Attack* (New York, 2004)

COLD WAR OVERVIEWS

Aldrich, Richard J., *The Hidden Hand: Britain, America and Cold War Secret Intelligence* (Woodstock, NY, 2002)

Barlow, Jeffery G., *The Revolt of the Admirals: The Fight for Naval Aviation, 1945–1954* (Washington, DC, 1994)

Black, Jeremy, *War since 1945* (London, 2004)

Carroll, James, *House of War: The Pentagon and the Disastrous Rise of American Power* (New York, 2006)

Crile, George, *Charlie Wilson's War: The Extraordinary Story of the Largest Covert Operation in History* (New York, 2004)

Freedman, Lawrence, *The Evolution of Nuclear Strategy* (New York, 1989)

——, *Kennedy's Wars: Berlin, Cuba, Laos, and Vietnam* (Oxford, 2002)

Friedman, Norman, *The Fifty Year War: Conflict and Strategy in the Cold War* (Annapolis, MD, 2000)

——, *Terrorism, Afghanistan, and America's New Way of War* (Annapolis, MD, 2003)

Gacek, Christopher M., *The Logic of Force: The Dilemma of Limited War in American Foreign Policy* (New York, 1994)

Gaddis, John Lewis, *Strategies of Containment: A Critical Appraisal of Postwar American National Security Policy* (Oxford, 1982)

——, *We Now Know: Rethinking Cold War History* (Oxford, 1997)

Gilman, Nils, *Mandarins of the Future: Modernization Theory in Cold War America* (Baltimore, MD, 2004)

Keiser, Gordon, *The US Marine Corps and Defense Unification, 1944–47* (Washington, DC, 1996)

Kuklick, Bruce, *Blind Oracles: Intellectuals and War from Kennan to Kissinger* (Princeton, NJ, 2006)

Lebow, Richard Ned, ed., *Ending the Cold War: Interpretations, Causation, and the Study of International Relations* (New York, 2004)

Locher, James R., III, *Victory on the Potomac: The Goldwater-Nichols Act Unifies the Pentagon* (College Station, TX, 2002)

May, Ernest R., ed., *American Cold War Strategy: Interpreting NSC 68* (Boston, MA, 1993)

Pach, Chester J., *Arming the Free World: The Origins of the United States Military Assistance Program, 1945–1950* (Chapel Hill, NC, 1991)

Paterson, Thomas G., *On Every Front: The Making and Unmaking of the Cold War* (New York, 1992)

Record, Jeffrey, *Making War, Thinking History: Munich, Vietnam, and Presidential Uses of Force from Korea to Kosovo* (Annapolis, MD, 2002)

Reynolds, David, *The Origins of the Cold War in Europe: International Perspectives* (New Haven, CT, 1994)

Westad, Odd Arne, *The Global Cold War: Third World Interventions and the Making of Our Times* (Cambridge, 2005)

POST-COLD WAR OVERVIEWS

Bacevich, Andrew J., *American Empire: The Realities and Consequences of US Diplomacy* (Cambridge, MA, 2004)

Baer, Robert, *See No Evil: The True Story of a Ground Soldier in the CIA's War on Terrorism* (New York, 2002)

Berman, Morris, *Dark Ages America: The Final Phase of Empire* (New York, 2006)

Brune, Lester H., *The United States and Post Cold War Interventions* (Claremont, CA, 1998)

Clarke, Richard A., *Against All Enemies: Inside America's War on Terror* (New York, 2004)

Coll, Steve, *Ghost Wars: The Secret History of the CIA, Afghanistan, and Bin Laden* (New York, 2004)

Ferguson, Niall, *Colossus: The Price of America's Empire* (New York, 2004)

Gray, Chris Hables, *Postmodern War: The New Politics of Conflict* (New York, 1997)

Johnson, Chalmers, *Blowback: The Costs and Consequences of Empire* (New York, 2004)

——, *The Sorrows of Empire: Militarism, Secrecy, and the End of the Republic* (New York, 2004)

Kolko, Gabriel, *Another Century of War?* (New York, 2002)

Larson, Eric V., *Casualties and Consensus* (Santa Monica, CA, 1996)

Mann, James, *Rise of the Vulcans: The History of Bush's War Cabinet* (New York, 2004)

Naylor, Sean, *Not a Good Day to Die: The Untold Story of Operation Anaconda* (New York, 2005)

Nye, Joseph S., *The Paradox of American Power* (Oxford, 2002)

Oakley, Robert B., and John L. Hirsch, *Somalia and Operation Restore Hope* (Washington, DC, 1995)

Priest, Dana, *The Mission: Waging Peace and Keeping Peace with America's Military* (New York, 2003)

Shattuck, John, *Freedom on Fire: Human Rights Wars and America's Response* (Cambridge, MA, 2003)

Strobel, Warren P., *Late-Breaking Foreign Policy: The News Media's Influence on Peace Operations* (Washington, DC, 1997)

Van Creveld, Martin, *The Transformation of War* (New York, 1991)

ACKNOWLEDGEMENTS

Our greatest debt is to Jeremy Black, who saw merit in our proposal and recommended its publication. At Reaktion, Michael Leaman has been patient, trusting and firm – a perfect combination for stimulating independent thought. Emily Berry has answered our every e-mail with good cheer and helpfulness.

For advice and assistance we are most indebted to Tom Paterson, whose erudite and insightful suggestions for improvements prevented many a disaster. Branden Little edited, annotated and suggested improvements with tireless enthusiasm and precision. Marie McKenzie contributed her matchless bibliographical and editing skills. Tris Lovering, Bruce Clunies Ross, Dominic Kelly, Bunty Turner and Edward Mason provided encouragement and enthusiasm. Rose Drake made the office in Monterey run smoothly.

We began our book with an email from Sydney to San Francisco, and continued our trans-Pacific collaboration with trips to one another's country, and countless lengthy telephone (Skype!) calls. Many of the ideas we developed were first tested on the students of the Strategy and Policy course of the Naval War College in Monterey, California. We are grateful to them for hearing us out in the early stages of this venture. We also acknowledge the debt we owe to Geoffrey Perret and J.F.C. Fuller, two outstanding historians whose books we drew upon for insight and inspiration.

We wish to thank our wives, Vera and Jenny, who interrupted us often to proclaim their unwavering enthusiasm.

At the end, we reach across four decades to express our profound gratitude to Douglass Adair, the sage who understood that the thread of violence runs through the history of the United States, and to Charles Campbell, our mentor, who taught us that documents are the best source of history – both teachers now long gone from the Claremont Graduate School.

INDEX